NEGOTIATING ON BEHALF OF OTHERS

Sage Series on Negotiation and Dispute Resolution

SERIES EDITORS

Lawrence E. Susskind, *Massachusetts Institute of Technology*
Robert H. Mnookin, *Harvard University*

This series is designed to promote applied research in negotiation and dispute resolution. Drawing on the multidisciplinary efforts of scholars and practitioners in the social sciences, humanities, law, public policy, psychology, urban planning, and management science, the **Sage Series on Negotiation and Dispute Resolution** seeks to examine the next round of research questions, including various challenges to interest-based models of conflict management originating at the Program on Negotiation at Harvard Law School and other research centers. Taking a distinctly cross-cultural perspective, this series aims to broaden and deepen the dialogue between scholars and practitioners and to establish the highest possible standards for reflective practice.

Volumes in this series . . .

Negotiating on Behalf of Others
Edited by Robert H. Mnookin and Lawrence E. Susskind with Pacey C. Foster

Edited by
Robert H. Mnookin
Lawrence E. Susskind
With Pacey C. Foster

NEGOTIATING ON BEHALF OF OTHERS

Advice to Lawyers, Business Executives,
Sports Agents, Diplomats, Politicians,
and Everybody Else

NDR
Negotiation and Dispute Resolution

Sage Publications, Inc.
International Educational and Professional Publisher
Thousand Oaks ■ London ■ New Delhi

For information:

Sage Publications, Inc.
2455 Teller Road
Thousand Oaks, California 91320
E-mail: order@sagepub.com

Sage Publications Ltd.
6 Bonhill Street
London EC2A 4PU
United Kingdom

Sage Publications India Pvt. Ltd.
M-32 Market
Greater Kailash I
New Delhi 110 048 India

Printed in the United States of America

Library of Congress Cataloging-in-Publication Data

Main entry under title:

Negotiating on behalf of others: Advice to lawyers, business executives, sports agents, diplomats, politicians, and everybody else / edited by Robert H. Mnookin and Lawrence E. Susskind with Pacey C. Foster
    p. cm.—(Negotiation and dispute resolution)
    Includes bibliographical references (p.   ) and index.
    ISBN 0-7619-1326-2 (cloth: alk. paper)
    ISBN 0-7619-1327-0 (pbk.: alk. paper)
    1. Negotiation in business—United States. 2. Negotiation—United States.
3. Agency (Law)—United States. I. Mnookin, Robert H. II. Susskind, Lawrence. III. Foster, Pacey C. IV. Series.
    HD58.6 .N4334 1999
    302.3—dc21   99-6667

This book is printed on acid-free paper.

99 00 01 02 03 04 05 7 6 5 4 3 2 1

Acquiring Editor:	Marquita Fleming
Editorial Assistant:	MaryAnn Vail
Production Editor:	Diana Axelsen
Editorial Assistant:	Karen Wiley
Designer:	Lynn Miyata
Indexer:	Virgil Diodato
Cover Designer:	Michelle Lee

Contents

Preface   ix
Abram J. Chayes

Introduction   1
Robert H. Mnookin and Jonathan R. Cohen

PART I: Negotiation Theory Revisited

1. Toward a Theory of Representation in Negotiation   23
Joel Cutcher-Gershenfeld and Michael Watkins

Commentary
The Shifting Role of Agents in Interest-Based Negotiations   52
Lawrence E. Susskind

2. Authority of an Agent: When Is Less Better?   59
Roger Fisher and Wayne Davis

Commentary
Rational Authority Allocation to an Agent   81
Max H. Bazerman

3. Minimizing Agency Costs in Two-Level Games:
Lessons From the Trade Authority Controversies in the
United States and the European Union   87
Kalypso Nicolaïdis

Commentary
Minimizing Agency Costs: Toward a Testable Theory   127
Gordon M. Kaufman

PART II: Agency in Context

4. Challenges for International Diplomatic Agents   135
   Eileen F. Babbitt

   Commentary
   The Role of Agents in International Negotiation   151
   Bruce M. Patton

5. Law and Power in Agency Relationships   157
   Jeswald W. Salacuse

   Commentary
   Law and Power in Agency Relationships   176
   Janet Martinez

6. Agency in the Context of Labor Negotiations   181
   Robert B. McKersie

   Commentary
   Agency in the Context of Labor Management   196
   Kathleen Valley

7. Legislators as Negotiators   203
   David C. King and Richard J. Zeckhauser

   Commentary
   Turning the Tables: Negotiation as the Exogenous Variable   226
   Jonathan R. Cohen

8. First, Let's Kill All the *Agents*!   235
   Michael Wheeler

   Commentary
   Unnecessary Toughness: Hard Bargaining
          as an Extreme Sport   263
   Brian S. Mandell

PART III: Prescriptive Implications

9. Major Themes and Prescriptive Implications   275
   Lawrence E. Susskind and Robert H. Mnookin

10. Agents in Negotiations: Toward Testable Propositions   283
   Terri Kurtzberg, Don Moore, Kathleen Valley,
   and Max H. Bazerman

   Annotated Bibliography of Selected Sources   299
   Pacey C. Foster and Jonathan R. Cohen

   Index   317

   About the Authors   326

Preface

Abram J. Chayes

This book is the product of the first of a series of seminars conducted by the faculty of the Program on Negotiation at Harvard on "complicating factors" in negotiations. The animating idea of the projected series was that it was time to move beyond the simple one-on-one negotiation format that has explicitly or implicitly been the focus of much of the work in negotiation theory to date, beginning with Roger Fisher and William Ury's seminal *Getting to YES* (1981). It was time to begin identifying and addressing elements in the setting or evolution of the negotiating process that might complicate or qualify the descriptive and prescriptive propositions developed in the study of the simple, "normal" situation. The first of these "complicating factors" selected for study was the effect of the presence of an agent in the negotiating process. The seminar was held during the spring of 1997, and, as the roster of participants shows, included many of the legendary greats in the pantheon of negotiation theory.

The most important conclusion to emerge was that the traditional object of academic study and analysis in the field—the dyadic two-person negotiation, with each person representing and bargaining for his or her own interest—was not the "normal" situation at all, at least in a practical sense. It is instead a construct, a simplification, an abstraction from the realities of negotiating practice. Such constructs are, as Thomas Schelling remarked long ago in *The Strategy of Conflict* (1960), extremely important for generating theoretical propositions and, one might add, for teaching them, but their relation to the real world remains problematic. What emerged from the seminar was that the conduct of negotiations through agents, far from being a special or occasional "complicating factor," was the norm. Indeed, it is hard to think of situations in the real political, commercial, or even personal world that fit the dyadic paradigm. In bargaining for a rug in the *souk*, or even in purchasing a car, one of the parties, the seller, is almost always represented by an agent, a salesperson. For practical purposes, every negotiator is an agent, accountable to somebody or some body, even if it is an amorphous constituency or membership.

In law and economics, academic work has proceeded from another simplified dyadic conception of the relationship between "a principal" and "an agent." It has addressed questions of the authority, information, and incentives involved in the relationship. When, how, and how much authority and information should the principal provide *to* the agent? What are the agent's incentives in a rationally calculating world, and how can the principal modify them to align them more closely with his or her own? Even at this rather straightforward level, the elements of the relationship are not as fully within the control of the two parties as might appear in what is essentially a consensual relationship. The law has always recognized that, in certain circumstances, the agent will have power to bind the principal without his or her consent, and even against his or her instructions. Nor is this a rare circumstance. Agents acting for corporations and other collective bodies—and how can such bodies act *except* through agents?—are almost always vested with relatively broad powers to bind that cannot be traced back to any positive action of the principal other than participating in the system.

The mention of corporations and collective bodies—which includes states—widens the horizon of inquiry even further and reveals an even stranger landscape, as compared to the "normal" negotiation that has been the familiar object of theoretical study. An overwhelming portion of contemporary economic and social life, and a good deal of our personal lives too, is conducted by or with such collectivities. In this setting, the simple notion of *a* principal and *an* agent, with lines of authority running from the former to the latter, begins to evaporate. We enter a world of multiple principals and multiple agents, and oscillations between the two, where one person or entity is at times a principal and at times an agent, and at times both, with respect to the same subject and even the same negotiation. Often, the parties to the negotiation are not two but many, and the participants work across party lines to help shape the authority, information, and incentives of their negotiating partners. In such situations, anything approaching unified control of these dimensions of the relationship, proceeding in a straight line from principal to agent, is illusory. It is not only that all of them are ambiguous. Even more important, they are constantly being constructed and tested and contested—*negotiated*—between and among the participants in the negotiating process: "Everything has suffered a sea change into something wondrous strange" (William Shakespeare, *The Tempest*, Act I, Scene 2).

The complicating factor, then, is that the world of negotiation, like most of human endeavor, is complicated. It is fraught with ambiguities and shifting relationships and changing environments. This book embarks on the quest for insight and understanding in an environment where complication is normalcy.

REFERENCES

Fisher, R. and W. Ury. 1981. *Getting to YES.* New York: Penguin.
Schelling, T. C. 1960. *The strategy of conflict.* Cambridge, MA: Harvard University Press.

Introduction

Robert H. Mnookin
Jonathan R. Cohen

A ttorneys structuring settlements for clients, diplomats drafting treaties on behalf of governments, sports agents representing athletes, managers bargaining with union representatives—agents participate in many negotiations. At times, this is a matter of practical necessity. How could nations, companies, and unions negotiate if not through agents? At other times, a principal has the option of negotiating directly but elects to use an agent, believing that the agent will produce better results. A professional athlete may know little about high-stakes salary negotiations. A lawyer might be willing to push harder on an issue than the party directly involved. How *do* agents affect negotiations? How *should* principals and agents act when negotiations involve agents? The purpose of this book is to systematically explore the impact of agency on negotiation and how parties should respond to it.

 ## THE BACKDROP

Over the past two decades, principal-agent analysis has blossomed within economics.[1] The central question this field addresses is how

---

AUTHORS' NOTE: We thank Lawrence E. Susskind for his helpful suggestions. All errors are ours alone.

one party (the principal) can get another party (the agent) to do its bidding. Suppose an employer hires an employee to inspect products for quality control. How can the employer ensure that the employee performs, rather than shirks from, the task? Variables such as the employer's ability to monitor the employee (information), the degree to which the employee wants to accomplish the task (preferences), and how the employee is paid (incentives) are central elements.[2]

What if, instead, the agent's task is to *negotiate with other parties on the principal's behalf*? What factors should the principal now consider? No doubt, information, preferences, and incentives remain important, but other factors also come into play. Questions arise from the principal's perspective. Should I use an agent at all, or, assuming I have the option, should I negotiate on my own behalf? If I use an agent, what sort of agent should I use? Should I select a "hard" bargainer or someone who is more cooperative? If I have a particular negotiating style, should I pick an agent with a similar or a different style?[3] What instructions should I give my agent? Should I tell him or her everything that I know and want, or should I hold some things back? For example, will my agent bargain harder for me if I pretend that my "bottom line" is higher than it actually is? When should I allow my agent to make commitments on my behalf? Questions also arise from the agent's perspective. What information do I need from my principal before entering a negotiation? What authority to make commitments should I seek from my principal, and when should I seek it? What should I do if we cannot reach an agreement because my principal, rather than the other side, is being unreasonable? How far should I go in trying to persuade my principal to accept a deal? Questions also arise from a theoretical or scholarly perspective. Are parties more or less likely to reach agreement if they negotiate through agents?[4] In what cases can an agent negotiate more effectively than a principal, and why?

In the main, the negotiation literature has concerned itself with negotiations conducted directly by principals. This is not to say that agency in negotiation has never been addressed: Many pioneering works analyzing labor-management, international, and legal negotiations, to name but a few topics, have stressed the tensions of agency.[5] The dominant perspective within the negotiation literature, however, has been that of principals negotiating directly. This was a natural place to begin, for without some understanding of the "basic" case of principals negotiating directly, one stands little chance of understanding the more complex case of negotiation through agents.

Below, we present what we see as some *key issues* to understanding negotiation through agents. We do not attempt to resolve these issues in this introduction—the ensuing chapters take up that task—we merely raise them. To introduce these issues, we use as springboards two well-known works on negotiation: *Getting to YES* (*GTY*) by Fisher, Ury, and Patton (1991) and *Barriers to Conflict Resolution* (*Barriers*) by Arrow, Mnookin, Ross, Tversky, and Wilson (1995). For each work, we ask what challenges agency poses to its central messages.

We chose these works for several reasons. First, the negotiation literature has long straddled two overlapping domains: *prescriptive* advice on how to negotiate successfully and *descriptive* analysis of negotiation.[6] *GTY* exemplifies the finest of the former and *Barriers* the finest of the latter. Second, both *GTY* and *Barriers* are comprehensive in their outlooks: *GTY* presents an overarching view of "principled negotiation," and *Barriers* systematically explores why negotiations often fail when mutually beneficial agreements were possible. Third, as is typical within the negotiation literature, both *GTY* and *Barriers* focus on direct negotiations between principals.[7]

▤ GETTING TO YES

In *GTY*, Fisher and colleagues offered four main pieces of advice for those entering a negotiation: (1) separate the people from the problem; (2) focus on interests, not positions; (3) invent options for mutual gain; and (4) insist on using objective criteria. The authors contended that these at-the-table steps would help parties reach "wise agreements amicably and efficiently" (Fisher et al. 1991:83). In *GTY* and subsequent writings, Fisher also stressed three away-from-the-table factors critical in negotiation: the best alternative to negotiated agreement (BATNA), the relationship between the parties, and commitment.[8] How are these "seven elements" of negotiation affected by the presence of agents? We consider each in turn.

Separate the people from the problem. A great benefit of agents is to do precisely this (Rubin and Sander 1988). Principals' emotions frequently interfere with their abilities to negotiate effectively. Neighbors feuding over who should pay to repair a common driveway may be so antagonistic that they cannot talk without shouting. If each gets a representative, however, a settlement may be struck. More detached from the conflict than the principals, agents often communicate more effectively. Such communication raises the likelihood of finding a mutually beneficial agreement.

Focus on interests, not positions. Without agents, focusing on interests rather than positions is, at least conceptually, a straightforward step. With agents, that step is more complex. Although an agent is supposed to, and is usually legally obliged to (see Clark in Pratt and Zeckhauser 1985; Salacuse, Chapter 5, this volume) represent the principal's interests with fidelity, as the principal-agent problem reflects, an agent might focus instead on his or her own interests. Even assuming that the agent wants to represent the principal's interests, how is the agent to know the principal's interests? Many principals have unclear, inchoate, or multifaceted interests. Furthermore, principals often instruct agents by telling them what deals they will and will not accept. Yet such instructions are positions, not interests. Focusing on interests requires richer discussions between principals and agents than commonly occur.

Invent options for mutual gain. Who are better at generating options, agents or principals? On one hand, principals know more about their own interests and resources than agents, and such information is needed in generating options. On the other hand, agents can foster a more relaxed and open negotiating environment, which often is critical to brainstorming. Agents also see options that principals do not. A buyer, fearing that the product will malfunction, and a seller, confident of the product's quality, may be unable to reach a deal directly, but if their lawyers suggest a warranty, a deal may ensue (see Mnookin, Peppet, and Tulumello forthcoming: chap. 14). Agents bring "fresh eyes" to disputes. If two heads are better than one in generating options, four heads should be better than two.

Insist on using objective criteria. Who is more likely to insist on and be effective in using objective criteria, the principal or the agent? Agents, expert in a particular area of negotiation, frequently invoke objective criteria. Real estate agents use fair market appraisals to strike deals.

Sports agents and management representatives use other players' salaries as benchmarks. Lawyers base settlements on estimates of how courts will decide cases (see Mnookin and Kornhauser 1979). Principals also invoke objective criteria, but agents, expert in a field, may do this more naturally.

BATNA. Can negotiating through an agent change one's BATNA? At first, one might think that an agent would do little to change one's BATNA: If I use an agent to negotiate with party P, what difference should that make to my alternatives if I fail to reach an agreement with party P? Yet agents can alter one's BATNA. Agents frequently know of alternatives of which the principal is unaware. If I try to sell my house myself, I may find few prospective buyers, but if I hire a real estate agent, that agent may know of dozens. Even where an agreement is reached with party P, negotiating through an agent can still change the outcome. Some deals, even deals that *ex ante* were good deals, turn out to be bad deals. Suppose a baseball team signs a multimillion-dollar contract with a "star" pitcher, but the pitcher proves ineffective the following season. If the deal was negotiated by the team's general manager (an agent), the team's owner can readily blame, if not fire, the general manager. If the owner negotiated the contract, however, the owner will have no ready scapegoat.

Relationship. How do agents affect the principals' relationship? Principals often turn to agents because their relationship with the opposing party has soured. The ability of agents to reach an agreement, however, does not mean that the underlying relational conflict between the principals has disappeared: It is common for agents to broker an agreement, only later to have the principals break that agreement and resume their hostilities. As Edmond Rostand's *Cyrano de Bergerac* (1898) illustrates, tenuous is the relationship where the parties cannot speak without agents.

Commitment. When entering negotiations, parties must consider commitment. Is my goal at the upcoming meeting to sign a contract, to reach a tentative settlement, or merely to agree to meet again? If I think that the price is too high, should I walk away? If I think that the price is reasonable, should I accept it, or should I haggle to see if an even better price might be forthcoming? With agents, commitment is far more complex. What authority, if any, does an agent have to make commitments? When should a principal grant an agent authority to make commitments, and when should a principal withhold it?

When it comes to authority, more is *not* always better (see Schelling 1960). Take an example like wanting to delay reaching an agreement. If a buyer has a meeting lined up with a potential seller but wants to "shop around" before committing to an agreement, the buyer might send an agent with little authority to commit in lieu of meeting with the seller directly. If the seller says, "Our price is $X. Do we have a deal?", the agent may respond, "Thanks for your offer. I'll have to check with my boss and then get back to you." If the buyer were to have met with the seller, however, or if the buyer had given the agent full authority to commit, delaying could be awkward.

 ## BARRIERS TO CONFLICT RESOLUTION

"Why do negotiations so often fail even where there are possible resolutions that obviously would serve the disputants better than protracted struggle?"[9] Mnookin and Ross suggest three general categories of barriers to conflict resolution: (1) tactical and strategic barriers, (2) psychological barriers, and (3) organizational, institutional, and other structural barriers (see Mnookin 1993; Mnookin and Ross in Arrow et al. 1995; Ross and Stillinger 1991). Each is rich for examination through the lens of agency.

Tactical and strategic barriers. A central tension in negotiation is between creating and claiming value. As Lax and Sebenius (1986) argued, negotiation tactics that promote one goal are likely to harm the other (see also Mnookin et al. forthcoming). When agents negotiate, several questions arise.

Will parties create more value or less value by using agents? Usually, we think that agents help in finding value-creating solutions; however, this is not always the case. In some negotiations, the transactions costs of using agents are high, thereby shrinking the "pie" available to the principals.[10] More fundamentally, whether agents will be more capable than their principals in finding value-creating solutions depends on the negotiating approaches taken by the agents. Many a business agreement has been ruined by "nit-picking" lawyers.

In contrast, many a child custody agreement has been reached by lawyers who can explore possible solutions more cooperatively than the divorcing parents.[11]

Do agents help in claiming value? Can a skilled agent help the principal get a larger slice of the pie than the principal could get for him- or herself? In some cases, the answer is surely yes. For a professional athlete, a multiyear contract negotiation can be a one-shot deal, but his or her agent will likely be a repeat player in that market. If in direct negotiations the athlete says, "I'll take no less than [an extremely high figure]," the statement may lack credibility; however, if the agent, who has a reputation to protect, says, "We'll take no less than [an extremely high figure]," the demand may be credible (see Wheeler, Chapter 8, this volume). One need not even invoke reputation to see distributive advantages to using agents. If I'm a soft bargainer, I may well do better in distributive negotiations by hiring an agent who is a tough bargainer.

Psychological barriers. People have systematic biases in assimilating and construing information: Parties tend to see the world in ways favorable to their positions (see Kahneman and Tversky in Arrow et al. 1995). Might agents dampen such biases and thereby promote settlement? Less enmeshed in the conflict than their principals, agents may be more objective in assimilating and construing information. For example, a lawyer may see the other side's argument more readily than the client does and thus play a useful role in "reality checking" with the client. Parties' biased views of what is just or equitable also can be a barrier to resolving a conflict (see Bazerman and Neale in Arrow et al. 1995), a barrier that agents might again help overcome. So too with other cognitive biases that contribute to conflict, such as loss aversion, dissonance reduction, and avoidance. Agents may, however, suffer from other cognitive biases, such as reactive devaluation and judgmental overconfidence, just as strongly as the principals. Agents, like principals, may discredit an offer that comes from the opposing side and overestimate the strength of their own position (Kahneman and Tversky in Arrow et al. 1995:47).

Organizational, institutional, and other structural barriers. When a principal negotiates through an agent, how is the principal to ensure that the agent does its bidding? As the principal-agent problem stresses, the interests of principals and agents frequently diverge. This applies in negotiation as much as in any other domain. Can the principal find an agent whose preferences are similar to the principal's? If not, can the agent's incentives be modified (e.g., via contract incentives[12]) so that the agent will act as the principal desires? Can the principal monitor the actions of the agent?

Many principals are caught in a structural trap of fearing to look weak to an internal constituency if they negotiate directly with the "enemy." Heads of opposing organizations, be they nations or unions and management, may find direct negotiations, let alone option generating, politically infeasible. Agents may worry less about such risks. Agents, however, also encounter structural challenges. When entering a negotiation, an agent faces a Janus-like task of keeping one eye trained on the other party and one eye trained on the agent's own principal (see Walton and McKersie 1965; Mnookin et al. forthcoming). How can I reach an agreement that *both* the other party and my own principal will accept? If I strike a tentative deal with the other side, can I sell it to my principal? This tension is particularly challenging when one's principal is not a single person but a multifaceted entity.

A final note: There may be a tendency to think that agents can overcome many, if not all, of the barriers to effective negotiation. If principals are biased in acquiring and construing information, let their agents correct those biases. If principals will not negotiate directly because of internal political pressures, let them send agents. If principals cannot commit to cooperative negotiation tactics that "expand the pie," let them select agents who can. *We caution against an overly simplistic view.* Agents too possess cognitive biases, agents too must worry about pressures from internal constituencies, and agents too face irreducible tensions between creating and claiming value. Agents will not make the tensions of negotiation entirely disappear; rather, these tensions will be recast in a new system. For example, an agent, like a principal, may worry about his or her internal standing if he or she appears "too chummy" with the "enemy." Furthermore, the presence of agents necessarily adds at least one new dynamic to the negotiating environment: the principal-agent tension. Agents frequently help parties reach agreement, but they are no panacea to the tensions of negotiation.

THE ORGANIZATION OF THIS VOLUME

To investigate these issues, this book proceeds in three stages. Part I (Negotiation Theory Revisited) explores ways of reworking negotiation theory to take account of agency. Part II (Agency in Context) examines five specific arenas—international diplomacy, agency law, labor-management relations, professional sports, and the legislative process—in which agents play central roles in negotiation. Part III (Prescriptive Implications) synthesizes the theoretical insights and practical wisdom of the earlier chapters, offering testable propositions for future research and extracting "take-away" lessons for practitioners.

Negotiation Theory Revisited

How should negotiation theory adjust for the fact that negotiations frequently occur through agents? Part I explores three topics central to this reworking: representation, authority, and two-level games.

Representation

At times, an agent is simply an agent, obediently following the expressed wishes of a principal. At other times, agents do much more. In "Toward a Theory of Representation in Negotiation," Joel Cutcher-Gershenfeld and Michael Watkins present a new framework for understanding the diverse tasks of agents involved in negotiations. They argue that negotiating agents must be understood along three distinct dimensions: (1) To what extent does the agent represent the agent's interests and to what extent does he or she represent the principal's interests (the agent/principal continuum); (2) to what extent does the agent accept the principal's stated interests and to what extent does he or she seek to transform the principal's interests (the agent/visionary continuum); and (3) to what extent does the agent represent a principal with internally unified interests and to what extent does he or she represent a principal with internally divided interests (the agent/partisan continuum)?

Cutcher-Gershenfeld and Watkins argue that these three tensions give rise to three inescapable, though not unmanageable, dilemmas:

the trust dilemma, the transformation dilemma, and the flexibility dilemma. The *trust dilemma* is that the more an agent is trusted by the principal, the more able he or she will be to create value through negotiation, but the more the agent cooperates with the opposing party, the harder it will be for the principal to trust the agent. The *transformation dilemma* is that the more an agent can transform the principal's stated interests, the more likely the agent will be to find innovative agreements; however, seeking to transform the principal's interests creates risk for the agent. The *flexibility dilemma* is that an agent needs sufficient internal agreement among his or her constituents to protect against divisive bargaining tactics by the other side, but the more consolidated is that internal agreement, the less flexibility the agent will have in external negotiations. The authors illustrate these tensions with two case studies: a labor-management negotiation at the Ford Motor Company Sterling Plant and former Israeli Prime Minister Shimon Peres's efforts to facilitate the Middle East peace process. They challenge us to see the multidimensional representational tasks of agents, highlighting ramifications for negotiation practice and theory building.

Lawrence E. Susskind takes issue with a challenge that Cutcher-Gershenfeld and Watkins pose to the practice of interest-based bargaining. More specifically, Susskind argues that the key to interest-based bargaining is to free the participants to move through the panoply of roles and tensions that Cutcher-Gershenfeld and Watkins describe. Rather than viewing the three dilemmas as obstacles, Susskind sees them as indicators of the opportunities inherent in all negotiations, no matter how bitter the controversy.

Authority

What authority should a principal grant an agent? In a provocative essay, "Authority of an Agent: When Is Less Better?," Roger Fisher and Wayne Davis argue that asking *how much* authority a principal should grant an agent is the wrong question. Instead, Fisher and Davis contend that the critical issue is *when* a principal should grant an agent authority. More specifically, they argue that a principal should grant an agent very little authority to commit to a deal at the outset, but full authority to explore interests and options with the other side. Authority to commit to a deal should be granted only later.

Good negotiations, reason Fisher and Davis, are *interest-based* rather than positional. If a principal gives an agent authority to commit at the outset, this is likely to be done through positional instructions (e.g., "Don't sell at any price below $X. Definitely sell at any price above $Y. If the price is between $X and $Y, do your best to negotiate it upward."). Such positional instructions will likely produce positional negotiations between the agent and the opposing party. In contrast, if agents are given little authority to commit at the outset, they are more likely to engage in interest-based negotiations and find value-creating solutions. This view is a natural extension of the earlier emphasis of Fisher et al. (1991) on interest-based negotiation. Fisher and Davis also offer an illustrative set of instructions that a principal might give an agent at the outset of a negotiation. These are "open" instructions that can be shared with the other side. This template is sure to be a practical aid to many principals and agents.

In "Rational Authority Allocation to an Agent," Max H. Bazerman responds to Fisher and Davis's approach. Fisher and Davis's main argument is that principals should think more about *when* to give authority to an agent, rather than *how much* authority to give. Bazerman argues that principals must also think carefully about *what kind* of information to give the agent. For example, should the principal share her interests, her priority trade-offs, and her BATNA with her agent? (Bazerman's answers: Yes, yes, and generally no.)

Two-Level Games

Often, one agent represents multiple constituents who disagree with one another. When entering a negotiation, how should the agent proceed? How should the constituents instruct the agent?

In "Minimizing Agency Costs In Two-Level Games," Kalypso Nicolaïdis argues that optimal mandates in two-level games involve balancing *external efficiency* (i.e., getting the best agreement one can from the opposing party) with *internal equity* (i.e., getting an agreement that fairly suits the differing interests of the agent's multiple principals). She offers three prescriptive implications, and concomitantly positive hypotheses, about such two-level negotiations: (1) The more the constituents' interests align internally, the less flexible the agent's mandate should be; (2) the more the constituents' interests align with the agent's, the more authority the agent should be granted;

and (3) the more the constituents' interests conflict either internally or with the agent's interests, the less autonomy the agent should be granted.

Nicolaïdis applies this theory to trade negotiations of the European Union (EU) and the United States. She contrasts the mandates given to EU and U.S. negotiators, problems engendered by those mandates, and how those mandates evolved over time. She distinguishes between three stages of negotiations through agents—before, during, and after the agents meet—and suggests three related concerns for principals: how much *flexibility* to give the agent going into the negotiations, how much *autonomy* to give the agent during the negotiations, and how much ratification *authority* to give the agent after the negotiations are completed.

In "Minimizing Agency Costs: Toward a Testable Theory," Gordon M. Kaufman frames Nicolaïdis's analysis through an operations research lens, his central concern being how to test the robustness of Nicolaïdis's analysis. Against that more formal backdrop, Kaufman also calls attention to the complexities added by strategy, uncertainty, and iteration to determining optimal mandates.

Agency in Context

Part II ("Agency in Context") examines the impact of agency on negotiation in five specific arenas: international diplomacy, agency law, labor-management relations, the legislative process, and sports negotiations. Important domains in their own rights, these topics provide fertile grounds for exploring the theoretical concerns posed in Part I and for raising new questions as well.

International Diplomacy

In international diplomacy, agents face special challenges. Often they represent amorphous principals (e.g., the United States) or multiple principals (e.g., the president, the State Department, and domestic trade groups), the mandates from their principals can shift rapidly, and principals use multiple agents simultaneously to carry out their agendas. International diplomacy also involves role conflicts. At times, a foreign service officer merely relays the interests of a foreign nation to his or her principal(s), and at other times the same officer must negotiate with that foreign nation on behalf of his or her princi-pal(s). Complicating matters further, some principals depend heavily upon their agents for information about foreign countries, again alter-ing the dynamics of traditional principal-agent roles, though advances in information technology have mitigated this somewhat.

In "Challenges for International Diplomatic Agents," Eileen F. Babbitt argues that to produce better diplomatic practice, such com-plexities of international negotiation must be addressed more effec-tively. For example, when different messages are being conveyed by multiple principals using multiple agents (e.g., the State, Treasury, Commerce, and Defense departments all sending different repre-sentatives to post-Dayton, Bosnia negotiations), it may be impossible to reach an external agreement until those constituents negotiate an internal agreement about how they will conduct external negotiations. Similarly, the role conflicts with which agents grapple should be faced openly. Peppering her analysis with examples from U.S. foreign policy over the past several decades, Babbitt argues persuasively that by em-bracing, rather than ignoring, the complexities inherent in inter-national diplomacy, we can produce better diplomatic practice.

In his commentary on Babbitt's chapter, Bruce Patton addresses aspects of what, in his view, is the more fundamental question of how an international agent should conceptualize his or her role in meeting the challenges Babbitt raises. He offers five general ideas to guide the thinking of proactive agents.

Agency Law

What controls the agency relationship in negotiation? Jeswald W. Salacuse explores two central variables: law and power.

From a legal viewpoint, agent-negotiators fall into one of three categories: independent contractors, employees, or partners. These different legal relationships involve both real and legal trade-offs. When the agent is a partner, the agent's interests are likely to align with the principal's; however, the principal loses control over the agent (e.g., partner Q can commit partner P to a contract without P's approval.) When the agent is an employee, the principal gains control over the agent but risks greater divergence of the agent's interests from the principal's own. By hiring the agent as an independent contractor, the principal may reduce overhead costs but further loses ability to control the agent. Commenting on Salacuse, Janet Martinez nicely summarizes such trade-offs, helpfully charting different consequences arising from different agency relationships. She points to the dynamic nature of the agency relationship and the possibility of iterative design of contractual relationships between principal and agent.

Salacuse also argues that power dynamics, although irrelevant from a legal viewpoint, are key to understanding agency relationships in practice. He stresses the importance of the agent's personal relationship with the principal (e.g., making Mickey Cantor a strong negotiator for Bill Clinton), the unavailability of other suitable agents (e.g., which made Henry Kissinger a powerful agent for Richard Nixon), and the agent's ability to use his or her own network to influence the principal.

Labor-Management Relations

In their pioneering book *A Behavioral Theory of Labor Negotiations*, Richard Walton and Robert McKersie (1965) introduced the idea that when a union or management representative bargains with the opposing side, the representative must simultaneously keep an eye trained on his or her own constituency and how to achieve agreement within it for any tentative deal the negotiators might strike. In "Agency in the Context of Labor Negotiations," McKersie delves deeper into the interaction between the representative and his or her organization. He describes critical challenges such representatives face and offers "best practice" advice.

Challenges faced by representatives are many. The players may be concerned not only with what happens at one particular plant but also with setting a precedent for the industry as a whole. Agents and principals can have different time horizons, the union president worrying about an imminent election and the union's negotiator envisioning years of ongoing contact with his or her negotiating counterpart. McKersie responds to such challenges with deep contextual analysis, reviewing responses that have worked well. For example, where labor and management have developed a cooperative negotiating relationship, management ought to think twice before resisting a union's organizing campaign. Parallel to Nicolaïdis's suggestion, McKersie recommends that agents view their actions as involving three conceptually distinct stages: (1) the initial phase during which "negotiations take place within each organization," (2) the main negotiations with the other party, and (3) the phase during which "the agent works for understanding and acceptance of the proposed settlement" within his or her organization.

Kathleen Valley evaluates many of McKersie's specific insights, highlighting differences in incentives between principals and agents. She also suggests that labor negotiations are a fertile ground for empirical research on how personal relationships influence negotiations. Two problems with laboratory studies of the influence of personal relationships on negotiations are that the participants in such studies play for small stakes and use short-term time horizons. In labor negotiations, the stakes are large and real, and the time horizons are much longer.

Legislation

"All laws," write David C. King and Richard J. Zeckhauser, "are born of negotiations" (Chapter 7, this volume, p. 203). This straightforward observation has profound implications. In "Legislators as Negotiators," King and Zeckhauser take a fresh and fascinating look at legislation and, by implication, politicians. Their thesis is clear: Much political behavior, especially legislation, can best be understood as the product of negotiation.

Through recognizing the centrality of negotiation to legislation, King and Zeckhauser unpack aphorisms like "politics makes strange bedfellows" and "in politics one has no permanent friends and no permanent enemies, just permanent interests" (p. 205). They help explain why congressional staffs, the press, and election deadlines strongly influence legislation. They offer a three-dimensional framework consisting of role, authority, and mission for characterizing legislators, and they assess different politicians within that framework.

Their chapter concludes with a pioneering empirical study of the selection of congressional party heads—the majority and minority leaders of the U.S. House and Senate. Simple models suggest that parties should choose leaders whose preferences reflect those of the median voter within their party. King and Zeckhauser posit a different model. They contend that, because a main aspect of being a party head is negotiating legislation with the opposing party head, parties will choose leaders who come from their "extreme" wings (e.g., if you're a

Republican and you know that your leader will be negotiating with a Democrat, it is best to pick a very conservative Republican to be your leader, because he or she will be a stronger bargainer for your side than would a moderate Republican). Using House and Senate data from 1901 to 1990, King and Zeckhauser find that the median voter model is rejected and that their model is supported.

In "Turning the Tables: Negotiation as the Exogenous Variable," Jonathan R. Cohen identifies a methodological shift used by King and Zeckhauser and suggests that this shift offers an important new avenue for negotiation research. Much negotiation research focuses on explaining the results of a negotiation in terms of external, or exogenous, variables (e.g., the parties' interests, relationship, BATNAs). A brilliance of King and Zeckhauser, suggests Cohen, is to reverse this approach and show how the fact of negotiation shapes external phenomena. Cohen illustrates this by considering the importance of negotiation to the judicial interpretation of legislation.

Sports Agents

In "First, Let's Kill All the *Agents*!," Michael Wheeler tackles the topic of agency in professional sports and simultaneously develops a critique of the standard approach of assuming that, if an agreement was reached, a zone of possible agreement (ZOPA) existed at the outset. Wheeler sees sports negotiations as overwhelmingly distributive, and thus dominated by confrontational tactics. He suggests that a model that assumes no possible agreement (NOPA) at the outset is more accurate in such circumstances. Within such a model, a party's main goal is to get the opposing party to change its reservation value, thereby creating the possibility of a favorable agreement.

Wheeler supports his view with a study of 50 National Hockey League managers in a simulated negotiation exercise, one half representing players and one half representing management. He finds that, in the vast majority of cases, the agents' reservation values did not overlap at the outset (i.e., no ZOPA existed), yet many dyads subsequently reached agreement. NOPA rather than ZOPA, argues Wheeler, should frame our analysis of highly distributive sports bargaining.

In "Unnecessary Toughness: Hard Bargaining as an Extreme Sport," Brian S. Mandell takes a different angle on agency in sports negotiations. Although Mandell concedes that underlying variables will continue to make sports negotiations tough and distributive, he contends that several steps could be taken to make sports negotiations value-creating as well. He argues, à la Fisher and Davis, that to foster more value-creating negotiations, players should at the outset reduce their agents' authority to commit on the highly distributive issue of salary. He also emphasizes the asymmetries between young athletes and their more experienced agents and suggests that athletes need to monitor and control their agents more effectively.

Prescriptive Implications

Part III ("Prescriptive Implications") synthesizes theoretical insights and practical wisdom found in the earlier explorations of agency in particular contexts. The emphases are two: (1) highlighting questions for future academic research and (2) extracting prescriptive "take-away" lessons for practitioners involved in negotiations through agents.

Prescriptive Advice

In "Major Themes and Prescriptive Implications," Lawrence E. Susskind and Robert H. Mnookin probe three central prescriptive ideas that emerge from the materials in this volume. They argue that agents should (1) presume that their counterparts (i.e., agents for the other side) do *not* have interests in portraying their principal's interests accurately; (2) assume that the interests of the other agent will diverge, at least to some extent, from those of their principal; and (3) think about trying to make the other agent(s) one's ally. Theoretically grounded, these practical insights illustrate well the significance of addressing agency when formulating negotiating strategy.

Agents in Negotiations: Toward Testable Propositions

Building on the earlier chapters, Terri Kurtzberg, Don Moore, Kathleen Valley, and Max H. Bazerman develop a set of 21 testable propositions on the effects of agents in negotiations. After briefly reviewing the scant existing empirical work on the effects of agents in negotiations, the authors turn to extracting empirically testable hypotheses from the insights of the previous chapters. Examples of such propositions include "Authority given to an agent will be positively correlated with ability to find integrative trade-offs" (p. 287), "Observable negotiations will limit the agent's search for solutions, and as such will be positively correlated with impasse" (p. 290), and "The stronger and longer lasting the relationship between the agent-negotiators, the more the final agreement will reflect long-term interests rather than short-term gains" (p. 293). The propositions nicely encapsulate many of the central analytical insights of the earlier chapters and provide a helpful framework for future research.

 CONCLUSION

Agents are a central feature of many negotiations. On the descriptive level, agents influence how negotiations occur. On the prescriptive level, forming optimal strategic behavior must also account for the presence of agents. In this introduction, we have outlined what we see as some key issues to understanding both descriptive and prescriptive dimensions of negotiations through agents. We have also briefly sketched the answers offered in the ensuing chapters. The proof, however, lies in the pudding. As your agents, we can attest that the pudding offered in the ensuing chapters is a rich one.

NOTES

1. For overviews, see Pratt and Zeckhauser (1985) and Sappington (1991).

2. Zeckhauser (1991:2) labels this triad of preferences, incentives, and information the "golden triangle" of principal-agent analysis.

3. See Lax and Sebenius (1986), chap. 15 ("Agents and Ratification").

4. For an experimental study suggesting that agents may enhance the likelihood of settlement, see Croson and Mnookin (1997).

5. See, for example, Walton and McKersie (1965) (labor-management negotiations), Putnam (1988) and Downs and Rocke (1994) (international negotiations), and Gilson and Mnookin (1994) (legal negotiations). See also Rubin and Sander (1988) (analyzing agency in negotiation generally) and Lax

and Sebenius (1991) (investigating the agent-negotiator's response to uncertainty).

6. Raiffa (1982:20-25) describes the mixed prescriptive/descriptive approach to studying negotiation. See also Sebenius (1992), who characterizes the development of the negotiation literature.

7. Gilson and Mnookin's chapter ("Cooperation and Competition in Litigation: Can Lawyers Dampen Conflict?") in Arrow et al. (1995) is an exception.

8. See Fisher and Brown (1988) (on relationship in negotiation) and Fisher and Ertel (1995) (specifying seven central elements in negotiation: communication, interests, options, criteria, BATNA, relationship, and commitment).

9. Civil litigation is one arena in which transactions costs have been found to be quite high. See Kakalik and Pace (1986:iii), who found that injured parties received only roughly half of gross payments in 1985 tort compensation cases. See also Conard (1993:292), who cites studies reporting similar findings. In other settings, such as international negotiations, transaction costs are negligible.

10. See Gilson and Mnookin (1994), who suggest that by hiring lawyers who can cooperate with one another, combative disputants may find mutually beneficial outcomes.

11. Levmore (1993) analyzes varying incentive arrangements used in different areas of agency as responses to principal-agent problems.

12. Mnookin et al. (forthcoming) suggest managing, rather than hoping to eliminate, inherent tensions found in negotiations through agents.

REFERENCES

Arrow, K., R. H. Mnookin, L. Ross, A. Tversky, and R. Wilson, eds. 1995. *Barriers to conflict resolution.* New York: W. W. Norton.

Conard, A. F. 1993. Who pays in the end for injury compensation? Reflections on wealth transfers from the innocent. *San Diego Law Review* 30:283-306.

Croson, R. and R. Mnookin. 1997. Does disputing through agents enhance cooperation? Experimental evidence. *Journal of Legal Studies* 26:331-345.

Downs, G. W. and D. M. Rocke. 1994. Conflict, agency, and gambling for resurrection: The principal-agent problem goes to war (How constituencies can control interventionist chief executives). *American Journal of Political Science* 38(2):362-380.

Fisher, R. and S. Brown. 1988. *Getting together: Building relationships as we negotiate.* New York: Penguin.

Fisher, R. and D. Ertel. 1995. *Getting ready to negotiate.* New York: Penguin.

Fisher, R., W. Ury, and B. Patton. 1991. *Getting to YES: Negotiating agreement without giving in.* 2d ed. Boston: Houghton Mifflin.

Gilson, R. J. and R. H. Mnookin. 1994. Disputing through agents: Cooperation and conflict between lawyers in litigation. *Columbia Law Review* 94:509-566.

Kakalik, J. S. and N. M. Pace. 1986. *Costs and compensation paid in tort litigation.* Santa Monica, CA: RAND.

Lax, D. A. and J. K. Sebenius. 1986. *The manager as negotiator: Bargaining for cooperation and competitive gains.* New York: Free Press.

Lax, D. A. and J. K. Sebenius. 1991. Negotiating through agents. *Journal of Conflict Resolution* 35(3):474-493.

Levmore, S. 1993. Commissions and conflicts in agency arrangements: Lawyers, real estate brokers, underwriters, and other agents' rewards. *Journal of Law and Economics* 36:503-539.

Mnookin, R. H. 1993. Why negotiations fail: An exploration of barriers to the resolution of conflict. *Ohio State Journal on Dispute Resolution* 8(2):235-249.

Mnookin, R. H. and L. Kornhauser. 1979. Bargaining in the shadow of the law: The case of divorce. *Yale Law Journal* 88:950-997.

Mnookin, R. H., S. Peppet, and A. Tulumello. Forthcoming. *Bargaining in the shadow of the law: How lawyers help clients create value in negotiation.*

Pratt, J. and R. J. Zeckhauser, eds. 1985. *Principals and agents: The structure of business.* Boston: Harvard Business School Press.

Putnam, R. D. 1988. Diplomacy and domestic politics: The logic of two-level games. *International Organization* 42:427-460.

Raiffa, H. 1982. *The art and science of negotiation.* Cambridge, MA: Belknap Press of Harvard University Press.

Ross, L. and C. Stillinger. 1991. Barriers to conflict resolution. *Negotiation Journal* 7(4):389-404.

Rubin, J. Z. and F. Sander. 1988. When should we use agents? Direct vs. representative negotiations. *Negotiation Journal* 4:395-401.

Sappington, D. 1991. Incentives in principal-agents relationships. *Journal of Economic Perspectives* 5(2):45-66.

Schelling, T.C. 1960. *The strategy of conflict.* Cambridge, MA: Harvard University Press.

Sebenius, J. 1992. Negotiation analysis: A characterization and review. *Management Science* 38(1):18-38.

Walton, R. and R. McKersie. 1965. *A behavioral theory of labor negotiations.* New York: McGraw-Hill.

Zeckhauser, R. J., ed. 1991. *Strategy and choice.* Cambridge: MIT Press.

Negotiation Theory Revisited

Toward a Theory of Representation in Negotiation

Joel Cutcher-Gershenfeld
Michael Watkins

If I am not for myself, who will be for me?
If am not for others, what am I?
If not now, when?

—Hillel (*Pirke Avot*)

A union leader and a plant manager are engaged in a discussion about potential outsourcing of jobs. Clearly, both are representing the interests of others, but what do we mean when we say that the union leader is representing the membership? What do we mean when we say that the plant manager is representing the corporation? The union leader also brings to the table the interests of the international union, a particular caucus in the local union's political structure, her own political aspirations, and a broad vision of where the union needs to go in the future. Similarly, the plant manager brings to the table a concern for the lives and livelihoods of people in the plant, awareness of competing factions within management, aspirations for his own career advancement, and a broad vision of where the plant needs to go in the future to remain competitive. Given this complexity, each is inevitably playing multiple representational roles in the negotiation.

Existing scholarship on representation is only partly helpful in understanding this complexity. The principal-agent literature is valuable in highlighting the importance of informational asymmetries and the risks of incentive incompatibility—both of which play an important role understanding representation (see, for example, Pratt and Zeckhauser 1985). Much of the existing principal-agent literature, however, is written from the point of view of a monolithic principal whose well-specified interests are assumed to have primacy. It focuses on concerns that the agent will illegitimately seek to advance her own interests at the expense of the principal.[1] The presence of distinct interests on the part of the agent and distrust of the agent's motives on the part of the principal gives rise to the classic problem of information and control known as the principal-agent problem:[2] It is not possible for a principal to design an incentive system that perfectly aligns an agent's interests with her own, nor is it possible for the principal to perfectly observe or control the actions of the agent, because the agent has access to information unavailable to the principal.

One difficulty with applying the principal-agent model to real-world negotiations is that principals' interests often are not the only legitimate ones. Individuals at the table may have legitimate concerns of their own—distinct from those of their constituents. They are, in effect, acting as a mix of agent and principal. A second difficulty is that representatives rarely represent principals whose interests are fixed and static. Instead, interests are constructed in interactions between representatives and those they represent, interactions informed by the representatives' superior knowledge of external realities. Representatives may therefore play an indispensable role in reshaping constituent's perceptions of their interests. The ability to do this arises from relationships between representatives and constituents, relationships in which substantial trust may have been developed. A third difficulty is that the interests being represented often are not monolithic: The representative may have multiple constituents. For this reason, more attention should be focused on looking at representation from the perspective of the representative, on exploring the broader range of interests that representatives seek to advance in negotiations, and on the impact of relationships between representatives and constituents. This, in turn, draws attention to diverse representational roles that do not map easily onto classic models of agency.

The literatures from industrial relations, international relations, and organizational theory help somewhat by highlighting the multiple stakeholders and interests that are at play, as well as the complexity of decision making between representatives and internal factions (see, for example, Allison 1971). These institutional perspectives, however, tend to view the interactions of representatives and constituencies from a structural point of view, with relatively fixed conceptions of the roles that representatives play.

The negotiations literature provides a more dynamic perspective on internal and cross-table interactions—highlighting the importance of ratification, commitment, and problem-solving processes (see, for example, Raiffa 1982). This perspective does not always capture the nuances of the institutional context or the interplay of the multiple representational roles.

In this chapter, we integrate important insights from these three literatures to begin the process of constructing a new theory of representation in negotiation. It is an approach that builds on the concept of intraorganizational negotiation developed by Walton and McKersie (1965) but focuses specifically on the issue of representation. To illustrate the potential scope of such a theory, consider three ubiquitous representational scenarios. The first is a classic principal-agent relationship in which a lawyer represents a single client in a divorce case. Here the lawyer may have her own views about the divorce situation, but she will primarily focus on understanding the stated and implied interests of her client. Contrast this with the case of an elected union leader negotiating with management over the introduction of new technologies, a case in which the discussions inevitably involve matters not anticipated by a fractious union membership. In a third scenario, consider the case of a manager attending a budget planning meeting, making commitments on behalf of her organizational unit to productivity improvement targets for the year. Here the manager has both independent authority as a principal to enter into agreements and concerns about getting buy-in for implementation from key subordinates.

These three individuals are representing diverse interests and playing multiple roles; each may be shifting among roles in various ways. Our objective in this chapter is to clarify understanding of the range of interests that get represented and the multiple roles that representatives play. We begin by defining a representational matrix constructed from three distinct dimensions characterizing the interests represented in the negotiation. The three dimensions are conceptually distinct, although any given representative role will fall somewhere along all three dimensions. The first dimension is a continuum involving the representation of others' interests at one end and the representation of one's own interests at the other end, which corresponds to ideal or pure types for "agents" and "principals." Then we present a continuum running from advancing stated interests (also characteristic of a "pure" agent) to the transforming of constituent interests (which places the representative in the role of a "visionary"). Finally, we present a continuum centering on the degree to which internal interests are unified or divided (again beginning with the classical agent and extending to a role we have labeled "partisan"). The representational matrix is constructed by combining these three interest dimensions.

We also focus on three core dilemmas associated with representation—the trust dilemma, the transformation dilemma, and the flexibility dilemma—one associated with each of the three dimensions of the matrix. Building on these dilemmas, we discuss the challenges that representatives face when they seek to change their roles. Finally, we analyze the implications of role complexity with two case study examples, one in the workplace and the other in an international peace-making context. We conclude with implications for theory and practice regarding representation in negotiation.

Underlying this chapter are some key assumptions and distinctions. It is assumed that all negotiations—internal and external—are mixed-motive in nature. Even in highly adversarial or highly cooperative interactions, there will be a mixture of common and conflicting interests, although the mix will vary. As a result, representatives always face a threefold challenge. First, any representative faces the challenge of reconciling a diverse mixture of internal interests, both common and competing. Second, the representative faces a challenge in negotiating externally with other parties around the processes of creating and claiming value (Lax and Sebenius 1986). Third, the representative faces a challenge attending to his or her own interests, which will always be distinct, at least to some degree, both from the interests of the parties he or she is representing and from the interests of other parties to the negotiations.

Ultimately, this analysis points to new insights about interests and representation in negotiations. In particular, we suggest that the roles representatives play, the interests they represent, and their scope for transforming these interests arise out of *relationships* between representatives and those they represent—relationships that may be long-standing and involve substantial trust. In our focus on the social construction of interests and the central role that relationships play in representation, we reach beyond traditional economic models of agency. This focus also helps to illuminate the particular challenges that representatives face when bargaining becomes interest-based.

UNDERSTANDING REPRESENTATIONAL ROLES

We define a representative as an individual who is negotiating on behalf of other parties. We will not be using the terms "agent" and "representative" interchangeably. We will define agency as but one type of representational role and the point of departure for our analysis.

In the principal-agent literature, an agent is a party who represents the interests of a principal in negotiations with a third party. The principal retains the authority to ratify proposals, is responsible for implementing any agreement, and is concerned about ensuring that the agent faithfully represents her interests. This definition highlights a particular aspect of the way "agent" is used as a term of art in the law and in the economics literatures on principals and agents (Reuschlein and Gregory 1979). This is what might be thought of as the "classic" situation, in which the principal seeks to minimize interest incompatibility through monitoring and the use of incentives. The primary benefits of the classic principal-agent relationship are the ability of the principal to distance herself from the negotiations (and if necessary, the agent), the ability of the agent to bring focus and expertise, and the potential for both to use ratification tactics.[3]

The Principal-Agent Continuum

As a first step in creating a new framework for thinking about representation, we take issue with the practice of treating the roles of principals and agents as dichotomous and mutually exclusive. Rather than thinking of principals and agents as distinct types, we think of

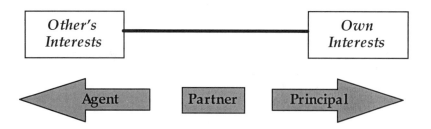

Figure 1.1. The Agent-Principal Continuum

them as being located at opposite ends of a continuum characterized by the mix of interests being advanced by representatives in negotiations. At one end of the continuum, a "pure" agent will strive only to represent the interests of the principal. In this case, just one set of interests are on the table—those of the party being represented. At the other end of the continuum, a principal might represent herself. Once again, just one set of interests are on the table.

What makes this continuum interesting is what happens in the middle. Here we find parties who are legitimately representing their own interests—effectively acting as principals—while at the same time representing others—effectively acting as agents. The result is a mixed set of interests being represented, with the consequent tensions and complexities. We have drawn this continuum in Figure 1.1 based on the mix of interests being represented with the other's interests at one end and one's own interests at the other.

In reality, all representatives will have some independent interests. To the extent that they legitimately seek to advance these separate interests, they move up the continuum from the agency role, ultimately toward acting just on their own interests, in effect becoming a principal. In the middle of the spectrum, representatives act as partners, acting both to serve the priorities established by the principal and to advance their own, though these two goals are inherently in tension.

In the three scenarios outlined in the introduction, the lawyer, union official, and manager are enacting roles that are broadly centered at the three points in this continuum. The lawyer is primarily at the agent end, with a potential range that might reach to the partner role (but rarely beyond that). The elected official often acts as a partner, simultaneously representing the interests of the membership and her own political aspirations. Depending on how this individual enacts her role, it could move closer to the classic agent role or closer to the independent principal role, but it would rarely reach either extreme. Finally, the manager primarily acts as a principal, but her authority over subordinates is incomplete. She must still be concerned about subordinate commitment to any agreement reached, which will involve movement toward some degree of partnership.

In part, the range of roles representatives play on this dimension is shaped by the legal duties, formal positional authority, and customary powers associated with being a lawyer, an elected official, or a manager. The responsibilities of lawyers acting in the role of agent, for example, are well defined as fiduciary duties in the law, and this places strict limits on a lawyer's range of movement on the principal-agent continuum (Reuschlein and Gregory 1979). Similarly, the union official acts within a framework constituted by bylaws that establish the formal powers of elected officers and federal laws concerning a legal duty of fair representation, as well as customs concerning the use of that office. Likewise, the manager comes to the table with considerable authority to make commitments on behalf of subordinates, authority defined by the legal framework of corporate law and the hierarchical structure of the organization.

The Agent-Visionary Continuum

Defining a continuum between agents and principals does not exhaust the range of roles that representatives play in negotiations. In addition to representing a mix of personal and constituent interests, representatives must also seek to align stated constituent preferences with the external constraints and possibilities visible to the representative. When a representative sees a gap between what is possible to achieve in negotiations and the stated desires of constituents, she faces a core strategic choice. At one extreme, she could continue to act in a classic agent role and seek to advance the stated interests articulated by those she represents while knowing full well that this may produce no agreement or a suboptimal one. At the other extreme, she will work to transform constituents' perceptions of their interests.

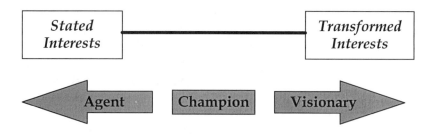

Figure 1.2. The Agent-Visionary Continuum

To the extent that she begins to try to reshape the priorities, perceptions, and even core underlying concerns of those she represents, she is beginning to move along a continuum to a place where she is acting less like a classic agent and more like a visionary leader. This continuum is presented in Figure 1.2, where the range begins with representation of the stated interests of constituents and extends to representatives who are seeking to radically transform constituents' perceptions.

Movement along this continuum involves a twofold process in which constituents voluntarily cede increasing authority to their representative and, at the same time, the representative assumes increasing responsibility for outcomes. If only one of these two processes take place, movement will be constrained. Constituents may cede authority, but a representative has to be willing to assume responsibility. Conversely, a representative can try to take on responsibility but will be able to do so only to the extent that authority is ceded. At one extreme, which we have termed "agent," the authority resides almost entirely with constituents. At the other extreme, which we have termed "visionary," the responsibility has been almost entirely been assumed by the representative. Note that movement along this continuum could involve education or persuasion of constituents by representatives.

In the middle of this continuum, representatives can act as "champions" who advance a mixture of stated constituent priorities and perceived "best interests" of constituents. As the representative moves along the continuum toward the visionary role, she will be increasingly envisioning desirable outcomes, reframing negotiations, and shaping constituent perceptions. At the midpoint, the representative as champion does not act solely on the narrowly stated interests of constituents, but neither does she seek to totally transform these interests.

Implicit in the agent-visionary continuum is a fundamental assumption about the very nature of interests. From a functional/ structuralist perspective, the individual preferences are derived from structural circumstances. Although different sets of interests may be evoked by the way an issue is framed, the core underlying interests are assumed to be fixed. Our analysis takes these structural circumstances into account, but it is also informed by a social constructionist perspective, in which interests are assumed to emerge in a social context. As such, interests are constructed through social discourse, learning, and reflection. In a very real sense, interests can be identified only in retrospect, and these emergent interests may evolve or change dramatically as new realities become salient. Thus, the structural circumstances establish what might be thought of as boundaries within which interests are configured, but the exact alignment within these boundaries is socially constructed.

Recall the three scenarios involving a lawyer, a union official, and a manager. In each of these cases, representatives can move along the continuum from a classic agency role toward that of visionary— increasingly transforming the perceptions of those they represent. In handling a divorce case, the lawyer might move along the continuum from a classic agent role toward being a champion for new ideas by, for example, focusing the attention of her client on the consequences of a protracted battle for the well-being of children. If the client had previously defined the case around retribution, this would involve significant reshaping of the client's perception of his interests.

In the case of the elected union official, realization of the threats of new competition or the inevitability of new technologies may lead the official to focus members on issues of job security and retraining rather than economic gains. As the union official begins to act as a champion for change, she takes on new risks but also increases her potential to enable members to successfully adapt to new realities.

Finally, the manager may go into the budget negotiations and find that the issue at hand is how to implement a plan to reengineer and radically downsize operations. To succeed, the manager will have to realign the perceptions and priorities of subordinates, some of whom may be leaving.

The Agent-Partisan Continuum

The first two dimensions are sufficient to map representational roles when the interests of the represented are monolithic. Naturally, the representative may still represent a mix of her own interests and those of the person she represents (i.e., be somewhere on the agent-principal dimension), and be working to transform their perceptions (i.e., be somewhere on the agent-visionary dimension).

In many representational situations, however, internal interests are more fractious. As the number of people being represented increases, the likelihood that internal interests will be monolithic declines. There may even be multiple internal factions with interests so divided that no agreement can satisfy them all. In such cases, agreement can be reached only if an internal coalition emerges that can enter into an agreement with the other side (or with a compatible coalition in the other side). As a result, positions in the external negotiations emerge from internal negotiations among constituents. When there is serious internal division, representatives may work as partisans in the sense of "colluding" with a subset of constituents to build coalitions around potential agreements (see Putnam 1988 for a discussion of internal-external interactions as a "two-level game").

We therefore can define a third continuum of interests being represented. At one extreme, the representative could be acting in the traditional agent role, representing the interests of a monolithic principal. At the other extreme, the representative acts as a partisan, actively working to build an internal coalition in support of agreement. Movement to the right along this continuum, shown in Figure 1.3, is characterized by increasingly fractious internal negotiations and increasingly active involvement by the representative in the process of coalition building.

In the middle of this continuum, the representative acts as a mediator seeking to build consensus. The goal of the internal mediation is to reach consensus on a negotiating mandate that naturally evolves over time. As the representative moves along the continuum toward the partisan role, she will be taking an increasingly active and partisan role in the process of coalition formation.

Returning to the three scenarios, the divorce lawyer tends to be located toward the left end of the spectrum because she is representing a single (we assume reasonably unconflicted) client. The manager

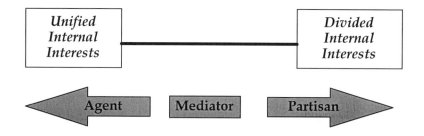

Figure 1.3. The Agent-Partisan Continuum

often plays roles in the middle and upper end of the spectrum, seeking to build consensus among subordinates but potentially having to build coalitions when interests diverge. Because of the size of her constituent base and corresponding internal politics, the union official will tend to play roles on the right end of the spectrum, seeking to mediate an internal consensus if possible and to build coalitions when necessary.

A Representational Matrix

The three continua each share a common anchor around the classic agent role in which the stated interests of a monolithic principal have primacy. Few representatives actually match this ideal or pure type for three reasons. First, some of their own legitimate interests are at play. Second, they work, at least to some degree, to transform stated interests of constituents. Third, they rarely deal with a completely unified constituency.

As a result, it is possible to put the three dimensions together—forming a representational matrix. This matrix allows for the reality that representational roles may vary along multiple dimensions. The matrix, which is presented in Figure 1.4, allows us to map many different representational roles. In fact, the matrix also serves to illustrate some of the dimensions on which interests can vary and thus complicate the work of representatives.

Movement along the first continuum—from representing another's interests to representing one's own—is strongly constrained by

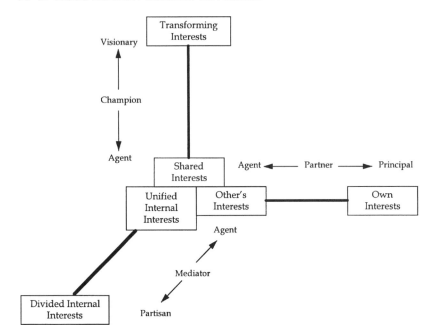

Figure 1.4. The Representational Matrix

structural circumstances. Laws, customs, and role definitions all serve to establish relatively well-defined ranges along the continuum within which a representative will balance personal and constituent interests. More extensive movement along this dimension will primarily happen with restructuring of these laws, customs, and role definitions.

Movement along the second dimension—from representing stated interests to transforming interests—is a consensual process between constituents and representatives. A representative's ability to move along this continuum is a function of motivating external circumstances and informal authority that is rooted in personal capabilities, including expertise, the ability to persuasively reframe issues, charisma, political support, and vision. Constituents' willingness to support their representative's move along this continuum is a function of their understanding of motivating external circumstances, flexibility, and the trust they have in the representative.

Movement along the third continuum—from representing unified interest to representing divided internal interests—is shaped both by the structure of relationships between representative and constituents and by the social construction of internal decision-making processes. Here norms and expectations concerning the representative's role will enlarge or constrain her scope for participating in internal negotiations as a partisan.

In moving within the matrix, representatives may pursue a rich mix of stated constituent interests, perceived underlying constituent and institutional interests, and their own distinct interests. They also may represent monolithic interests or seek to advance the interests of an internal coalition—all depending on the representative role that is being enacted. Often, we can know that they are occupying this role only in retrospect, by observing the patterns of interaction. This means that the roles are not preordained. Instead, they are socially constructed over time and may shift as the negotiations progress (see Rubin and Sander 1988).

 ## FUNDAMENTAL DILEMMAS OF REPRESENTATION

Using the representational matrix as a point of reference, we now turn to some fundamental dilemmas faced by representatives. Given the complex matrix of interests that we have constructed, it is no wonder that representatives face numerous dilemmas. Focusing on underlying dilemmas provides insights into effective strategies for meeting the core challenges of representation. By *dilemma*, we adopt the three-part definition from Ford and Cutcher-Gershenfeld (forthcoming) in which a dilemma involves (1) a choice that is (2) irreversible and (3) has important consequences.

Viewed from the perspective of the representative, movement on each of the three dimensions of our matrix gives rise to an important dilemma. We have termed these

- the trust dilemma,
- the ratification dilemma, and
- the mandate dilemma.

The Trust Dilemma

Every negotiation involves a tension between the integrative and distributive dimensions of an issue, which calls for negotiators to be effective in both creating and claiming value (Lax and Sebenius 1986).

This tension is heightened when representatives enter the picture. As a representative moves horizontally along the grid from the role of classic agent to the role of partner, the representative can be creating or claiming value in ways that focus more on advancing her own interests or those of her partners who are not at the table.

As discussed at the beginning of this chapter, we assume that relationships between representatives and those they represent are mixed-motive in nature. Consequently, some actions in external negotiations will advance shared interests, whereas some will favor the interests of the principal or the representative. The representative may well use her ability to control the process and flows of information to the disadvantage of those she represents, giving rise to the classic principal-agent problem.

The representative also may experience the mirror image of this problem—she may be restrained in her ability to effectively create and claim value for her side because of distrust on the part of those she represents. Her superior access to information about what is going on at the table may paradoxically turn out to be a problem. She cannot convey the full nuance of what happens at the table to those she represents, and the more intensive these efforts to create value are, the greater the likelihood of generating doubt in constituents. Ironically, because she knows more, she is trusted less.

The dilemma can be stated formally as follows:

> *The Trust Dilemma*—If representatives are trusted by constituents, they will be better able to create value, but the more extensively they are involved in creating value, the harder it is to persuade constituents that these activities are appropriately advancing their interests.

This dilemma become more acute as the representative moves from agent to partner and less acute as the representative moves from partner toward being the principal. As a result, the dilemma is most problematic when a representative openly represents a mix of personal and constituent interests.

The Transformation Dilemma

When moving along the vertical continuum from agent through champion to visionary leader, representatives face a second dilemma.

To the extent that the representative is perceived as being *unable* to reshape the interests and positions of her constituents, she is able to portray these needs as rigid and use ratification requirements to support her position and claim value in external negotiations. The problem is that mismatches between stated constituent interests and external realities may lead to no agreement or a suboptimal one, when reshaping would have created joint value.

To the extent that the representative seeks to reshape the interests of her constituents, she will come under increasing pressure from her negotiating counterparts to do so and may be vulnerable to internal criticism. Although she is better able to create value, it is more difficult to support her positions and claim value.

This second representational dilemma might be expressed as follows:

> *The Transformation Dilemma*—The more that a representative seeks to transform the stated interests of constituents, the greater the likelihood of producing an agreement that is responsive to external realties; however, the same efforts to transform stated interests also increase the risk to the representative, either from internal constituents who question legitimacy or from external counterparts who assume yet more capability.

The difficulty in creating value effectively is most acute for the traditional agent. As representatives move vertically toward the champion role, they may be better able to balance creating and claiming because their influence over constituents can be portrayed externally as limited and contingent. As representatives move toward being visionary, their ability to credibly use ratification and internal rigidity to claim value declines, although this may be counteracted by their ability to credibly make commitments that "stick" with constituents.

The Flexibility Dilemma

When moving along the third continuum, from agent through mediator to partisan, the representative confronts the need to understand and reconcile the divergent interests of constituents. This reflects the adage that an overall agreement between sides actually requires three agreements—one between the parties and two within the parties. The dilemma facing a representative is that a broader internal consensus can impose rigidity on external negotiations, while internal disagreement leaves the party vulnerable to being divided and conquered.

If a representative does not push for internal consensus, she will have more flexibility in negotiations but more internal disagreement around a proposed settlement. If the representative pushes for strong internal consensus, she will have less flexibility in bargaining but more internal agreement about a proposed settlement.

The dilemma might formally be stated as follows:

> *The Flexibility Dilemma*—Representatives require sufficient internal agreement to understand the interests they represent and protect against divisive power tactics, but increasingly specific and focused internal agreements will constrain flexibility in external negotiations.

This dilemma becomes more acute as the representative moves along the third dimension from agent to mediator. A pure agent will be least likely to be constrained by this dilemma because she represents monolithic interests. Of course, the agent still needs to have room to bargain and will not want those she represents to serve up nonnegotiable positions. The agent will always want constituents to be more clear about their interests.

A representative who has to reconcile diverse internal interests as a mediator may not want to see internal agreements become too firm or too clearly defined. Rather, she may seek the flexibility to learn about external realities before pressing for internal consensus. At the same time, however, she risks looking unprepared in external negotiations.

As a partisan, the representative may not want an internal consensus at all—preferring instead to build an internal coalition sufficiently supportive to give her flexibility in negotiations. The risk is that success in building the coalition will come at the cost of a broader consensus that would facilitate subsequent implementation of agreements.

In summary, representatives experience different tensions depending on the roles they enact. All relationships between representatives and those they represent are complicated by asymmetrical access to information and limits on control. To the extent that a representative moves from agent toward partner, the trust dilemma becomes more salient. Likewise, a move from agent to champion leads to challenges in balancing value creation and claiming. Finally, the move from agent to mediator results in tension between flexibility and positional strength.

CASE STUDY IN WORKPLACE REPRESENTATIONAL DILEMMAS[4]

To illustrate some of the dilemmas associated with multiple representational roles, we will examine a case example. In this case, we will focus on labor-management relations in the workplace.

The case highlighted here involves a private sector manufacturing plant—the Ford Sterling Plant, which is the company's largest producer of car and truck axles. The plant has more than $1 billion in annual sales, produces more than 10,000 axles a day, and spans more than 3 million square feet of enclosed space. Approximately 3,500 hourly and salaried people work in the plant, with the hourly workers represented by UAW Local 228.

We will examine some of the key representational roles associated with a multiyear initiative in this facility to foster continuous improvement in the work system in the context of what is now termed the Ford Production System. This approach to manufacturing involves organizing production around teams or work groups rather than individual jobs, empowering workers to do their own quality inspection, reducing in-process inventory and other "waste" in the system, moving toward just-in-time delivery with customers and suppliers, and closer integration between new product engineering and manufacturing. These are substantial changes that highlight many representational dilemmas.

Table 1.1 presents three key representatives and their primary roles with various constituents. Each of the three groups—the union bargaining committee, the plant operating committee, and the organizational development group—is a champion, agent, or partner for some stakeholder group. In the analysis that follows, a series of situations will be examined in which some of the dilemmas associated

TABLE 1.1 Selected Representative and Constituent Roles in a
Manufacturing Facility

Representative	Selected Constituents
Bargaining committee	Champions for union membership
	Agent for the region and international union
	Partner with plant operating committee
Plant operating committee	Agent for corporate and divisional management
	Champions for plant employees (hourly and salaried)
	Partner with the union bargaining committee
Organizational development	Agent for union bargaining committee
	Agent for plant operating committee
	Agent of policy decisions associated with the change
	Champions for departments in the change process
	Partner with other resource/change groups

with these multiple concurrent roles are at play. These do not represent all possible combinations of these roles or of the dilemmas, but they illustrate the various ways they interact with one another.

The Trust Dilemma

The union and management pair that serve in an organizational development capacity are constantly confronted with variations on the trust dilemma. The union appointee is seen by a number of outspoken union leaders and members as having moved "into bed" with management. At the same time, his management counterpart is accused by senior managers as being "in the union's hip pocket." These charges are typically intensified whenever either one of these individuals tries to hold his or her own constituents accountable for commitments they have made or otherwise is aggressive in advancing the change process.

In this regard, their roles as internal champions of change are in tension with their roles as agents of their respective organizations. This is a product of the trust dilemma. The more intensively these two individuals do their jobs, the more their own constituents raise questions around the degree to which they can be trusted as representatives advancing the constituent's interests.

The Transformation Dilemma

The management leadership—especially the Human Resource Manager—encountered the transformation dilemma in 1994, shortly after launching the continuous improvement initiative. At that time, the plant was in negotiations with the corporation over possible investment associated with the awarding of a contract to build a new product. As the product was about to be awarded to the plant, the Human Resource Manager was instructed to link the investment to the negotiation of what is termed a "Modern Operating Agreement" (MOA) with the union. This sort of agreement would represent a comprehensive commitment to compressing job classifications, eliminating work rules, imposing a plantwide team-based structure, and linking an ability-based pay system—all highly controversial issues in the union.

Although the proposed investment was large, both union and management leaders in the plant were in agreement that the investment (and the alternative fear of disinvestment) was not sufficiently large to have a plantwide MOA be ratified. As a result, the Human Resource Manager successfully argued with corporate officials that it was better to follow a five-year plan for movement to a new work system, on a department-by-department basis, in which key aspects of the system would be adapted to the specific circumstances of each department.

By transforming the MOA demand from corporate headquarters into a multiyear framework for continuous improvement, management served as an effective champion for the employees and as a reliable partner with the union. At the same time, management assumed a much greater risk in its role as an agent for the corporation. If there were problems with the MOA, corporate officials would have to temper any criticism with the awareness that it was originally a corporate mandate. On the other hand, if there were problems with the continuous improvement approach, the plant leadership would be held to a much higher level of responsibility. There is no right answer in this situation.

The Flexibility Dilemma

The transformation from an MOA into a framework for continuous improvement did not, in itself, create a dilemma for the union. It had few internal or external constituents who favored the MOA concept over a more flexible arrangement. The very flexibility associated with the continuous improvement approach, however, has revealed what we have termed the flexibility dilemma for the union.

Keeping the framework for continuous improvement flexible was preferred by the union precisely because it avoided divisive internal splits among the union members. A vote on an MOA would pit high-seniority workers against low-seniority workers because some of the advantages of seniority around job assignments are eliminated under most MOAs (primarily because of job rotation). Such a vote would also pit workers in departments receiving new products and investment against workers in older departments.

At the same time, the union is now faced with the complicated reality that a more flexible structure requires a constant revisiting of the need for change each time a new department moves into the new work system. Because there isn't a single MOA to point to, the union has to educate people about a long list of policy decisions reached in the course of the multiyear phases of the continuous improvement system. Flexibility prevented splits among constituents, but it also means that ongoing change efforts must be constantly reanchored by demonstrating the need for change.

These three illustrations from the case example help us see the way multiple representational roles are interwoven with the dilemmas. By acting on one representational role—say, that of a champion—a representative may be triggering a dilemma associated with another concurrent role, such as that of a more traditional agent.

▨ SEQUENTIAL AND CONCURRENT REPRESENTATIONAL ROLES

Not only do most representatives play a mixture of roles, but these roles also will often shift as time passes. For example, the head of a governmental agency will sometimes be a champion of the mission of that agency, sometimes an agent protecting taxpayer dollars from waste, sometimes a partner in pursuing her interests jointly with the heads of other agencies, and sometimes a mediator reconciling internal differences.

The sequence in which multiple roles are filled makes an enormous difference. For example, making the transition from agent to champion is very different from the reverse. For an agent to become a champion, that individual shifts from the passive presentation of constituent interests to more aggressive shaping of these interests. This may be seen favorably by constituents, if they see the process as legitimate and as likely to best advance their interests (even as their perception of these interests may be changing). Of course, constituents may find the process uncertain or threatening—all of which will constrain the ability of an agent to become a champion.

The shift from champion to agent can be even more complicated because it involves a scaling back of interactions and affirmative behavior. A champion who is losing political support as a result of being seen as too far out in front of constituents, for example, may be forced to shift into a more passive agency role of merely restating constituent demands. If the champion is no longer actively shaping internal interests and stressing the importance of value creation, then others may emerge to assume the mantle of leadership or the group may descend into a divisive internal claiming game.

The shift from being an agent to being a partner can happen for a number of reasons. An incentive structure designed to align agent interests with those of the principal, for example, can transform a classic agent into a partner with distinct interests of his or her own that are now part of the negotiations. By making an agent into a partner, the principal has more confidence in the vigor that will be exercised by the representative, but the principal must also contend with the reality that no incentive structure will perfectly align principal and agent interests. In this case of the shift to being partners, the mixed-motive nature of the principal-agent relationship becomes more salient.

The shift from mediator to partisan can occur when the representative concludes that internal consensus is not possible but that less-than-unanimous agreement is still more desirable than no agreement. Once a representative has chosen to side with a particular internal coalition, however, it is impossible to return to being a neutral mediator.

The rate and timing of the shifts in representational roles are also important. For example, the leader of a consumer or civil rights movement may shift over many years from being a champion for protective legislation to being an agent, protecting new legal rights. Contrast this with the rapid change required when this same champion leaves a protest demonstration outside the doors of a corporate headquarters to meet with top executives and negotiate a strategic partnership to address the issue.

 ## CASE STUDY IN INTERNATIONAL PEACE MAKING[5]

Efforts to resolve complex international disputes provide a rich context for exploring the dynamics of representation over time. To illustrate this, consider the multiple roles that Shimon Peres played in the Middle East peace process. At various stages in the process, he served as a champion, agent, partner, and partisan.

Champion for Peace

Beginning in the late 1970s, Peres acted as a champion for peaceful accommodation between Israel and its neighbors. In the early 1980s, Peres began to develop the idea of Gaza First as a basis for settlement with the Palestinians and attempted to sell the idea to Anwar Sadat, but he failed. Throughout the 1980s, Peres and his aides worked to develop relationships with moderate Palestinian leaders on the West Bank. In 1987, while foreign minister in the joint Labour-Likud government of "national unity" (1984-1990), he initiated negotiations with King Hussein of Jordan and developed a framework for comprehensive talks, only to see the process undermined by Prime Minister Yitzhak Shamir. In raising the idea of Gaza First and in initiating talks with King Hussein, he was not acting with a firm mandate from constituents but exploring options that he judged to be in the interest of his constituents.

Following the Labour victory in the 1992 elections, Peres resurrected Gaza First, raised the possibility with Prime Minister Yitzhak

Rabin, and, on his own authority, floated the idea in a series of meetings with Egyptian officials. The Egyptians transmitted the idea to the Palestine Liberation Organization (PLO) leadership in Tunis, who subsequently raised it in the secret meetings in Oslo. Gaza plus Jericho First eventually became the foundation for phased transfer of authority from Israel to the Palestinians. In these ways, the efforts to champion peace began to bear fruit.

Agent at the Table

Once Peres had successfully initiated secret negotiations, he had to balance his role as a champion for peace with his role as agent of the Israeli government of Yitzhak Rabin. In a series of tough negotiations, Peres proved himself capable of driving a hard bargain on behalf of his constituents. At the table, Peres was no longer working to frame the agenda as a champion; he was acting as a partisan agent representing his government with a formal mandate. For example, the talks focused on issues such as safeguarding Israeli security, and Peres pressed Yassar Arafat to accept severe restrictions on PLO control over entry into the Gaza and Jericho enclaves and on travel between them.

Partner in the Process

Peres also had to balance his own political and personal interests with those of Yitzhak Rabin and others in the Labour party. Although they were historic rivals for leadership of the party and both had an eye on history, Peres and Rabin successfully forged an alliance to pursue the Oslo agreement. The two men were more powerful together than either might be on his own—this was the key to the partnership. Peres could push the envelope while Rabin served as the reluctant skeptic who would then guarantee that an agreement addressed the security concerns of the Israeli public. Peres later attributed the success of this partnership to the secrecy surrounding the talks, secrecy that permitted the two men to work together without the "echoes" of media commentary to fan the flames of their rivalry. As a result, the commonality of interests in this alliance were strengthened, rather than their differences.

Partisan in Selling the Agreement

Having entered into an agreement, Peres (along with Rabin and others) had to sell it to a highly polarized Israeli polity. There was no chance of gaining broad consensus, and that is why the agreement had been negotiated in secret and presented as a *fait accompli*. Although they succeeded in building a political coalition sufficiently strong to ratify the agreement, this coalition proved very fragile. Having been excluded from the process, hard-line groups on both sides felt justified in using any necessary means to undermine implementation.

Managing Shifting and Overlapping Roles

Peres's ability to balance the roles of agent, champion, partner, and partisan was critical to his success in fostering the Oslo peace process; however, as effective as he was in shifting among representational roles, his early image as a champion and partisan cast a shadow over his subsequent efforts to build internal support for the peace process. His work as a champion left him open to criticism that he was too willing to reach accommodations with Israel's adversaries. While working in partnership with Yitzhak Rabin, a great war hero, Peres was effective as a partner playing the role of strong champion. In the aftermath of Rabin's death, Peres was forced to forestall criticism by abandoning his champion role and defining himself in a particularly narrow, partisan agent role. In initiating severe restrictions on movement in and out of Gaza following the Hamas suicide bombings, in publicly pressing Arafat to crack down, and in aggressively intervening in Lebanon, Peres undoubtedly knew that he was undermining the credibility of the Palestinian National Authority. He was forced, however—for the sake of the survival of his government—to take strong actions to address Israel's security concerns.

Thus, we see that one individual can play multiple roles concurrently and can shift roles over time. Moreover, each of the roles serves to both constrain and enable the enactment of other roles. Some sequential and concurrent patterns of role enactment reinforce the power of the representative, and some undermine it.

CONCLUSIONS

Representation is at once a complicating factor in negotiations and a commonplace occurrence. Most negotiation analysis treats representation from the perspective of the principal or constituent. In making representation the focus of the analysis, we have highlighted a broad range of representational roles that can be mapped on a matrix constructed along three dimensions—each defined around interests. A set of three dilemmas are associated with the dimensions of the matrix, and important considerations are noted around the dynamic shifts that are possible among roles.

By taking a close look at representation along three dimensions, we see that these representational roles both facilitate and constrain the effectiveness of negotiators. The roles provide a framework within which it is possible to assess effectiveness and identify areas for improvement. The roles also may tie the hands of representatives as they face circumstances that call for shifts in behavior.

This analysis should be considered as exploratory. We are just beginning to map the territory required for a full theory of representation. Further research is needed, for example, into common sequences of representational role enactment and the implications of these sequences for both enabling and constraining the ability of representatives to serve effectively in their multiple roles. Even at this stage, however, there are some implications of the analysis for practice and for theory building.

Implications for Practice

Our analysis helps to clarify the challenges representatives face when they enact particular roles. To the extent that representatives move horizontally on the grid from being an agent to being a partner, they can expect to confront the trust dilemma—and have to balance personal gain against relationships with partners. For representatives who enact the role of champion, the central challenge is the transformation dilemma—managing the tensions inherent in being a "double agent" and attempting to shape the perceptions of counterparts and constituents. A move from agent to mediator brings with it the associated flexibility dilemma—the challenge of retaining flexibility internally while bargaining effectively externally and of avoiding perceptions of favoring one faction over another.

In moving from role to role, representatives must be aware that some shifts are much more difficult to achieve than others. The move from agent to champion is not easy but can be accomplished if the representative is prepared to deal with the associated internal tension and questions concerning resolve and ability. By contrast, the move from partisan to mediator may be impossible because the choice to support one internal faction over another is irreversible.

Implications for Theory Building

In the process of examining representational roles, we have defined representation in terms of interests. In this context, it is important to note that this approach points to some complex nuances associated with the classic advice from *Getting to YES* (Fisher and Ury 1981) to "focus on interests, not positions." This concept is a valuable antidote to narrowly conducted positional bargaining, but we have seen that perceptions of interests are in fact a subject of negotiations. We also have seen that when constituents clarify their interests, this can create its own dynamics that facilitate the work of agents but (beyond a certain point) complicate the work of champions. In many ways, the entire concept of principled negotiations is premised on representatives acting as champions, not just as agents and not just as self-interested partners.

Thus, the more interest-based that bargaining becomes, the more complicated are the roles of representatives. In fact, research on interest-based bargaining is increasingly identifying representation issues as a leading cause of their failure (Friedman 1994). Our analysis helps to clarify why this is so. Where representatives attempt interest-based bargaining without complete understanding by constituents, they risk having their "creative" agreements rejected. When they seek the mandate to attempt interest-based bargaining, they risk rejection.

As representatives seek to create and claim value, internally and externally, they face numerous decisions as to what interests are at stake and which interests will be given primacy. The key question of what it means to focus on interests becomes most problematic in the middle of the matrix—when representatives play a role that is a mix of partner, champion, and mediator. This is the common situation in which representatives seek to advance some mix of their own interests and constituent interests, while at the same time attempting to transform constituents' perceptions of their interests and to build internal consensus in support of agreement.

By mapping representative roles along three dimensions, each defined with respect to interests, we may also have raised some deeper questions about the very nature of representation. In the fields of economics and decision sciences, interests are assumed to be fixed, defined by the structure of the negotiation. In the classic principal-agent model of representation, this is manifest in a focus on issues of observability, control, and incentives. There is a further normative assumption that "good" representation primarily consists of fidelity on the part of the agent in pursuing the stated interests of the principal. Our analysis suggests that traditional concepts of agency are an important but incomplete framework for understanding representation in negotiation. Indeed, some of the implications of our analysis may be unsettling to people operating within the principal-agent framework. For example, we highlight the way in which interests are negotiable and socially constructed (via representative roles). We also suggest that the efficiency of outcomes can be increased when interests are transformed by representatives. Efficiency may also be undercut when multiple interests are present or when interests are a source of internal division.

Finally, the very nature of being a representative in negotiations involves the ever-present tension associated with three core dilemmas. Representatives must constantly address ambiguity about whether they are advancing their own interests or those of constituents. They face a continuing challenge around whether to advance interests as stated by constituents or attempt to transform them. Finally, they must balance their desire for internal consensus with the harsh realities of internal splits and the external need for flexibility.

▓ NOTES

1. In some cases, such as sports or entertainment agents, these interests are highly visible. These agents may even court controversy or engage in other behaviors designed to attract future clients—with neutral or negative impli-

cations for the present clients they ostensibly represent. In other cases, agents will go to great lengths to demonstrate the degree to which their interests are aligned with those of their constituents. In international diplomatic negotiations, for example, governmental representatives would reject any charge that they are advancing their personal interests or even the interests of their agency instead of the interests of their government or their nation.

2. As we will see later, the focus on creating options in *Getting to YES* (Fisher and Ury 1981) implicitly promotes a process of shaping the way constituents perceive their interests that reaches far beyond traditional notions of agency.

3. Sometimes representatives are chosen because they are perceived as having greater skill or expertise. Sometimes they are believed to have deeper resolve or commitment. Sometimes the choice reflects the structure of power and authority relations. Sometimes physical distance, time pressure, or sheer numbers of constituents makes it more practical to have representatives negotiate. Sometimes the constituents are at the table—accompanied by their representative.

4. These case data are derived from the past three years, in which Joel Cutcher-Gershenfeld has worked with the parties as a consultant in the change process. Aspects of the case have been presented in a number of public forums, including the 1995 Work In America annual conference. The intervention is being conducted as "action research," in which the organizational development group and the external consultant are maintaining a "road map" record of progress and insights during the change process. Although the data are presented here only for illustrative (not confirmatory) purposes, caution should still be exercised in interpreting the data given the close connection of one coauthor with this change process.

5. These case data are from a study by Michael Watkins and Kirsten Lundberg of the Oslo peace process. For more details, see Lundberg (1996) and Watkins and Lundberg (1998).

REFERENCES

Allison, G. 1971. *Essence of decision: Explaining the Cuban missile crisis.* Boston: Little, Brown.

Fisher, R. and W. Ury. 1981. *Getting to YES.* New York: Penguin Books.

Ford, K. and J. Cutcher-Gershenfeld. Forthcoming. *Reflected learning: New perspectives on the bold visions and harsh realities of organizational learning.* New York: Oxford University Press.

Friedman, R. A. 1994. *Front stage, backstage: The dramatic structure of labor negotiations.* Cambridge, MA: MIT Press.

Lax, D. A. and J. K. Sebenius. 1986. *The manager as negotiator: Bargaining for cooperation and competitive gain.* New York: Free Press.

Lundberg, K. 1996. *The Oslo channel: Getting to the negotiating table. Case #1333.0.* Cambridge, MA: John F. Kennedy School of Government.

Pratt, J. W. and R. J. Zeckhauser, eds. 1985. *Principals and agents: The structure of business.* Cambridge, MA: Harvard Business School Press.

Putnam, R. 1988. Diplomacy and domestic politics: The logic of two level games. *International Organizations* 42(3):427-460.

Raiffa, H. 1982. *The art and science of negotiation.* Cambridge, MA: Belknap Press of Harvard University Press.

Reuschlein, H. G. and A. Gregory. 1979. *Handbook on the law of agency and partnership.* St. Paul, MN: West.

Rubin, J. and F. Sander. 1988. When should we use agents? Direct versus representative negotiations. *Negotiation Journal* 7(4):395-401.

Walton, R. and R. McKersie. 1965. *A behavioral theory of labor negotiations.* Ithaca, NY: ILR Press.

Watkins, M., and K. Lundberg. 1998. Getting to the table in Oslo: Driving forces and channel factors. *Negotiation Journal* 14(2):115-135.

The Shifting Role of Agents in Interest-Based Negotiations

Lawrence E. Susskind

In "Toward a Theory of Representation in Negotiation," Joel Cutcher-Gershenfeld and Michael Watkins argue that "where representatives attempt interest-based bargaining without complete understanding by constituents, they risk having their 'creative' agreements rejected. When they seek the mandate to attempt interest-based bargaining, they risk rejection" (p. 48). If they are right, this is cause for serious concern. Those of us trying to encourage individuals and organizations to shift away from positional bargaining toward a "mutual gains approach" to negotiation would have to think twice about pushing in this direction when agents or representatives are involved.

Cutcher-Gershenfeld and Watkins suggest that representatives or agents face three dilemmas, and these are the cause of "role confusion" that, in turn, makes it hard for agents involved in mutual gains negotiations to succeed. As they say in their chapter, agents must constantly address the ambiguity about whether they are advancing their own interests or those of their constituents. Second, they face a continuing challenge around whether to advance interests as stated by constituents, or instead attempt to transform those interests. Finally, they must balance their desire for internal consensus with the harsh realities of internal splits and the external need for flexibility. I explore each of these dilemmas and argue that they are not really as difficult to handle in practice as Cutcher-Gershenfeld and Watkins suggest.

I think there is substantial evidence that skilled agents deal with these pressures quite effectively most of the time. Moreover, I do not agree with the assertion that "agency" or "representation" is, in and of itself, a particularly significant cause of difficulty in interest-based negotiations. Perhaps the reason we see things so differently is that Cutcher-Gershenfeld and Watkins concentrate heavily on distinguishing among the roles that representatives play in each negotiation, when, in my experience, representatives actually move through a range of roles in each negotiation precisely because that is the way to handle the tensions Cutcher-Gershenfeld and Watkins describe.

WHOSE INTERESTS IS AN AGENT WORKING TO ADVANCE?

Cutcher-Gershenfeld and Watkins frame the "trust dilemma" as follows: If representatives are trusted by constituents, they will be better able to create value, but the more extensively that they are involved in creating value, the harder it is to persuade constituents that these activities are appropriately advancing their interests. This is an extension of what Lax and Sebenius (1986) first called "the negotiator's dilemma"—how to handle the tension between creating and claiming value.

Based on my own practice as a mediator, I've always felt that this tension was overdramatized by Lax and Sebenius as well as by other commentators. If the parties in a negotiation (of any kind) can create sufficient value—well beyond what any of the parties expected at the outset and well above what each of them requires beyond his or her best alternative to negotiated agreement (BATNA)—why should there be a problem working out an acceptable distribution of the value created? It is only when the parties fail to create much value and settle for a total that prevents one or both from exceeding their BATNAs by very much that the task of distributing value becomes difficult.

So, in a simple two-party negotiation (involving agents), the agents are always conscious of how much value they are creating because they are really involved in two simultaneous negotiations—a real one with the parties/agents on "the other side" and a putative negotiation between themselves and their principal(s) about how much of the value created will go to the agent. Thus, agents are always working to advance the interests of their principals because it is in their own interest to do so.

When there is a real trade-off between advancing the interests of the agent and advancing the interests of the principal, I would argue that the agent has no choice but to put the interests of the principal first. If agents fail to do this, they won't be agents for very long. The impact on an agent's reputation of being seen as working to advance his or her own interests at the expense of a principal's interests could be devastating. Working to do this in a surreptitious way would be unethical.

I therefore do not accept the trust dilemma as being particularly difficult. Agents make their reputations by helping their principals "get more" than they ever expected, not by meeting their own needs at the expense of their principals but by working hard to expand the pie. There should not be a substantial conflict between the agent's interests and the principal's interests.

▓ ARE INTERESTS OF PRINCIPALS GIVEN, OR CAN (AND SHOULD) THEY BE TRANSFORMED?

Cutcher-Gershenfeld and Watkins define the "transformation dilemma" as follows: "The more that a representative seeks to transform the stated interests of constituents, the greater the likelihood of producing an agreement that is responsive to external realities; however, the same efforts to transform stated interests also increase the risk to the representative, either from internal constituents who question legitimacy or from external counterparts who assume yet more capacity" (p. 37). Why would an agent or a representative try to transform the stated interests of his or her constituents? I can think of two reasons. First, the agent might acquire new information that leads the agent to realize that the principal has made a miscalculation. Perhaps a key assumption on which the principal's priorities were based is wrong. Second, the agent might realize that his or her own (unstated, selfish) interests can be met only by convincing the principal to recalibrate his or her interests.

Cutcher-Gershenfeld and Watkins talk about representatives who see themselves as champions or visionaries (as opposed to traditional agents), but I question the significance of these distinctions. Either you represent someone or you don't. A union negotiator must (by law) represent the interests of the rank and file. A diplomat represents the interests of his or her country (or, at least, the government in power). Representatives who think they know better what the interests of their constituents are than do the constituents themselves probably should run for office. At the very least, they should seek a different role.

If the principal has made a miscalculation, it is the agent's responsibility to help the principal see that such is the case. If the principal (or the constituency) doesn't agree with the agent's analysis, I believe the agent must either resign or move forward in a fashion consistent with the mandate he or she has received. Any attempt to subvert the interests of the principal in favor of the selfish interests of the representative would, I believe, be unethical and entirely unacceptable, regardless of how ennobled the agent believes his or her vision to be.

To some extent, I think that Cutcher-Gershenfeld and Watkins are really talking about positions, not interests. I can imagine a great many situations in which an agent quickly realizes that his or her principal's interests will be better served if the principal will back off from a publicly stated position and give the agent more room to maneuver. This is not, however, about transforming interests. Although interests can be informed through the give-and-take that occurs during the process of negotiation, it is not usually the case that information is revealed that causes the hierarchy of basic interests and values to shift. More often than not, interests (i.e., priorities) are static. For these reasons, I don't think the transformation dilemma is a serious problem.

HOW SHOULD INTERNAL DIFFERENCES WITHIN A CONSTITUENCY BE HANDLED?

Cutcher-Gershenfeld and Watkins frame the "flexibility dilemma" in these terms: "Representatives require sufficient internal agreement to understand the interests they represent and protect against divisive power tactics, but increasingly specific and focused internal agreements will constrain flexibility in external negotiations" (p. 38). I see this problem as the most serious of the three they raise. I think they are exactly right in their formulation of the difficulty facing any representative or agent; however, there are several things that agents and representatives can do to handle this tension.

First, agents need to do what all skilled negotiators do (and what Roger Fisher and Wayne Davis spell out in their chapter in this volume). They must segment the negotiation into at least two parts: an inventing phase that is primarily cooperative and a committing phase that is more likely to be predominantly competitive. During the early stages of any negotiation, agents should be willing to explore wildly different options without implying any commitment. This is best accomplished by agreeing to ground rules that clearly distinguish between the exploration of alternatives and the formulation of binding commitments. Once such ground rules are in place, an agent should have complete flexibility during the early stages of a negotiation.

As the negotiation comes to a close, it is natural to move toward a narrow formulation of the final agreement. By this time, however, if an agent has done his or her job, internal disagreements within the constituency should have been worked out or bridged, usually by adding to the overall package that the agent must have to reach agreement with the other side. Prior to starting the negotiation, an agent should have worked with his or her principal(s)—regardless of how internally diversified—to formulate a clear statement of the principal's (i.e., constituency's) BATNA and its interests. Options considered along the way should be presented for review by the principal (or the constituency). Before any final agreement is reached, internal disagreements within the constituency (and with the agent) should be worked out. Such differences should not be allowed to compromise the agent at the point at which commitments must be made.

A second way of handling the flexibility dilemma is to insist on a contingent agreement. If there are disagreements within the principal's side (i.e., constituency) based on different forecasts of what is likely to occur in the future (or different risk orientations), contingent agreements can be used to cover a range of possible futures. In this way, internal disagreement within the principal's side can be handled without undermining the flexibility the agent requires.

A skilled agent or representative knows how to broker agreement internally on what the principal's BATNA and interests are. With internal agreement in hand, the agent enters the value-creating stage of a negotiation with substantial flexibility. As interesting options and a provisional package begin to take shape, the agent takes these back to the principal for review. Further internal mediation may be necessary. Contingent agreements may be used to bridge remaining internal disagreements. In the end, there should not be a need to constrain flexibility in the external negotiations as a means of coping with internal disagreements.

THE SHIFTING ROLE OF AGENTS IN INTEREST-BASED NEGOTIATION

At the outset of any negotiation, an agent needs to be a clearheaded analyst, helping his or her principal deal with internal disagreements, examining the BATNA, and clarifying interests. The agent and the principal ought to talk honestly about overlaps and possible divergences in their interests. During negotiations, an agent ought to be unabashedly partisan on behalf of his or her principal's interests, in part because the agent's interests will almost always be well served by such a strategy. Because the early phase of any negotiation should be focused on creating as much value as possible, however, agents ought to be collaborative in their styles, each helping the "other side" create as much value as possible.

During the later stages of a negotiation, an agent must be in close contact with his or her principal(s). When commitments are sought (whether in a contingent form or not), these must be clearly understood by the principal (or factions in the principal constituency). Commitments must be made by the principal and not just the agent. For example, if the agent thinks the principal is making a mistake (or clinging to misguided interests), that should be discussed. In the end, an agent (of whatever type) must be accountable to his or her principal and must put the principal's interests first. These are the key steps in an interest-based or mutual-gains-style negotiation. In the final analysis, I see nothing to suggest that interest-based negotiations will be more difficult if agents are involved.

I am impressed with Cutcher-Gershenfeld and Watkins's effort to broaden and deepen our thinking about the roles that representatives play in various types of negotiations. All told, they examined seven different roles: advocate, partner, principal, agent, champion, visionary, and mediator. I think it will help us build a more robust theory of negotiation if we keep all these roles in mind. I do not believe, though, that the involvement of agents makes it particularly difficult to move toward a more interest-based approach to negotiation or dispute resolution. Although agents or representatives can, and probably should, play a variety of roles, all the roles described by Cutcher-Gershenfeld and Watkins call for behaviors that are consistent with the key steps in a mutual gains approach to negotiation.

 REFERENCE

Lax, D. A. and J. K. Sebenius. 1986. *The manager as negotiator: Bargaining for cooperation and competitive gain*. New York: Free Press.

Authority of an Agent

When Is Less Better?

Roger Fisher
Wayne Davis

This book proceeds from the premise that negotiations through an agent are the norm, not the exception. We can safely assume that in most such cases, the principal expects to get better results through use of an agent or at least to incur lower transaction costs than if he handled the negotiation personally. Principals carry this optimistic expectation, in most cases reasonably so, despite the considerable risks and difficulties discussed elsewhere in this volume.

Nevertheless, every principal faces the challenge of how to instruct the agent so as to maximize the agent's prospects of achieving on behalf of the principal the best possible results in the negotiation. Although there are many dimensions to the challenge of instructing agents, in this chapter we focus on the subset that often produces the most anxiety for principals and agents alike: the authority of the agent to make commitments on the principal's behalf.

Conventionally, most principals ask themselves the question, "How much authority should I grant the agent?" We believe that this framing of the instruction question is counterproductive, leading principals down a path that yields unhelpful answers. Instead of seeing authority as an essentially static instruction given at the outset of the negotiation, we suggest that a principal should calibrate and recalibrate an agent's authority over the course of the negotiation, in proportion to the level of learning achieved by both agent and principal around the interests, options, standards of legitimacy, and alternatives to agreement that shape the eventual outcome of the negotiation. We develop an illustrative template to demonstrate how this concept could work in practice.

In addressing this question, we will assume that the situation is one in which the answer to the authority question is *not* easy or obvious. We can, for example, imagine a variety of conditions in which a principal might readily grant the agent broad authority. These include, for example, low stakes or simple, one-issue transactions; time-urgent transactions in which the principal is unreachable; or transactions in which the principal and agent have extensive experience with each other and the principal has a high degree of trust in the agent.

Conversely, there are times when the principal obviously should grant very narrow authority. Such might be the case where the agent is inexperienced (as is frequently the case when employees, new to a position or situation, negotiate on their firm's behalf) or where there is obviously a strong divergence of interests between principal and agent. The latter situation occurs every time a car salesman offers to be the buyer's agent in negotiating with the sales manager for another $300 price concession.

We are concerned with the more complex situation where the principal faces a genuine dilemma about how best to instruct the agent.

THE TWO DIMENSIONS OF AUTHORITY

A principal typically grants authority to an agent along two critical dimensions: commitment and communication. First, the principal may authorize the agent to make some class of commitments on his behalf that the principal will honor. The class is defined by subject matter (e.g., purchase of real estate lot X), quantity or quality of the medium of exchange (e.g., up to $120,000), and degree of commitment (e.g., tentative, subject to the principal's approval). Of course, this quickly gets complicated as the number of possible issues expands.

The granting of such authority implies its limits. The agent's authority to make a contingent offer to buy Lot X does not include the authority to buy Lot Y, or to offer an equity share in the principal's business in lieu of cash payment, or to make a binding commitment.

Additionally, the principal implicitly or explicitly authorizes the agent to disclose or directs the agent specifically not to disclose certain information. Such instructions frequently revolve around possible commitments (e.g., whether the principal would be willing to consider a long-term lease in addition to outright purchase) and the principal's interests, priorities, intentions, financial condition, or identity.

In this chapter, we focus primarily on commitment authority as the critical variable and consider what kind of communication strategy might flow from it.

THE AUTHORITY INSTRUCTIONS DILEMMA

The essence of an agency relationship is that the principal gives *some commitment* authority to the agent. Principals thus tend to frame the practical question: How much authority should I give the agent? This framing poses dilemmas for both the principal and the agent, and even for the other side.

From the Principal's Perspective

The principal fears granting both too much and too little authority. If the principal grants the agent broad authority, the principal runs several risks. The agent may not try hard to understand the interests and preferences of the principal, because a broad range of solutions seems to be acceptable. The agent may not negotiate vigorously for a better deal once he finds a solution within the range of acceptability. The agent may feel less constrained about pursuing his own interests that conflict with the principal's, because he may well be able to do so and still "deliver" an acceptable solution. Thus, if the principal grants broad authority, the principal may get a deal that is minimally acceptable (i.e., better than the principal's best alternative to negotiated agreement, or BATNA), but far from the most favorable that might have been achieved.

On the other hand, the principal should be wary of granting too little authority. The agent may reject solutions that were not within the scope of his authority, thereby ending the negotiations without agreement, even though the proffered solution was in fact better than the principal's BATNA. Narrow instructions may also limit the agent's practical ability to explore creative solutions outside the scope of the original information and thinking that informed the instructions. Finally, an agent with narrow authority may be seen by the other side as lacking credibility; the other side may therefore decline to deal seriously with the agent.

From the Agent's Perspective

The agent also fears being accorded too little authority. The agent, of course, does want to be taken seriously by the other side. Moreover, the agent does not want to be prevented from exercising his creativity, flexibility, and professional judgment to get the best possible deal. After all, a not-so-great deal is more likely to be blamed on the agent and his performance (and thereby damage the agent's reputation) than it is to be blamed on the principal for giving overly restrictive instructions. The agent may also fear that narrow instructions evidence the principal's lack of trust or confidence in the agent. The agent may fear that the principal intends to micromanage the agent and that the agent will have to endure a series of difficult and high transaction cost renegotiations of instructions over the course of the negotiations.

Although at first thought the agent may wish for broad authority, the agent may upon reflection recognize that broad authority can be dangerous too. The agent may be getting set up: Whatever he agrees to will be roundly criticized by the principal, and he will be blamed for having agreed to it. Indeed, the principal may go further and repudiate the agreement, which could be particularly damaging to the agent's reputation, credibility, and future effectiveness.

From the Other Side's Perspective

The other side, whether represented directly or by an agent, also has a stake in this question. If our agent has been given too broad authority, the other side runs what might be termed a compliance risk. Our principal may repudiate the deal or may not fully implement it if the principal feels the agent went too far. Nor does the other side want our agent to have narrow authority. The other side may fear, justifiably, wasting time and effort with an agent who appears to lack information and cannot "speak authoritatively," that the negotiation will need to be repeated anyway directly with the principal, or that the principal will demand a "second bite at the apple."

Thus, the principal faces a dilemma in trying to answer the question, "How much authority should I give the agent?" Any answer seems to require a delicate balancing act. The principal can, at best, attempt to strike the best balance and rely on the good judgment of the agent. For example, the principal might tell a highly trusted agent, "You have as much authority as you think you ought to have." In the absence of that level of trust, however, the principal can avoid the dilemma in the first place by reframing the authority question.

 ## DIAGNOSES: TOWARD A DIFFERENT QUESTION

Before suggesting a different question, let us first consider how the conventional question leads both principals and agents astray. We must do so by examining the type of answer it produces. Typically, a principal will answer the question, "How much authority?" by directing the agent along the following lines:

> *Sales manager to sales representative:* "List price for the machinery is $83,000. You can settle for anything above $78,000. Reject anything below $75K; come back and check with me first if it's going to be in the $75-$78K range."

> *Baseball player to sports agent:* "I'd like a long-term deal—preferably 4 or 5 years, but no less than 3. See if you can get me $2.5 million a year. They've got to pay me better than $2M—that's what the Dodgers just signed Jackson for, and my numbers are better than his. I'll go for free agency if they can't beat that."

This fairly typical answer can be generalized as

> "My ideal solution would be value I. You have authority to settle for any package whose value to me is better than A; anything between R and A, please come back and check with me first. Anything less than R should be rejected. It is simply unacceptable—I'll go to my BATNA."

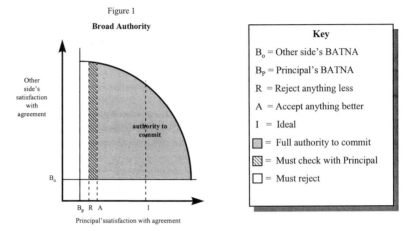

Figure 1

Broad Authority

Figure 2.1. Broad Authority

"Broad authority" means that, at the time instructions are given, out of the set of reasonably anticipated possible solutions, many would appear to be at least as good as A, and the agent may commit to them. "Narrow authority" means that many of those possible solutions are excluded—the agent may not commit. In the conventional depictions relative to the Pareto, or Possibilities, Frontier, these might be represented graphically as in Figures 2.1 and 2.2.

Point B_p represents the value satisfaction equivalent of the principal's BATNA—the point at which the principal would be indifferent between an agreement and his BATNA. In setting the reservation value of R and the "check-back" range between R and A, the principal is attempting to manage what we might call *judgment risk*: the possibility that the agent will commit to something that the principal would not have, had the principal been there at the negotiation. For example, if our machinery salesman is paid a commission based on revenue rather than profitability, we might surmise that a wily sales manager is thinking along the lines of Figure 2.2. She sets a reservation value ($75,000) that is high relative to her true walkaway point (perhaps $68,000) out of fear that the salesman will too quickly lower the price to close the deal, rather than negotiate more vigorously and maintain a better profit margin. Conversely, if the sales manager perceives no judgment risk (i.e., she has total trust in the salesman's intentions and

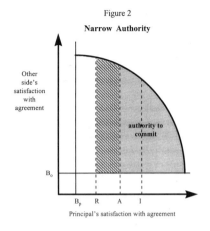

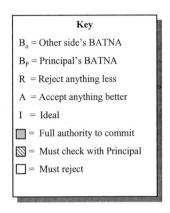

Figure 2.2. Narrow Authority

confidence in his abilities), then she should set the reservation value at her BATNA. In Figure 2.1, Point R would move to Point B_P.

For our purposes, it does not matter whether the judgment risk arises from misaligned incentives, the agent's incomplete knowledge of the principal's preferences, the principal's incomplete understanding of the stakes being negotiated on his behalf, or some other reason. Whatever the cause, the principal's attempt to moderate the judgment risk by giving this type of instruction produces a potentially more severe risk: that of making premature, ill-informed decisions that diminish the likelihood that the agent will produce outcomes more favorable to the principal.

In any but the most simplistic, one-issue negotiations, any description of the various settlement points R, A, and I requires the principal to make assumptions about the vast array of options (possible terms and conditions that might be agreed to), choose trade-offs among them, and then express those in the relatively simple form of discrete positions on a few key, typically quantifiable, issues.

Intelligent prediction of the options and how they will play out requires, in turn, a good understanding of the interests of both sides, the alternatives to negotiated agreement available to each, and some tactical prediction of how the other side is likely to negotiate. The more complex the negotiation, the less likely the principal and agent *early in the negotiation process* are to possess good information and insight on these factors. When the principal is ignorant in this way, the conventional form of instructions can be dangerous.

Consider our machinery sales example. The instructions address, logically enough, what appears to be the obviously most important issue of price. Such situations, however, often have hidden subagendas around timing. The purchasing company may want delivery earlier or later to fit into production schedules; it may prefer payment to be made earlier or later—independent of delivery and installation—to fall in or out of a budget cycle or to match available cash flow. On the seller's side, both the salesman and the sales manager may have interests around the timing of when the sale is booked, relating to their sales plan. None of these interests would likely be "more important" than price in a roughly $70,000 transaction, yet they could easily swing the deal a few thousand dollars in either direction—a significant proportion of the possible variance between "broad" and "narrow" instructions. The impact could be even greater with the addition of other issues such as warranties, service, and financing.

Such nuanced, interest-based possibilities are not captured in the original instructions as given. Because the principal worries about the risk of an improper commitment, his instructions focus naturally on commitment around the most salient issue, price. Much less salient for the principal—and therefore less likely to find its way into instructions—are the nonobvious interests of the other side. Unfortunately, any negotiation, with or without agents, is *more* likely to produce a positional bargaining process and *less* likely to produce Pareto optimal outcomes to the extent that the negotiators make and commit themselves to early decisions about the specifics of an "acceptable" agreement. With an agent, the more specific the principal in articulating the position, the more likely the agent is to try to satisfy that term—rather than to satisfy the underlying interest. In essence, positional instructions given from principal to agent tend to beget positional negotiations.

Such positional instructions are counterproductive in other ways. They tend to subvert or at least handicap the information or expertise advantages of the agent. Presumably, the principal is expert on the *what* of his or her own interests, whereas the agent is expert (or more cost-efficient) on *how* to satisfy those interests. The more specifically the principal instructs the agent on possible terms, however, the

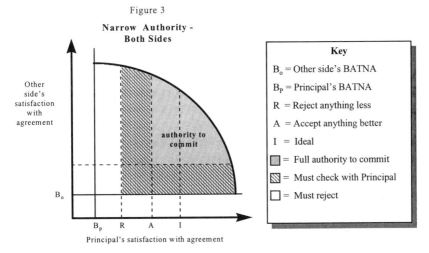

Figure 3

Narrow Authority - Both Sides

Figure 2.3. Narrow Authority on Both Sides

more the principal discourages the agent from exploring creative, value-generating ways of satisfying those interests. When the agent learns new information that suggests the original instructions ought to be reconsidered, he is likely to consider the risks and transaction costs of seeking new instructions from the principal. The more specific—and positional—the original instructions, the greater the transaction costs of renegotiation the agent may anticipate. This, in turn, is likely to inhibit the agent's creativity in the course of the negotiation. In effect, the agent declines to explore even modestly "out of bounds" ideas because he considers it likely that the principal will reject them anyway.

Finally, all these risks get multiplied when the other side negotiates through an agent as well. As Figure 2.3 illustrates, if both sides use agents, give positional instructions, and try to mitigate the judgment risk by giving narrow instructions, the range of solutions that will seem "acceptable" to them will be far fewer than is actually the case, considering the BATNAs of the respective principals.

Although the remaining acceptable solutions in Figure 2.3 are better for one or both principals than those excluded, they will likely be more difficult to find. The search may be complicated if both agents adopt a positional, rather than interest-based, approach to the negotiation. The result may be no agreement, even though many agreements were possible that would have been better for both sides than their respective BATNAs.

In summary, the problem with the conventional question "How much commitment authority should I give?" is that the answers it tends to produce push both principal and agent into "early" commitment, prior to sufficient learning in and from the negotiation process.

▨ GENERAL APPROACH

Our analysis suggests that the principal needs to add two dimensions to his thinking about instructing the agent: learning and timing. A more useful framing of the authority question might be along these lines:

> How should I adjust the commitment authority level of the agent over the course of a negotiation?

We believe that the principal should generally grant the agent no authority to make a binding commitment on any substantive issue at the outset and then grant increasing levels of authority, over time, in proportion to the level of learning (information development and strategic and tactical insight) developed by the agent and shared with the principal. The details of this approach are elaborated below.

1. *At the outset of a negotiation, the agent should have no authority to make a binding commitment on any substantive issue in the negotiation.* It is our current belief that the first stages of a negotiation are most likely to be constructive if it is understood by both sides that *nothing* said constitutes a binding substantive commitment. We believe this to be true for principals. It is also true—and somewhat easier to arrange—for agents.

Why remove commitment authority completely? Commitment authority imposes a heavy strategic and tactical burden on the negotiators. When either side possesses such authority, there is a strong, natural tendency for the negotiators to frame their communications in terms of what would and would not be acceptable terms of an offer. They focus on careful calibration of their own words and deeds to communicate the right nuance about acceptable settlements without inadvertently "giving anything away." Simultaneously, they vigilantly attend to the other negotiator's words and deeds to try to fathom the shape of a possible offer. This introduces a level of formality and tension to the negotiation that is not conducive to the development of an effective working relationship between the negotiators and an environment in which flexibility and creative problem solving occur. Removal of substantive commitment authority enables the agent to focus on other aspects of the negotiation process that will yield better results.

2. *At the outset, the agent should have discretion to design and begin to develop an effective overall negotiation process.* Here, we suggest giving the agent wide latitude to exercise his best professional judgment to design an effective negotiating process, subject only to the constraint that the process commitments not be inconsistent with the overall approach recommended here.

Because the basic approach is predicated on an evolving negotiation with considerable learning occurring, we would expect the agent to devise with the other side a structure for the negotiations that would proceed thorough a series of stages appropriate to the subject matter. For a complex, multi-issue negotiation, these stages might include the following:

■ Initial exploration—identification of issues and exploration of interests

■ Option generation—creation of a range of possible agreements or parts of an agreement that might accommodate the interests of the principals on a given issue

■ Template development—preparation of a single draft of a complete agreement with lots of blanks in it as the skeletal structure of a possible agreement

■ Contingent approval of some details—the negotiators fill in the blanks with numbers, dates, or other specific terms, with acceptance of any one term contingent on acceptability of all other terms and approval of the final draft by the principals

■ Closure—the agents settle on a draft final package to recommend jointly to their principals

■ Ratification—exchange of binding commitments

This breakdown is, of course, illustrative and would be modified to meet the exigencies of a particular situation. For example, an agent for an author who has written a potential blockbuster novel may well begin the negotiations with an auction among competing publishers to fix the commitment around basic financial terms, followed by staged negotiations to complete the details of the agreement.

Besides structuring the negotiation in this formal sense, we would expect the agent at the outset to work on the communication and relationship aspects of the negotiation process. Specifically, the agent would establish unconditional, two-way communication that is easy, open, regular, and frequent. We would also expect the agent to build and continue to improve a side-by-side working relationship with his counterpart.

3. *The principal should focus the substantive portion of the instructions on his interests, priorities, and alternatives, rather than on "settlement points."* As we have seen, the principal's premature commitment to specifying acceptable and unacceptable solutions tends to misdirect the agent's attention. Instead, the principal should articulate his interests as clearly as he can and indicate relative priorities among the interests. The principal will also want to give some indication of the available alternatives to agreement and assess how well they do (or don't) meet his interests. Of course, this aspect of the instructions is not just a one-way street of the principal "telling" the agent. Often, the principal will rely on the agent to help the principal understand exactly what alternatives might be available, assess the interests that might be implicated, and pose questions to help the principal think through priorities and trade-offs.

Some principals may worry that, by merely stating interests and not providing a specific target point, the agent will not be sufficiently motivated to negotiate vigorously and aggressively on the principal's behalf. We believe this concern may best be met by establishing firm expectations around meeting interests, rather than by setting an artificially aggressive bottom line. To the extent that the principal still feels uneasy, more frequent checks with the agent would be appropriate.

4. *The principal should establish clear expectations about the quality and frequency of reporting from the agent.* Because the agent's authority in subsequent stages depends on the *principal*'s learning, a key element

of the initial instructions must be the what and when of further principal-agent interactions. Although such midnegotiation discussions are fairly typical, they too often revolve around reporting the offers and counteroffers and planning more of the same. Instead, we recommend a broader discussion, with the agent reporting on the other side's interests and alternatives, any information that might lead the principal to reconsider his interests or BATNA, possible options and template(s) for agreement, persuasive standards, expected process to completion, and the agent's recommendation of how much authority would be useful to have in the next stage and why. Such a report provides the principal with a much richer understanding of the negotiation so that further instructions can be more nuanced and interest-based, rather than blunt and positional.

5. *As the agent and principal gain information and insight through the negotiation process, the agent's authority should gradually expand.* Neither the principal's agent nor the other side will want to continue the negotiations for very long unless the agent has the authority to disclose what he is prepared to recommend to the principal and what weight he expects the principal to give a joint recommendation. As both principal and agent learn more about what is and is not possible to achieve in the negotiation, the principal can grant greater authority to the agent, with greater confidence that bad decisions will not result. In complex negotiations, the ultimate limit of the agent's authority should probably be authorization for the agent to commit with the other side jointly to recommend a package to their respective principals, with the agent specifically authorized to indicate his genuine belief that the principal is likely to accord the recommendation great weight. At first glance, this seems like relatively limited authority, because the principal can reject the recommendation; however, in a complex negotiation that has stretched out over some period of time, with known (to the other side) consultations between principal and agent, such a joint recommendation carries the implicit message that the agent believes the package is both better than the principal's BATNA and likely to be accepted. Rejection at this stage carries potential reputation costs to both principal and agent and may make subsequent negotiations fairly difficult. Hence, this granting of authority, although limited in the sense of not being complete, is real and significant. Table 2.1 illustrates how this overall approach operates.

TABLE 2.1 Possible Instructions to an Agent

Negotiation Element	Negotiation Phase				
	Interest Exploration	Option Generation	Template Development	Contingent Approval	Closure
Interests	— Disclose principal's (but not principal's priorities) — Seek information on other side's		Discretion to disclose principal's priorities if: — Sufficient trust *and* — Necessary to find joint gains		Not applicable
Options	Partial exploration of possibilities	— Propose without commitment — Explore without commitment any standard proposed by any party	— Explore — Reject — Advocate for any option		Not applicable
Legitimacy	Explore possible standards	— Propose without commitment — Explore without commitment any option proposed by any party	— Explore — Reject — Advocate for any standard		Not applicable

	Explore other side's	— Explore other side's / — Disclose own as appropriate	— Improve own / — Diminish other side's, as appropriate		Not applicable
Alternatives	Explore other side's				Not applicable
Substantive commitments	None	— Recommend that principal consider certain options or — Commit to a single negotiating text to be submitted to all principals for criticism	Provisionally agree to a working template, subject to later changes and filling in blanks	Provisionally agree to specific terms, contingent on acceptability of all other terms and approval of final draft by principal	— Personal commitment to recommend package to principal or — Maximum legal authority (but not to be exercised unless transaction costs of final check with principal exceed benefits)
Process commitments	Discretion to commit to negotiating processes not inconsistent with overall approach				

NOTE: Degree of learning increases across the table from left to right.

6. *The instructions should be put in writing and shown to the other side.* To reduce the risk of misunderstanding and confusion, the agent should be given clear, written instructions to define what he should do and the kind of commitments he has authority to make. Table 2.1 provides a useful starting point for such instructions. To reduce the risk of misunderstanding, these basic instructions should be shown, and a copy given to the other side. This should help allay the other side's justifiable concerns about being "set up" by dealing with someone who appears to lack authority.

Of course, the principal may also want to give the agent other instructions which would be kept confidential. These might include the principal's priorities and trade-offs among interests and information about his alternatives. Whether and when to disclose such information is a critical tactical decision that will vary from situation to situation, whether or not agents are involved. Illustrative written instructions are contained in the Appendix.

7. *Establish disclosure authority.* The other great fear that the principal may have is that the agent will inappropriately disclose information to the other side. Much of that fear revolves around disclosure of "bottom lines" or reservation values. For example, a seller may fear that her real estate agent may encourage a buyer to submit a bid at $5,000 less than the asking price, saying "I think she [the seller-principal] will accept it." The principal worries that the agent will "give away the store" (or most of it) simply to get a quick deal—knowing that the principal will take it because it is slightly better than his bottom line.

Both principals and agents should recognize that in multi-issue negotiations, there is no one "bottom line." The minimum figure acceptable on one issue, such as price, will depend on what is proposed on other issues, such as credit, interest rate, closing dates, warranties, and restrictions. The principal should resist any temptation to simplify the agent's task by specifying a single figure on one issue as representing what would be an acceptable outcome. Instead, the principal should at the outset explain *what* her walkaway alternatives are, but should avoid quantifying those alternatives or reducing them to a single dimension.

Later, as the shape and possible terms of an agreement emerge and the principal gains greater confidence in the negotiating stance of the agent, the principal can be more specific in comparing proposed terms and an emerging package to the alternatives to agreement. If the principal is still concerned that, notwithstanding such interest-based instructions, the agent might still inappropriately "estimate" the principal's "bottom line," an explicit warning against such disclosure would be appropriate.

Sometimes, principals will use an agent for the express purpose of hiding the principal's identity. As a general rule, we would advise principals not to seek to hide their identity behind the veil of an agent. Such tactics may cause needless fear and anxiety for the other side that, in turn, can make it more difficult for the agent to establish an effective working relationship in the negotiation. The tactic can also impose higher transaction costs, both by making the negotiation more difficult and in implementation of an agreement, because the other side may reasonably demand assurances or guarantees that the hidden principal can and will deliver on whatever commitments are being given. Nevertheless, there will be situations where the benefits of nondisclosure of the principal's identity may outweigh such risks and costs. The most common benefits principals seek to achieve are these:

■ *To avoid a situation where the other side might be induced to negotiate differently, based on the principal's identity.* For example, a wealthy individual buying property may be concerned that a seller might demand a higher price simply because he thought the buyer could afford it.

■ *To avoid causing harm in related activities or linked negotiations.* For example, a developer trying to assemble a contiguous parcel from several adjacent lots may need to have a series of negotiations with individual property owners and could reasonably fear that disclosure in early negotiations would increase the risk of holdout tactics in subsequent negotiations. In other situations, premature disclosure of a move would cause public relations or competitive harm.

Under these types of circumstances, the principal may wish to instruct the agent to keep his identity hidden. To minimize the potentially negative impact on the agent's ability to build a sense of trust with his counterparts, it helps to give the agent the discretion to explain that the principal prefers to keep his identity confidential, to acknowledge that that may cause some concern for the other side, and to offer to work with them to allay whatever concerns they may have.

Even with these cautions, the cost-benefit analysis for a principal considering such secrecy can be tricky, as Harvard University recently learned. Over the past nine years, it remained hidden behind an agent while it acquired a series of properties in a neighborhood adjacent to the Harvard Business School. Harvard used the agent both to purchase and to manage the properties, so that sellers would not demand too high a price from their "rich neighbor." Although the strategy appears to have accomplished that tactical objective, it produced a public relations nightmare when the university's holdings were publicly revealed. Harvard's public relations officer was described in *The Boston Globe* as admitting that "the school was guilty of a 'breach of trust.' " Boston Mayor Thomas Menino sent a letter to Harvard President Neil Rudenstine pledging to protect the neighborhood from "major disruptions due to rampant institutional expansion" ("Harvard Says," 1997, p. A1). If and when Harvard begins to develop these properties, it may face a hostile and mistrusting neighborhood, backed by the mayor, capable of delaying the project and driving up Harvard's costs. These costs could erode any of the savings achieved through use of the agent to hide Harvard's identity.

WHY THIS APPROACH IS IN EVERYONE'S BEST INTERESTS

We began by showing how the conventional question of how much commitment authority should be given to an agent produces unsatisfactory answers for the principal, the agent, and the other side. The approach described above reduces or eliminates most of those difficulties.

From the Principal's Perspective

The principal's greatest fear—that the agent will commit to an unwise deal—is substantially mitigated. The principal can calibrate the agent's authority as he sees how the negotiation is proceeding, what the agent is doing, and how well he is doing it. By gradually expanding the agent's authority, the principal also protects against the risk of being too restrictive and denying the agent the flexibility and credibility needed to be effective. Most important, this approach tends to encourage the agent to pursue an interest-based rather than positional approach, which should itself help produce a better out-come for the principal.

From the Agent's Perspective

The agent worries that he will have too little authority to be able to do his job well, or be given too much authority that might lead to an embarrassing repudiation by the principal. In the suggested ap-proach, the agent lacks authority when that is tactically most useful—during early-stage information exchange and brainstorming of options—and gains greater authority as the ultimate agreement takes shape, when that is tactically most useful. Frequent consultation with the principal and the use of interest-based instructions reduce the like-lihood that the agent will produce an agreement that the principal will reject.

From the Other Side's Perspective

In negotiating with an agent, the other side worries that the agent may lack the flexibility to bargain and that the agent's lack of authority will necessitate further negotiations directly with the principal. If the principal follows the approach suggested here—especially the advice concerning sharing of written instructions to the agent—then the other side has greater assurance that it is dealing with "the right person." The other side's time and effort are being well spent with an agent who *will* be able to speak definitively when the time comes. There will be much less likelihood that the other side will need to endure a "second bite at the apple."

Appendix

Illustrative Written "Open" Instructions to an Agent

Purpose. These instructions are intended to help both you and me clarify what things you should do in the negotiation and the kind of commitments you have authority to make.

Open to the other side. These instructions are also intended to help reduce the risk of misunderstanding with your counterpart. You should, therefore, give a copy of these instructions to him or her.

Note to the Other Side: In addition to these instructions, I have given my agent some confidential instructions that disclose such things as my present thinking on how I rank various of my interests, some ideas on comparative values, relevant criteria, my possible alternatives to a negotiated agreement with you, and so on. Nothing in the confidential written instructions is inconsistent with these open instructions, and my agent has some discretion as to if and when to disclose such information. I simply do not believe it wise to try to disclose at the outset of a negotiation all the inner thoughts that it might be useful to share with my agent.

Communication. You are free to communicate with the other side without preconditions and at times and places in your discretion. I will be available on short notice to listen to anything you have to say. You may communicate to me any message that the other side gives you for that purpose, but you need not do so. You are also authorized, in your judgment, to commit yourself to keep confidential from me things that the other side wants you to keep confidential. Should you believe it appropriate, you are authorized to go over my head and communicate directly to my superior or superiors with or without informing me of that fact, leaving it to their discretion whether to inform me. You may make recommendations to them as well as to me.

Relationship. Although you are free, in your discretion, not to disclose everything you may know or think, you are authorized at all times to be honest and to tell the truth. You are not authorized to lie. Rather, you should honestly disclose that there are some things you are not disclosing.

Process commitments. In general, you have authority to commit to any negotiation process that you believe will best enable a successful negotiation, so long as that process is not inconsistent with these instructions.

Interests. You are authorized to—and should—disclose the nature and quality of my interests, but you need not disclose their intensity or your current estimate of the value I might place on a given interest. Later in the negotiation, you have discretion to disclose that information, if you believe you have developed sufficient mutual trust with the other side and to the extent that such disclosure will help both of you find joint gains.

Options. At the outset, you are authorized to participate in brainstorming all sorts of options, including ones that we have not considered and ones that you believe are grossly unfair or do not meet my minimal interests. As the negotiation proceeds, you should try to put together a package of options that meets my interests and those of the other side. At those later stages, you should feel free to reject options whose inclusion would render the overall package unacceptable.

Legitimacy. You are free to explore precedents and other criteria of legitimacy that might apply, regardless of whether you believe them to be fair or appropriate in these circumstances. Particularly at the outset, give a fair hearing to any criteria suggested by the other side. Of course, I do expect you also to advocate for those criteria you find most persuasive.

Alternatives to a negotiated agreement. You are free, in your discretion, to explore the alternatives that might be pursued by either principal in the event that no agreement is reached.

Substantive commitments. You may participate in designing and drafting language for substantive commitments that you or the other agent, or both, believe may be worth recommending to one or both of the principals. You have an obligation to design carefully any important substantive commitment before you recommend it. My current thinking is that I would like you and the other agent to attempt to formulate a package that both of you would recommend to your respective principals. If you can achieve such a joint recommendation, I would give it very serious consideration; however, *unless and until you receive from me contrary instructions in writing that you have shared with the other agent, you have no authority to make any substantive commitment on my behalf or on behalf of any organization or person other than yourself personally. Unless and until so authorized, you must make clear that nothing you say or do constitutes such a commitment.*

Notwithstanding the above instructions, you may at any time receive instructions and authority to make a firm offer on my behalf or some other limited commitment. You are authorized to tell the other agent that should you receive such special instructions, they will be accompanied, in writing, by a statement of your special authority.

Further consultations with me. You should consult with me periodically as the negotiations proceed. During those meetings or conference calls, I will expect you to update me on what you have learned about the other side's interests and alternatives, the options and standards that you have discussed, your assessment of what type of package may be possible, and your advice to me on how much authority you ought to have in subsequent stages of the negotiation. I will, of course, answer any questions you might have and discuss whatever strategic or tactical issues you wish.

▦ REFERENCE

Harvard says its purchases violated trust. 1997. *Boston Globe*, January 12, p. A1.

Rational Authority Allocation to an Agent

Max H. Bazerman

In their chapter, "Authority of An Agent: When Is Less Better?," Fisher and Davis address a critical question facing individuals who manage negotiators: What should be the nature of the authority given to an agent? In this fascinating and provocative chapter, Fisher and Davis provide compelling arguments against even asking the question "How much authority should I grant the agent?" and instead argue that the question should be "When should I grant authority to an agent?" Although I generally agree with the shift from "how much" to "when," I will argue for an additional shift to "what kind of information should I give to an agent?"

My comments are guided by my underlying view of what constitutes a good negotiation strategy. Coming from a decision analytic view (Bazerman 1998; Bazerman and Neale 1992; Lax and Sebenius 1986; Raiffa 1982), I think that a rational procedure (i.e., the best advice to achieve the principal's goals) should increase the likelihood of parties reaching an agreement if a positive bargaining zone exists, create Pareto optimal outcomes when agreements are reached, and lead to "fair" resolutions. It is within this context that I comment on the Fisher and Davis chapter.

Fisher and Davis provide the general argument that principals should grant the agent no authority to make a binding commitment at the outset and then grant increasing levels of authority over time, as a learning process occurs. Central to their chapter are seven principles that constitute a general approach for agent authority management. As I considered these, I thought about three agent problems to see if their principles provided me with rational advice. The three contexts were (1) being a seller of a house, (2) hiring an agent to represent me as the author of a book that I am writing, and (3) managing a corporate sales force. The following provides my analysis of the rationality of the seven principles in these three contexts.

Fisher and Davis (p. 68): *"At the outset of the negotiation, the agent should have no authority to make a binding commitment on any substantive issue in the negotiation."* Although I agree with the basic concept of providing authority to an agent over time, the pure form of this principle fails a practicality test. In "listing" the house for sale, you must provide an asking price that you are willing to accept. In this instance, "no authority" is an overstatement, at the least. The advice works fine in the book agent context; however, a salesperson who can make no commitment in front of a customer is at a distinct disadvantage. Again, I see "no authority" as too extreme.

Fisher and Davis (p. 69): *"At the outset, the agent should have discretion to design and begin to develop an effective overall negotiation process."* I agree and would argue that Fisher and Davis nicely point out the importance of team building between principal and agent.

Fisher and Davis (p. 70): *"The principal should focus the substantive portion of the instructions on his interests, priorities, and alternatives, rather than on 'settlement points.'"* I like the emphasis that this principle places on moving the discussion away from price and toward the underlying interests and the development of creative alternatives; however, the real estate agent and the sales force generally need to have a price available for the customer. It will often be impractical or impossible to have the discussion of interests, priorities, and alternatives if no price is provided. Again, this principle works much better in the book agent context.

Fisher and Davis (p. 70): *"The principal should establish clear expectations about the quality and frequency of reporting from the agent."* This is a good idea in all three cases—real estate, book contract, and sales force.

Fisher and Davis (p. 71): *"As the agent and principal gain informa-tion and insight through the negotiation process, the agent's authority should gradually expand."* Again, I generally agree. I would add, particularly in the corporate sales force context, that this experience may occur across multiple different negotiations. As the salesperson and man-ager learn, the salesperson is given more authority to work on her or his own.

Fisher and Davis (p. 74): *"The instructions should be put in writing and shown to the other side."* This principle is likely to violate institu-tional norms and create havoc with the negotiation process, yet that is what Fisher and Davis intend in providing this counterintuitive ad-vice. I generally see it as not being practical for most contexts, includ-ing my three applications. At the same time, this advice provides a provocative idea to consider in specific situations.

Fisher and Davis (p. 74): *"Establish disclosure authority."* (They recommend that the principal provide information about walkaways but not reservation values.) Fisher and Davis implicitly disagree with the idea that multiple issues can be converted to utility (Raiffa 1982). Thus, they do not advocate giving away precise information about the desirability of trades. Precisely what I do want to convey to my real estate agent, my literary agent, and my sales force is that the price depends on a number of factors, which I can list and rank in impor-tance. This is exactly the logic that we teach in scorable exercises in negotiation courses and is relevant to what an agent should know. Fisher and Davis also advocate that a principal should provide infor-mation about his or her walkaways. My view here, and my view in negotiating in general, is to give away this information when, and only when, your walkaway is better than you think the other party believes it to be.

The cornerstone of the Fisher-Davis advice is to give away no authority to the agent on the front end and provide it slowly over time. Their seven principles are also presented in absolute form—with the implication that you should always follow this advice. Overall, their chapter provides far more good information than bad; however, rather than establishing absolute principles, I would consider the seven fac-tors that Fisher and Davis raise to be ideas to think about in the context of a decision-analytic determination of what information you want the agent to have.

In terms of content, throughout the Fisher-Davis principles, the focus is on timing. This is a serious limitation: I would argue that "what" information the agent should have the ability to share is as important as "when" he is allowed to share it. As a practical matter, many agents will need a price to act in a principal's interest. Of course, that price can come with other conditions (e.g., in the real estate case, the buyer might agree to accept the asking price if she can choose the closing date or make a cash deal). In addition, I advocate giving the agent pretty clear information about what factors would lead the principal to demand a higher price (e.g., closing in a month) and what factors would lead the principal to accept a lower price. Consistent with Fisher and Davis, I think that the precision of this information should increase over time as learning and trust develop.

Overall, my view is to think of negotiation through an agent as a variation on the general theme of negotiating. The agent should be viewed as an extra party to the negotiation. This means thinking carefully and systematically about the decision processes of the agent, as well as the decision processes of the other party. Generally, negotiators fail to sufficiently consider the decisions of others (Bazerman 1998). This failure leads principals to (1) give away too much information relevant to claiming a pie and (2) give away too little information relevant to creating a pie.

At the beginning of this response, I noted that I was thinking about three agent-mediated negotiations as I read the Fisher-Davis chapter. As I write this commentary, my house really is for sale. What do I conclude about what to tell Jim, the real estate agent? First, he should work on incentives to reduce principal/agent problems. Second, I should identify what Jim can do more effectively (e.g., finding customers) than Max and Marla (my spouse). Third, we should think clearly about, and communicate to Jim, the worth of specific issues (value of timing of closing, secondary financing, what goes with the house, and so on). Fourth, we should communicate our willingness to be unusually creative in creating a deal. Fifth, I should invite Jim to an open enrollment negotiation seminar at the Allen Center (I actually did this). Sixth, although Jim knows our aspiration level (asking price) and has a pretty good idea of our BATNA (an extra mortgage check each month), we do not need to tell him our reservation price or level of risk aversion.

The general discussion about agent authority has effectively moved us from a discussion of how much information to give an agent to the more relevant questions of when to give an agent information and what kind of information to give. I see this as a healthy shift in our prescriptions and concept development. I also see a need for rigorous empirical research to assess the relative merits of agent management advice, including "how much," "when," "what kind," and other dimensions that the research community have yet to identify.

REFERENCES

Bazerman, M. H. 1998. *Judgment in managerial decision making.* 4th ed. New York: John Wiley.

Bazerman, M. and M. Neale. 1992. *Negotiating rationally.* New York: Free Press.

Lax, D. A. and J. K. Sebenius. 1986. *The manager as negotiator: Bargaining for cooperation and competitive gains.* New York: Free Press.

Raiffa, H. 1982. *The art and science of negotiation.* Cambridge, MA: Belknap Press of Harvard University Press.

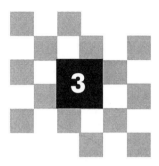

Minimizing Agency Costs
in Two-Level Games

Lessons From the Trade Authority
Controversies in the United States
and the European Union

Kalypso Nicolaïdis

We can only reach good deals when we go a bit beyond our instructions.

—Statement by a European trade ambassador

What is the optimal approach for delegating authority to a negotiating agent? The issue has been the object of intense policy debates on both sides of the Atlantic in the past few years. In the United States, the "fast track" procedure has become increasingly contested as members of Congress and the public at large question whether the executive branch is actually committed to taking the kind of stance in the international arena that they champion. In the European Union (EU), member states have recently succeeded in reasserting part of their individual competence over trade matters at the expense of the

European Commission, which is supposed to "speak with one voice" on their behalf.

To be sure, the standard procedures for delegating authority in these two contexts differ significantly. During the Uruguay Round, the United States trade representative was given a flexible initial mandate under the fast track procedure but was also able to use the threat of congressional veto at the end of the day to bully its partners. His European counterpart also held a flexible mandate on behalf of the member states of the EU, but his promise of ratification was much more credible than that of his U.S. colleague. On the other hand, throughout the negotiations, representatives of the EU member states were "breathing down his neck," in contact with him day in and day out. To better assess the policy debates surrounding "trade authority" in Europe and the United States, we need to develop conceptual lenses for systematic comparisons. We can then ask, Have these two different approaches been effective for those on behalf of whom the U.S. and EU representatives were negotiating? Could they be improved for future negotiation rounds?

These two cases illustrate the difficulty of shaping negotiation "mandates" that reconcile the requirements of all the parties involved and the importance of thinking about "optimal mandates" as problems of institutional design. This chapter develops a conceptual framework addressing situations in which one agent negotiates on behalf of several principals. To be sure, as discussed throughout this book, the question of optimal mandate arises in countless ad hoc principal-agent interactions. I am concerned here with examining ways of designing better relationships between principals and agents in contexts where such relationships are highly institutionalized. A whole host of factors can obviously affect the optimality of negotiating mandates. Above all, principals will ultimately need to take into account the interests and strategy of the other side in deciding how much margin of maneuverability to give their own agent. Although I recognize that such considerations are paramount, this chapter focuses on internal variables to seek some ways to generalize across cases for a given party.

I first present the relevant theoretical foundation and suggest that by disaggregating the notion of mandate into attributes that presumably can be traded off against one another, we can generate hypotheses as to what type of mandate better fits alternative patterns of the principal-agent relationship. I then lay out two case studies concerning the delegation of trade authority in the United States and the EU. Next, I present my analytical framework in three steps:

1. Describing the agency strategic dilemma, which consists of finding a balance between too broad and too narrow a margin of maneuverability for the agent at the negotiating table. Managing this dilemma is the central challenge for any agent negotiating on behalf of multiple principals.

2. Examining how this challenge is likely to be addressed in alternative interest configurations as a function of the degree of interest alignment between principal and agent and among principals. I suggest that each of these configurations is likely to lead to different types of agency costs, which will, in turn, suggest different remedies or types of constraints.

3. Asking how different characteristics of the negotiation mandate may affect the agent's capacity to minimize these agency costs by exploring the possible trade-offs between the attributes of negotiating mandates.

I conclude by testing the hypothesis generated by this framework against the prescriptions generated to deal with the two trade cases.

 **THEORETICAL AGENDA:
NEGOTIATION ANALYSIS, PRINCIPAL-AGENT
THEORIES, AND TWO-LEVEL GAMES
IN INTERNATIONAL RELATIONS**

"Agents" as Negotiators

This book is about negotiators as agents. The starting theoretical point, however, is to think about agents as negotiators, that is, to borrow from theories that examine agency in various organizational contexts unrelated to negotiations. Negotiation analysis can benefit greatly from the insights of principal-agent theories, not only because in practice most negotiations are conducted by agents negotiating on behalf of others (especially on the international scene), but also because the premises of the theory generally hold in a negotiation context. As Kenneth Arrow (1985) notes, the traditional literature on agency is concerned with cases in which the agent's action is not directly observable by the principal and the outcome that is of interest to the principal is affected but not completely determined by the agent's action.

The second assumption is to ensure that the principal could not infer the agent's action by observing the outcome (Arrow 1985:37). These two conditions are clearly met when the role of the agent is not to conduct a task (the focus of the principal-agent literature) but to negotiate on behalf of the principal. In this case, the agent's action—for example, the conduct and endpoint of the negotiation—is not directly observable by the principal and is certainly not inferable from the outcome that is the product of strategic interaction with external parties whose constraints, reservation values, and utility functions are usually only vaguely known to the principals. The state of the world—which, combined with the agent's effort, determines the negotiation outcome—is imperfectly observable.

To what extent can the prescriptive insights generated by principal-agent theories also be imported into the negotiation context? In any agency relationship, *agency loss* or *agency costs* arise either from differences in interests between agents and principals or from information asymmetries when "agents typically know more about their task than their principals do, though principals may know more about what they want accomplished" (Pratt and Zeckhauser 1985:3). In the context of negotiations, agency costs occur because the negotiator knows more about the external negotiations (the external zone of possible agreement, or ZOPA), whereas the principals know more about their reservation price and their utility function (i.e., the trade-offs they make among alternative resolutions of the issues). Agency costs also occur because the agent's interests might not be aligned with that of his principals, if, for instance, the fact of a deal matters more to him that its content.

The prescriptive challenge is to create institutional arrangements to minimize such agency costs. In the context of organizations, remedies require the creation of systems of control and systems of incentives that will minimize agency loss. Generally, economists have focused more systematically on inducement than on enforcement. In this chapter, I assume that the degree of alignment of interest between the agent and his principals is structurally given, through role definition, institutional mission, and incentives such as professional reputation, and other factors. I focus instead on the enforcement side or the "mechanisms of control," which, in the case of agents as negotiators, are the actual mandates under which agents must operate.

Such mechanisms of control serve a different function in negotiation and organizational contexts in two fundamental ways. First, in negotiations, constraining the agent not only serves to compensate for incentive and information asymmetries between principals and agents but also adds a strategic "signaling purpose" to the external game. (In some cases, the agent may even collude in being constrained or at least being perceived as constrained.) Second, although constraints in an organizational setting may interfere with the ability of an agent to perform the task at hand, such constraints in a negotiation setting may actually change the strategy of the negotiating counterpart. In this sense, two pitfalls—"too much" and "too little" constraint—may both be observed in negotiation contexts.

Multiple Principals

This chapter adds an additional layer of complexity to the consideration of principal-agent dynamics in negotiations by examining the class of cases where agents are negotiating on behalf of multiple principals (at least two) and where, therefore, delegation of authority involves negotiation both *among* the principals and *between* the principals and their agents, prior to or during the external negotiations between the agent and the external parties (defining three levels of negotiations rather than two). Mandates generally are not handed down as one-way instructions; they are negotiated with the agent. To be sure, the agent's role can vary from that of a passive messenger to that of a party in the internal negotiations (see Cutcher-Gershenfeld and Watkins, Chapter 1, this volume), but the existence of multiple principals enhances the potential for the agent to orchestrate such negotiations or even play a more proactive role in shaping the principals' aggregate interest. In some cases, and contrary to the assumption prevailing in the traditional literature regarding the one-principal case, the agent may be more certain about the internal ZOPA than each of the principals separately. Thus, when we have several principals, it becomes crucial to ask about the underlying pattern of relationship among principals as well as between the agents and the principals. In short, the move from one to two or more principals "creates" an internal game whereby the very definition of the interests of the "principals" needs to be rendered endogenous. The chapter does not venture into further fascinating complicating factors such as cases with multiple agents or the understanding that sometimes principals can themselves act as agents of an ultimate constituency (e.g., the U.S. Congress vis-à-vis voters).

The principal-agent framework has served international relations scholars in analyzing the delegation of power from sovereign units—considered as principals—to common institutions, as part of the broad issue of allocation of authority in systems of governance, be they federations or global regimes, characterized by multiple tiers. These studies, however, see the agent in terms of locus of "governance" rather than as a negotiator.[1]

The focus on negotiating on behalf of multiple principals points to another strand of international relations theory, namely the forays in "two-level games." For at least one school of international relations analysts, analyzing and predicting the actions of nations depends on understanding how multiple principals representing the domestic political, economic, and social spheres interact and how their diverging interests are reconciled and aggregated to form prevailing notions of the "national interest."[2] There has long been a constructive tension between the study of foreign policy making and of the international system. Recently, analysts have become increasingly interested in exploring the domestic-international interface; they have asked how political processes as well as institutional characteristics at the national level affect international diplomacy.

Robert Putnam has captured the issue through the metaphor of "two-level games," in an effort to convey the simultaneity between "Level 1" games at the international level and "Level 2" games at the domestic level. At stake is whether the Level 2 games will or will not result in the ratification of the deals reached in the Level 1 games and how expectations regarding the "win-set" (agreements that can be ratified domestically) might affect international dynamics.[3] This approach provides a textured and systematic analysis of the internal context and highlights the importance of domestic institutional factors (like modes of representation) in determining the two-level game dynamics.

To be sure, negotiation analysts have long highlighted the role of "negotiators in the middle" and the requirement of synchronization between internal and external negotiations (Lax and Sebenius 1986; Raiffa 1982). They have suggested guidelines for managing the two games simultaneously and have analyzed how characteristics of the external negotiations, such as the degree of conflict of interest, the number of issues, the potential for linkages, or the transparency of the internal game, may affect this interface. Along with international economists, some have also highlighted how the unequal distribution of gains domestically may constitute a structural barrier to the pursuit of joint gains externally (Mayer 1992). To relax this constraint, compensation mechanisms need to be devised at the domestic level that will reconcile the interests of the principals. Here again, the question is left open as to how the negotiating agent might facilitate this process.

Optimality

Drawing on insights generated in the fields of negotiations, principal and agents, and international relations, how should we think about the design of more "optimal mandates"? To start with, we need to define optimality. Optimal negotiation outcomes are defined here from the point of view of the principals and thus may or may not correspond to optimal outcomes from the viewpoint of the agent (the agent's interests are taken into account in this model only on the explanatory side). I measure the "optimality" of a mandate by the extent to which it maximizes the likelihood of achieving an optimal negotiation outcome that will maximize the expected value of the agreement for the principals.

More specifically, such value is assessed according to two generic criteria, external efficiency and internal equity. *External efficiency* obtains when gains in the external negotiations are maximized, both through value creation with the other side (Pareto optimal outcomes) and through the capacity to claim an "adequate" share of the value created externally for one's side. The model remains at a very abstract level and does not address how utility is actually measured. *Internal equity* is a secondary criterion in that it adds sustainability to the agreement reached externally by requiring some measure of fairness in allocation among principals of the side under consideration. This implies reaching external agreements that are not overly skewed in favor of one or a set of internal parties. The effect of the external agreement can be tested against some standard of fairness, such as a Nash equilibrium. This might imply that some principle of fair division needs to be negotiated among the principals themselves. To be sure, some would argue that this second criterion is not necessary.

In theory, an agreement only needs to be externally efficient to improve on the no-agreement alternative of all internal parties with veto power. In practice, however, parties can often refuse such a deal on the basis of relative as opposed to absolute advantage.[4] As Mayer (1992) points out, international agreements, no matter how much in the national interest, inevitably have differential effects on factional concerns. It may be preferable to devise internal compensatory schemes to ensure some degree of internal equity rather than fulfilling the equity criteria through the external deal (Mayer 1992).

Defining an Agent's Mandate

If external factors are exogenous, what are the variables that can be manipulated to maximize the likelihood of satisfying these efficiency and equity criteria? More specifically, how and to what extent should the principals—as a group or individually—seek to control their agent throughout the negotiation process? It is convenient to use a generic term such as "margin of maneuverability" to refer to the freedom of action of the agent, or conversely the extent to which the agent is constrained by the principal in the external negotiations. It is also useful to distinguish between attributes of negotiating mandates, which is akin to disaggregating this notion of margin of maneuverability. In the literature of two-level games, commentators often simply refer to "constraint" in general, without specifying how these constraints are exercised (Mayer 1992). Others may selectively refine the notion of constraints in particular by focusing on the use of internal veto, which I discuss below as part of an agent's authority (Mo 1995). More generally, constraints on negotiating agents can serve to define the boundaries of the negotiating space externally, to change the agent's incentives, or to channel information; they may also serve as signals to the other side. Can we classify these constraints?

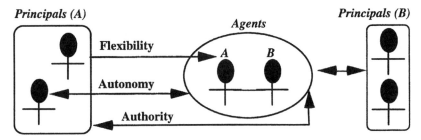

Figure 3.1. Flexibility, Autonomy, and Authority: The Three Attributes of Negotiation Mandates

In the agency literature, constraints or "agency ties" are the array of actual mechanisms that can link principals and agents and serve to frame the task of the latter. Agency relationships in the business world or the strength of agency ties can be arrayed along a spectrum from employee relationships (the strongest ties) to contracting out (the weakest). Similarly, the relationships of negotiating agents and their principals can be arrayed along a spectrum from the least to the most constraining for the agent (Coglianese and Nicolaïdis 1996). The mechanisms identified in the business world can be seen as attributes of mandates (i.e., as mechanisms that reflect different types and levels of constraint for the agent at different phases of the negotiation). I distinguish between three kinds of attributes as depicted in Figure 3.1.

Flexibility (Authorizing Stage)

First, agency studies highlight the importance of *strategic control*—control connected to the formulation of the agent's task and overall objectives. The specificity of this formulation constitutes the initial constraint on the agent's margin of maneuverability. A sales agent can be asked to act "in the best interest" of its firm or can be told to maximize the number of widgets sold in a given day. Similarly, the flexibility of the initial set of instructions under which negotiating agents operate is determined through negotiations between principals as well as between principals and their agents over the criteria that are to guide the negotiation strategy of the agent. The broadest, most flexible, or most vague mandate on the part of the principals would simply be "do the best you can" or technically "maximize our joint utility function." The principals may narrow the mandate by specifying their reservation value to the agent (including the existence of deal break-ers) or concessions that might be traded off with the other side. If there are multiple issues, they may further narrow the mandate by specify-ing the combination of resolution of issues that they would be ready to accept collectively, or they might create a broader mandate by indicat-ing only qualitatively the kinds of trade-offs they make between issues.

Finally, flexibility designates the formal character of the man-date, that is, the collective instructions to which principals are able to agree. A mandate can be given once and for all or can be updated on an ongoing basis to fit changing circumstances. In the latter case, it is an *iterated* mandate that acquires specificity over time. Only formal revisions of the mandate qualify as revision of flexibility; informal consultations between the agent and principals individually or collec-tively that do not result in a collectively defined set of instructions are captured below under the label of autonomy.

Autonomy (Representation Stage)

A second attribute of negotiation mandates has to do with the ongoing process of negotiation: To what extent are the principals actu-ally involved in the negotiation process itself, "at the table" alongside the agent? As opposed to the flexibility built into initial authorization, this dimension measures the propensity of the principals to influence agents individually, not collectively, because the interaction does not involve agreement between principals on a set of instructions. In con-sidering cases with only one principal, agency theories examine mechanisms of *operational control*, that is, control connected to the ongoing implementation of the task delegated to the agent and to the assessment of the agent's effort. These consist above all of monitoring techniques that range from obligations of reporting regularly to the principals to the standardization of task description according to specified categories. At one extreme, principals can reduce the agent's autonomy to the point where the principal shares in the activities of the agent. Thus, a joint venture with former suppliers strengthens agency ties by allowing the principal to become a party to the agent's operations. At the other extreme, the agent is left completely free until final ratification. Conversely, we can also ask to what extent the agent has a say in shaping the mandate given to it. In other words, does the agent sit in the boardroom? In all cases, the question is the degree to which the principal and the agent actually share their respective functions or participate in each other's deliberation and actions.

The autonomy of the negotiating agent is both a function of the principal's access to the negotiation process and a function of the agent's access to the principals during the negotiations. Questions include these: How transparent are the negotiation proceedings? Are there minutes of the discussions? Can the principals actually witness the discussions? What are the mechanisms for consultation that determine the extent to which the agent can exchange ideas and information with the principals about the new options proposed, generated, or received from the other side? A further measure of autonomy has to do with the extent to which the agent monopolizes contacts with the other side, be it the agent of the other side or the principals of the other side. If her own principals or a subset of principals start negotiating with the other side directly, the agent will completely lose autonomy as the role of the agent reverts back to the principal.

Authority (Ratification Stage)

Finally, principal-agent analysis asks to what extent the actions or pronouncements of the agent commit the principal and/or his resources (Does he act "in the name" or "in the person" of the principal?), and therefore the extent to which the principal can dissociate himself, if he so chooses, from his agent. The term *authority* refers to the authority of the agent to make commitments (or at least concessions) on the part of the principals on an ongoing basis regarding intermediary concessions and at the end of the negotiations regarding the final deal. Mandates can "authorize" agents to varying degrees. Robert Mnookin (with J. Cohen, Introduction, this volume) refers to this in legal terms as the contractual power of the agent. The assertion or reassertion of authority to commit is the ultimate, if blunt, measure of control on the part of principals. Withdrawal of authority to commit is a constraint introduced through the requirement that all commitments made by the agents be approved by principals. The authority for the agent therefore depends in part on the existence of formal and informal mechanisms by which the agency relationships can be suspended or severed at any future time. As a proxy, students of agency focus on the lengths of time of the agency relationship and the degree of entanglement implied.

In the realm of international negotiations, agents usually cannot be fired. Their authority is linked to the procedures for ratification of the negotiated agreement and the extent to which such procedures may lead to an uncertain outcome. This is the only one of my three attributes that is used in the analysis of two-level games. It is indeed the most visible and quantifiable constraint. Note that these three attributes can be associated with different phases of the negotiations. Decreasing the flexibility of the mandate is a constraint introduced *ex ante*. Narrowing agency autonomy is relevant to the *ongoing* conduct of the negotiation. Withholding of authority is a constraint operating *ex post facto* when a deal must be ultimately committed to (even if the procedure by which this authority may be granted can be determined *ex ante*). These analytical tools can now be applied to describe and assess the procedures in force in the United States and the European Union in the field of trade.

▓ CASE STUDIES: MECHANISMS FOR DELEGATING TRADE AUTHORITY IN THE UNITED STATES AND THE EUROPEAN UNION

The formulae for delegating trade authority in the United States and the European Union have very different historical origins but have tended to converge over time.[5] In the United States, the drafters of the Constitution were, above all, weary of unchecked executive power and sought to minimize foreign entanglements. The Constitution put the executive and legislative branches of the government in competition with one another, granting trade authority to the president through either one of two provisions: "treaty power" (Article 2.2), which calls for approval of treaties by two thirds of the Senate (i.e., policy making through diplomacy), and the "Commerce Clause" (Article 1.8), which gives Congress the authority to regulate commerce with other nations" (i.e., policy making as legislative revisions of tariffs).

In the European Union (EU), on the other hand, the founding fathers pursued the opposite objective (Meunier & Nicolaïdis, 1999).

The provisions of the Treaty of Rome reflected their fear of continuing the centrifugal force of individual state sovereignty and the ambition to provide those negotiating on behalf of Europe with broad authority. Thus, the common commercial policy was one of the few policy areas in which the European Community (which became the European Union in 1991) was granted "exclusive competence"—that is, in which authority was completely transferred from the state level to the supranational level (Article 113). At the supranational level, states retain control as an assembly through the role of the Council of Ministers in policy making, but it is the Commission (the embryonic executive branch) that negotiates on their behalf.[6]

With time, the two systems have evolved in the search for the best way to balance efficiency in the conduct of negotiations by the "executive agent" (president or Commission) and the assertion of sovereignty by the "principals" (Congress/Senate or member states). The history of U.S. trade policy can be portrayed as a struggle between the treaty power and the Commerce Clause, with increased predominance of variations on the latter (VanGrasstek 1997). The "fast track" is only the latest arrangement between Congress and the executive branch; it was preceded by at least four other main procedures.[7] The Reciprocal Trade Agreement Act of 1934 (the RTAA, extended until 1962) provided for the greatest ever freedom of maneuverability for the executive branch and even allowed it to negotiate executive agreements.[8] By the late 1960s, as trade agreements were starting to move beyond pure tariff issues, they started to require changes in domestic legislation, a power that Congress could not simply delegate to the executive branch. After a crisis over the ratification of part of the Kennedy Round, the "fast track" procedure was introduced in the United States in 1974 as a reassertion of congressional authority in trade matters. Since then, it has been used to approve five trade agreements, including the results of the last two trade rounds and the North American Free Trade Agreement (NAFTA).

In the EU, the reassertion of member state authority started a bit later, with the ratification of the Tokyo Round in 1979, and has been playing out ever since. That reassertion has taken two main forms. Some member states have refused the logic of two-thirds majority voting in the Council for ratification, asserting instead their right of veto over parts of the packages negotiated during trade rounds (e.g., France and agriculture during the Uruguay Round in 1993).

More fundamentally, a number of member states have argued successfully for dealing with "new issues" that have emerged under the global trade agenda (trade in services, intellectual property rights) under "shared competence" procedures, which require not only unanimous voting in the Council but above all ratification by the individual parliaments of the member states. In practice, however, and although contested, the "Article 113 procedure" continues to prevail.

In this way, the fast track and the Article 113 procedure became the two mechanisms that are currently used today in the United States and the EU. In both cases, the precise terms of delegation and coordination between principals and agent are formally determined, but the interpretation continues to evolve. In the United States, the delegation is between the legislative and the executive branch, whereas in the European Union, the delegation is between the individual member states and the Union, represented by the Commission.

In the United States, the U.S. trade representative (USTR) negotiates under the loose supervision of the White House after initial authorization by Congress. The agreements negotiated under fast track authority need to be translated into legislative bills. The fast track is usually characterized as a mechanism that gives Congress a simple choice between approving and disapproving the results of a negotiation by simple majorities in the House and the Senate, without any possibility of amendment, and within 90 days of submission. In fact, it gives Congress much more authority than is usually appreciated, including the capacity to add or alter provisions that affect the balance of concessions in an agreement.[9]

In the EU, the sole trade negotiator traditionally has been the Commission, acting on behalf of the member states under the Article 113 procedure. Committee 113—made up of national trade representatives at the ministerial or subministerial level who meet together and with the Commission—drafts the mandate to be formally granted by the Council and provides the Commission with ongoing feedback during the negotiations. The Council approves agreements by a two-thirds majority vote.

In contrasting the U.S. and EU procedures using the two classic approaches as a benchmark, three caveats are in order. First, as suggested above, we need to distinguish between the formal institutional design and practice. Ratification in the United States is not really up or down and in the EU not really by a qualified majority. Second, the way in which the procedures are applied may differ considerably from one instance to another. Third, and most important, there exist, both in the United States and in the European Union, competing approaches to delegating trade authority that have become more relevant as prevailing procedures have become increasingly contested on both sides. In the United States, initial fast track approval seems to have become almost impossible, leading, for example, to the failure in fall 1997 to ensure delegation of authority. In the European Union, there has been increased tension between the Commission and the member states over trade agreements that involve issues considered part of "shared competence." The Commission's last efforts to secure a revision of the treaties that would reassert the applicability of the classic Article 113 procedure over all trade matters was defeated during the negotiations over the Amsterdam Treaty in June 1997.

How can we better assess current debates on both sides of the Atlantic through the prism of agency mandates? Established modes of principal-agent relationships reflect different initial choices of emphasis between flexibility, autonomy, and authority as well as how trade-offs between these attributes have evolved with time. These trade-offs in turn reflect the prevailing balance between the practical requirements of international negotiations and the constitutional prerogatives asserted by the principals.

Flexibility (Authorization Stage)

Formally, the U.S. procedure is more focused on the endgame than is the EU procedure. It is even possible for the executive branch to initiate talks, negotiate, and reach agreement without prior authorization by Congress, whereas the Commission has no option of bypassing the member states initially. In practice, however, both sides rely on some sort of authorization. Trade negotiations have become increasingly complex, involving an array of issues that may be negotiated through linkages and package deals. Moreover, in the absence of visible and concrete gains offered by their counterparts, principals have a hard time agreeing on anything other than their lowest common denominator.

Thus, both the USTR and the EU Commission usually negotiate on the basis of very broad and flexible mandates. In the EU, Committee 113 draws one broad mandate at the beginning of any round of trade negotiation, but there is no procedure for updating the mandate (the EU negotiated the conclusion of the Uruguay Round in 1993 under a mandate written in 1985!). Attempts to use reduced flexibility as a mode of control have been more prevalent in the United States. In the past, procedures established before the fast track that gave the executive broad authority granted very limited flexibility.[10] During the most recent debates over fast track renewal, a majority in Congress favored reducing flexibility at the authorization stage by specifying extensively the terms of the negotiation mandate (especially regarding labor and environment clauses). It is disagreements over such terms that have led to the current stalemate over fast track.

Autonomy (Representation Stage)

The crafting of the fast track was in part a reaction to the inadequate internal consultation during the Kennedy Round, during which the RTAA procedure had allowed the executive branch to ignore oppositional warnings on the part of Congress. Thus, in addition to the ratification provisions, the 1974 Trade Act also served to curb U.S. negotiators' autonomy by requiring greater coordination between the branches during the negotiations, the designation of official congressional advisers, and the establishment of private sector advisory committees that were to be consulted throughout. In practice, the USTR does consult periodically with advisory groups, but representatives of these groups do not observe the process directly, and consultations are not systematic.

In contrast, when involved in formal multilateral negotiations, negotiators on behalf of the European Union enjoy much less autonomy.[11] To be sure, the Commission ensures the "unity of representation" of the member states, but Committee 113 acts on an ongoing basis during negotiations "to advise the Commission in the conduct of negotiations." Member state representatives meet with Commission negotiators before each important negotiation meeting, actually sit at the table (but remain silent) during World Trade Organization (WTO) negotiations, and may even participate more actively at more informal levels.

Traditionally, it can be argued that this lesser autonomy has bought both greater flexibility and authority for the agent: State representatives have their say during the negotiations. Member states have become extremely vigilant over this implicit deal. The dispute over competence in the EU crystallized over the so-called Blair House Agreement on agriculture negotiated secretly by the Commission with the United States in 1992 during the closing phase of the Uruguay Round. Neither the Committee 113 nor the individual state capitals were consulted about the deal, the results of which were leaked by the American side. This assertion of autonomy on the part of the Commission led to a major crisis with France, forcing a renegotiation of the deal and prompting France to proclaim its lasting loss of trust in the Commission. This was the first time an agreement already reached by the Commission failed to be approved by EU member states.

Authority (Ratification Stage)

The withholding of authority to commit and the practice of reneging on executive commitments has traditionally characterized U.S. trade policy, more than that of any other country in the world, as exemplified by the history of Senate failure to ratify treaties or to insist on extended amendment practices.[12] Initially, the fast track procedure was praised for giving U.S. negotiators more credibility with their foreign counterparts because the procedure made it less likely that Congress would unravel any deal (Low 1993). In practice, legislators have turned the fast track in their favor through backdoor amendment procedures.[13] The speed of ratification and thus the possible delay before actual coming into force of the agreement constitutes another component of the agent's authority; such delays can be lengthened even more if implementing legislation (and/or appropriation of funds) is required in addition to the ratification process itself, as is often the case in the United States.

There are two paths for relaxing the authority constraint. In the debates leading up to the establishment of the fast track, some legislators suggested the adoption of a legislative veto instead (i.e., adoption unless blocked) in exchange for decreased autonomy. Although the procedure was not adopted for generic purposes, it has been used for

TABLE 3.1 The U.S. Versus European Union Approach to Trade Mandates

Stages *Attributes of Mandates*	Authorization *Flexibility*	Representation *Autonomy*	Ratification *Authority*
United States			
"Fast track"	Medium	High	Low
Executive agreements	Low	High	High
European Union			
Exclusive competence	High	Medium	Medium
Mixed competence	Medium	Medium	Low

implementing bilateral free trade agreements under the requirement that negotiators consult with private sector advisory panels and the International Trade Commission, thus advancing the timing to express objections.[14] As discussed above, current debates over fast track renewal exhibit the alternative approach of buying authority with reduced flexibility.

As discussed above, ratification traditionally had been more of a formality in the EU, but recently it has been questioned whether the Commission actually has greater authority to commit than its U.S. counterpart. The Blair House crisis seriously hampered the credibility of the Commission. Under the current "shared competence" arrangement, individual member states formally have a right of veto in negotiation over new issues such as services. Nevertheless, when it comes to all other issues, although states like France would like to believe that they hold a de facto veto, the mere possibility that this veto can formally be denied by other member states does make a difference. Moreover, the procedure agreed to at Amsterdam in June 1997 would allow the Council to vote on a ratification procedure by a qualified majority, a bit like the fast track.

As shown in Table 3.1, principals control their agent in the United States mostly through the constraints on final authority. The EU clearly enjoys less autonomy but more authority. In both cases, there may be a bit of room for decreasing initial flexibility. As I elaborate on the conceptual framework in the pages that follow, it is plausible to assume that these two evolving patterns of delegation are often suboptimal, if only because they were designed through path-dependent developments that were not necessarily geared at ensuring external efficiency and internal equity but constituted temporary compromises reflecting prevailing domestic power games.

THE AGENCY STRATEGIC DILEMMA: MANIPULATING THE MARGIN OF MANEUVERABILITY TO MAXIMIZE GAINS EXTERNALLY

As described above, the degree of flexibility, autonomy, and authority enjoyed by negotiating agents in the field of trade may vary across settings. We can now turn back to a more abstract evaluation of these tools, taking into consideration the basic strategic objectives of the principals. These lead to what I call the agency strategic dilemma.

The three attributes discussed above together determine the margin of maneuverability available to the agent, along with the agent's own assessment of the bottom line of each of the principals. This margin of maneuverability is therefore based on subjective assessments under uncertainty.[15] It may be partially manipulated through the mandate design and partially given by interest assessment. At a general level, we can therefore ask, How much flexibility or margin of maneuverability should be given to the agent to maximize the expected value of the agreements to the principals (that is, to enhance his capacity to both create and claim value externally)? The received wisdom is that the principal generally wants the agent to have less flexibility, whereas the agent would like more; in their respective ideal worlds, the principal would be able to make the agent do exactly what he wants her to do, and the agent would be free to deliver whatever she considered an optimal deal.

There are clear reasons why these preferences may not be the case. Principals might have an interest in granting autonomy to their agent simply because creating agency ties might be costly inside organizations (e.g., costs of reporting and monitoring). Similarly, in negotiations, principals might not have enough at stake to invest in constraining the agent. They might also prefer to refrain from constraining the agent for strategic reasons. Howard Raiffa's (1982) suggestion that uncertainty (e.g., flexible mandate) might make the agents "bargain harder" is supported by experimental evidence, as well as having been derived formally on the basis of assumptions regarding agents' risk aversion (Lax and Sebenius 1991). As Fisher and Davis point out in Chapter 2 of this volume, "agents without authority" may simply not be able to extract concessions from the other side. More generally, sophisticated principals may realize that their agent will be unable to find ways to create value if that agent is not given leeway in the external negotiation to explore Pareto-improving options. This efficiency rationale was very much present both at the outset in Europe and in the establishment of the fast track.

Agents, on the other hand, know that without internal constraints, they might not be strong enough and might be less able to claim value on the external front. They also may find out that, without formal constraints, they have misjudged their actual margin of maneuverability and negotiated a deal that was not ultimately ratified or implemented by the principals. Thus, the EU Commission has been keen to obtain more specific (less flexible) mandates for its bilateral association agreements, including those negotiated after 1989 with East and Central European countries. Agents also know that if autonomy throughout the negotiations is combined with uncertainty in the endgame ratification, they risk (1) leaving good deals on the table given the uncertainty of the principal's reservation price and their own risk-averse behavior (Lax and Sebenius 1991) and (2) having to pay a "risk premium" to compensate the external party for the likelihood of nonratification (Putnam 1993).

The agency strategic dilemma can therefore be described irrespective of the viewpoint taken (principal or agent), although agents and principals are likely to disagree on how to handle this dilemma. To simplify, we imagine an agent negotiating on behalf of multiple principals with another agent. Two dimensions are relevant here, as shown in Figure 3.2. First, the agent must have two types of objectives. He wants to maximize the likelihood of reaching a value-creating agreement with the other side, while at the same time he wants to manipulate the relative strategic advantage between the two sides in his favor (claiming value). Second, the agent can target actions at either side to effect these objectives: He can act at home, or he can act on the other side. Four categories of strategies can be defined in this way, all mechanisms to maximize external gains from the viewpoint of one side.[16]

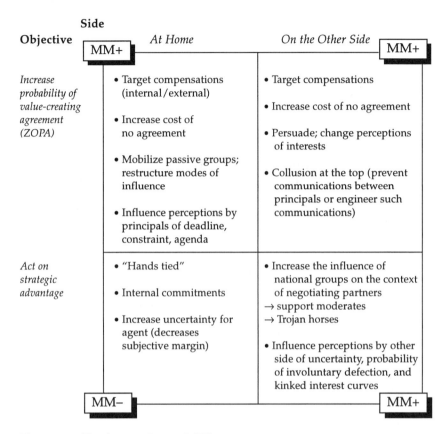

Figure 3.2. The Agency Strategic Dilemma

NOTE: MM+ = margin of maneuverability increases; MM– = margin of maneuverability decreases.

Each of these sets of strategies amounts to increasing or decreasing the margin of maneuverability of the agent or that of his counterpart, taking the preferences of the principals as given. The more the agent can increase his margin of maneuverability, the higher the likelihood of agreement, and therefore the greater his capacity to engineer value-creating agreement. The external ZOPA is widened by either agent increasing his margin of maneuverability; however, that margin is inversely correlated with the bargaining leverage that he may have, at least as the other side perceives it. For instance, a specific trade mandate can be seen as a tool to convey information to the agent as well as a mechanism to signal limits to the other side, but it clearly decreases the prospect of innovative deals. A more flexible mandate allows greater freedom in exploring issues with the other side, especially during the first phase of negotiations.

Nevertheless, because it represents an increase in uncertainty, it may represent a smaller subjective margin of maneuverability if the agent is risk averse than if his mandate had simply been truthful revelation of preferences on the part of the principals (Lax and Sebenius 1991). The strategic role of uncertainty about principals' preferences referred to above may be understood in this vein as a psychological mechanism to decrease the margin of maneuverability the agent allows himself to consider (although uncertainty implies a lesser objective constraint on the agent, a point to which I will return). More generally, early research in the 1960s and 1970s in social psychology investigated the ways in which negotiators behave while operating under both the expectations of their constituents and the influence of the outsider party.[17] The findings confirm the important impact of the existence of agents per se (whatever their strategies) on strategic advantage on the external front—that is, that accountability increases resistance to the other side's proposal. Experiments confirm that although representational roles increase competitiveness on the external front, they also decrease probability of agreement.

The principals therefore face a strategic dilemma between increasing the agent's margin of maneuverability as a means of increasing the likelihood of value-creating agreements and decreasing his margin of maneuverability to increase his strategic advantage. One way to reconcile the tension is to conclude that the agent must try to maximize his margin of maneuverability while minimizing it as perceived by the other side. An actual broad margin of maneuverability ensures that acceptable agreements are not left on the table, and a perceived narrow margin ensures a fair share from the value. Thus, EU trade negotiators can use their limited autonomy as an argument to resist concessions in the ongoing negotiations, by highlighting the resistance of one or two member states for instance, while ensuring that in reality a majority of member states stays on their side. The distinction between actual and perceived margin is not sufficient here to resolve the dilemma, especially in contexts of relatively high transparency of the internal process. This is a real tension that needs to be managed. Under what circumstances and how should the margin of maneuverability be narrowed or broadened? I now turn to analyzing how different configurations of principal-agent relationships may provide the basis for variation in circumstances.

▓ A TYPOLOGY OF PRINCIPAL-AGENT INTEREST CONFIGURATIONS AND CORRESPONDING AGENCY PROBLEMS

Agency costs vary according to circumstances. How does the design of mandates affect the attainment of the goals of external efficiency and internal equity that ought to serve as the benchmark of optimality? I argue here that it is important to examine how the configuration of internal interests ought to affect the way in which we think of negotiation mandates, even while ultimate prescriptions will also be affected by other independent variables.[18] Because principals cater to a range of different constituencies, the degree of conflict of interest between them may vary in the same way as interest alignment traditionally varies between principals and agents.

One of the core objectives of negotiation analysis is to identify factors that are likely to lead to suboptimal agreements (including no agreement when one would have been possible) and prescribe ways of reaching, or at least approximating, Pareto efficient results. To be sure, agency introduces not only costs but also benefits, which is why agency relationships are created in the first place. Agency situations may or may not create additional factors of suboptimality. As stated at the outset, agency costs arise from the differences in information and interests between principals and agents. On the *external efficiency* goal, information asymmetries imply that the agent is not able to work out the internal trade-offs between principals and is likely to miss a range of value-creating deals out of ignorance or restraints put on his capacity to "explore the Pareto frontier" with the other side. On the *internal equity* goal, asymmetries of interest between principals increase the likelihood of deals biased in favor of one principal. The principals might also have different incentives to manipulate the margin of maneuverability in suboptimal ways. Factors that affect agency costs should in turn be key determinants for the design of the mandate. The set of configurations under consideration here is distinguished according to two dimensions, the degree of interest alignment between principals and agents (P/A) and the degree of interest alignment among principals (P/P).

P/A: Degree of Interest Alignment Between Principals and Agents

This dimension differs somewhat from interest alignment between a single principal and its agent in that we need to ask, interest alignment with whom? What is measured here, therefore, is the extent to which the agent has his own agenda independent of that of the principals, be it to improve relations with a negotiating partner, to reach agreement as a goal per se, or to redefine the principals' interests in a way that he (the agent) finds attractive. This in turn influences the extent to which Principal 1 might trust him not to "defect" to Principal 2 and thus seek a biased external agreement (internal equity goal). The agent's interests are considered aligned with the principals' when the agent's sole purpose is to serve all of his principals (maximize their joint utility function) by simply aiming to fulfill the internal equity goal (although the internal weights may be determined by power relations among the principals or the internal rules of agreement between principals or other similar factors). The lower the interest alignment between principals and agents, the more likely the agent is to agree on outcomes unacceptable to his principals, all other things being equal. Conversely, greater alignment of interest can allow the principals to broaden the margin of maneuverability and thus increase the probability of value-creating agreements.

In both the EU and the United States, the agent generally tends to hold more liberal free-trade convictions than the majority of his principals, although he is flanked by principals on both extremes of the spectrum. This is in keeping with studies of agency in the regulatory realm (as well as commonsense observation) that show how regulatory agents are to a great extent guided by their own idea of the public good. Thus, principals on the protectionist end of the spectrum feel less represented by their agent. In relative terms, the degree of interest alignment between principals and agent is greater in the EU than in the United States simply because the Commission is a more neutral body than the executive branch in the United States. This may change as the Commission asserts its independence.

P/P: Degree of Interest Alignment Among Principals

This dimension—or its converse, the degree of conflict of interest among principals—determines the range of agreements that principals can collectively accept. Robert Putnam (1993) uses the notion of a "win-set" to describe the range of agreements acceptable at Level 1 (external negotiation) that can be ratified at Level 2 (internal negotiations). Focusing on internal interest alignment allows the principal to choose an independent variable that can be considered separately from what is acceptable to the other side. Internal interest alignment is the key determinant of the size of the ultimate internal ZOPA, although the latter can increase with a variety of factors that can be manipulated through the negotiation itself (including the existence of preexisting mechanisms for internal compensation; the reliance on majority voting rather than consensus, thus allowing alternative "winning coalitions"; the capacity of the parties to learn about alternative means to satisfy their interests; the degree of agreement on principles of just division; and the degree of certainty about reservation values and interests). Greater alignment of interest between principals makes it easier for them to collectively narrow the margin of maneuverability to increase their strategic advantage externally.

Typically, trade negotiations involve a high degree of conflict of interest between principals, given the well-known clash between free trade and protectionist interests and ideology. Interest alignment may increase if a given trade policy consists of implementing reciprocity threats or promises. In relative terms, interest alignment between principals may be greater in the EU, because each of its national positions is already a compromise between domestic free trade and protectionist forces. The enlargement of the EU, however, has decreased this cohesiveness. Pressures of globalization have also increased the degree of conflict over trade prevailing in the United States. This is all the more true when Congress and the White House are controlled by different parties.

On the basis of these two dimensions, one can think about likely factors of suboptimality under each of the four alternative configurations depicted in Figure 3.3. In short, starting with Configuration 1, which is the closest to a traditional two-party negotiation, agency costs are introduced along two directions. In this regard, it is useful to trans-

	Degree of Interest Alignment Among Principals		
Degree of Interest Alignment Between Agent and Principals	*High*	*Low*	*Error*
High	1. Strategic miscalculation problem: claiming drives out creating; poor corrective mechanisms due to lack of information; eschews range of more value-creating agreements	3. Trust problem: fear of biased agreement in terms of internal equity; ensure that one principal is not "sold out"; potential strategic behavior of agent implies that agent is not aware of value-creating trade-offs	
Low	2. Search problem: margin structurally small; agent risks "missing" agreement for lack of information; enhanced if risk averse; risk of involuntary defection	4. Entrepreneurship problem: Agents and principals most at odds; agents have risk of both "missing" agreements or striking deals in spite of internal constraints; risk of impasse and involuntary defection enhanced	Type I: Agents do not approve/ improve deals that are inside the internal ZOPA
Error		Type II: Agents approve deals that are not in the internal ZOPA	

Figure 3.3. Alternative Interest Configuration in Principal(s)-Agent Relationships and Corresponding Agency Problems

pose the distinction between so-called Type I and Type II errors used in organizational behavior. Type I errors are those committed when an agent is too conservative and imply that agreements are not struck when they could have been, or at least the search for a more optimal agreement is impeded by the agent's conservatism. Type II errors are committed when agents are too lenient and strike deals that are not in the range of internally acceptable outcomes.

Configuration 1: P/A and P/P interest alignment high. This configuration is closest to the traditional two-party situation and therefore involves the lowest degree of agency costs. As a result, the tension between decreasing and broadening the margin of maneuverability almost reduces to the classic tension between strategies for creating and claiming value, where the latter drives out the former. As with classical negotiation, a core barrier to conflict resolution is *strategic miscalculation* (Arrow 1985). Given the convergence of interests among principals, if the agent is fully informed on, and in line with, internal interests, he should have a correspondingly broad margin of maneuverability on the external front. This in turn suggests risks of exploitation and risks of strategic miscalculation in trying to protect against exploitation. Agency costs enter here because the agent still lacks full information about principals' interests and might therefore be less able to realize potentials for creating value through adapting positions as a function of interaction the other side.

Configuration 2: P/A interest alignment high and P/P interest alignment low. In this case, the main problem introduced by agency is a problem of information or a *search problem*. The agent wants to serve his principals, but he may not know how to serve them. Because his margin of maneuverability is structurally small, any strategic behavior on the part of a principal may simply wipe it out. If the agent is risk averse, he is most likely to miss the few possible agreements in the first place. Conversely, if he strikes a deal without being assured of ratification, he runs the risk of involuntary defection, that is, refusal of ratification by the principals acting collectively (majority against) or individually (veto power). The more conservative/risk averse the agent, the more likely he is to commit a Type I error and miss agreements that would have been acceptable for lack of accurate assessment of the bargaining space. Agency costs affect, above all, the efficiency dimension of optimal negotiation outcomes.

Configuration 3: P/A interest alignment low and P/P interest alignment high. This case may be the archetype of the principal-agent problem where the core source of cost is *lack of basis for trust* (interest alignment can be considered as a proxy for trust). The principals have a wide range of agreements on which they could agree among themselves, but they know that the agent has his own agenda and they do not trust him to act in their best collective interest. Experimental research has long shown that lack of trust in an agent induces more aggressive behavior on the part of the agent, both because she is trying to prove her "loyalty" and because she assumes that her principals are not revealing their true reservation value and thus does not want to take risks. This, in turn, decreases the likelihood of agreement externally, given information asymmetries (Valley, White, Neale, and Bazerman 1982). Because of interest misalignment with the agent and a degree of internal convergence that may induce cooperative behavior among principals, they may partially collude against their agent and provide a suboptimal amount of information. In turn, because agents have their own negotiation goals, while at the same time they know that internal alignment of interest is high, this may lead them to commit Type II errors (i.e., to approve deals that are not acceptable to some parties).

Configuration 4: P/A and P/P interest alignment low. Compounded conflict of interest induces costs in terms of efficiency (the agent is likely to "miss" potential external agreements, especially if he is risk averse) and internal equity (the agent is more likely to settle for biased deals). This configuration differs from Configuration 2 (search problem) mainly because the agent, acting on his own interest, may be "entrepreneurial," negotiating a deal externally in spite of an actually narrow margin of maneuverability. P/A misalignment is more likely to lead to impasse under P/P misalignment.

Entrepreneurship results in agency cost to the extent that it is a potentially suboptimal response to heightened internal conflict of interest between principals and increases the probability of the non-aligned agent striking a deal unacceptable to the principals (Type II errors). Knowing this, those principals that in addition have the greater degree of conflict of interest vis-à-vis the agent may be tempted to "nail down" the agent with a restrictive mandate. Collectively, principals are less likely to agree and may choose to reduce the agent's margin of maneuverability beyond even what is required by their narrow ZOPA. Costs associated with information asymmetries are enhanced in this configuration. The risks of involuntary defection are enhanced if deals on the outside are not accompanied by mechanisms to relax the internal constraint (such as side payments).

In all these cases, the source of suboptimal behavior is the gap between the theoretical agent of maneuverability that would actually best serve the efficiency and equity goals for the principals and the actual behaviors induced by the parties' incentives. In this gap lies a reserve of value lost that could be extracted from the potential deals of the other side. How can this gap be narrowed?

 ## GENERATING AND TESTING HYPOTHESES: MANIPULATION OF MANDATE

Attributes as a Function of Principal-Agent Interest Configuration

When agents negotiate on behalf of others, value is lost as principals fail to manipulate the agent's margin of maneuverability effectively. How should mandates be designed so as to minimize the agency costs that may arise in different kinds of situations? Arguments provided in the literature in favor of increasing or decreasing constraints imposed upon agents need to be fine-tuned according to the configuration of interests between the parties. Principals might be able to capture more value externally if they are able to choose more effectively between different mechanisms to deal with agency problems. Specifying the attributes of the mandate through which constraints ought to be imposed can provide a more nuanced picture of optimality in negotiations through agents. Although constraints may be necessary to minimize agency costs, we need to identify the "least restrictive" mechanism of control under each of the configurations. The different attributes of the mandate should vary to ensure that the agent is best able to explore neither more nor less than the range and type of outcomes acceptable to the principals. Clearly, this does not mean that she should refrain from exploring more than allowed by her set of instructions, as the negotiator quoted at the outset of this chapter prescribes.

Three hypotheses are put forth ceteris paribus. In practice, the prescriptions below should be combined with an assessment of the other side so as to devise an optimal margin of maneuverability. Figure 3.4 helps demonstrate these options.

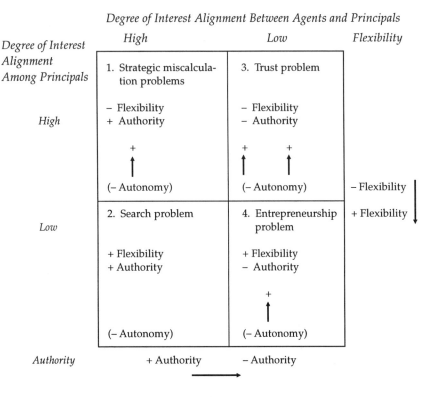

Degree of Interest Alignment Between Agents and Principals

Figure 3.4. Optimal Mandates as a Function of Principal-Agent Interest Configuration

NOTE: Constraints decrease, moving from top to bottom within the figure, and increase, moving from left to right across the figure.

> *Hypothesis 1:* The greater the degree of interest alignment among principals, the less flexible the mandate should be.

As we have seen, the presumption in favor of a flexible mandate is strong, especially at the outset of a negotiation.[19] Above all, many analysts have remarked that specifying the mandate at the outset cuts off part of the Pareto frontier by decreasing the options that can be explored with the other side.[20] At the same time, narrowing the mandate can serve informational and strategic purposes. On the information front, the agent gets a better sense of the structural margin of maneuverability available to her. Strategically, if the principals perceive that a large internal ZOPA may be a strategic weakness, specifying the mandate will strengthen the agent's hand.

My hypothesis here is that principals can most afford to constrain their agents through specific mandates when their interests are least in conflict. The starting point is the argument developed by Mayer (1992) regarding constraints in general: If internal parties do not have highly conflicting interests, increasing constraints is likely to cut off part of the externally feasible deals without ruling out all Pareto efficient deals. In other words, the costs in terms of possible loss in external efficiency are less likely to exceed the strategic gains provided by the additional constraints. Mayer's argument is operationalized here through the attribute of flexible initial mandate, which serves exactly the function of partial limitation of the bargaining space *ex ante* without impeding the agent's capacity to pursue external efficiency goals in the remaining space. Moreover, parties with less conflictual interests will be more capable of undergoing an initial internal negotiation and agreeing to a set of initial instructions approximating their internal ZOPA. In most cases, instructions ought to reflect reservation prices rather than aspiration values. Parties with highly conflicting interests may have a hard time "finding" the internal ZOPA and are likely to individually insist on a mandate that reflects a great deal of shading (overshooting their individual bottom line) because they are playing a strategic game among themselves.

Finally, if the mandate is renewed over time, the presumption should be—all else being equal—to start with broader mandates that will be progressively narrowed as more information about the state of the world and the other side's interests becomes available. Principals with less conflictual interests can choose to reduce the flexibility of the mandate over time rather than at the outset. Adaptable mandates are the least restrictive means of reducing flexibility to obtain strategic advantage over time.

> *Hypothesis 2:* The greater the degree of interest alignment between principal and agent, the more authority the agent should be granted.

Under what circumstances should the constraints put on the agent consist of decreasing his commitment authority as spelled out in the mandate? Decreasing authority is a costly constraint. Many negotiators argue that the use of "inability to commit" as a strategic tool is only window dressing that diminishes their credibility and thus their ability to pursue efficiency goals. With low interest alignment between agents and principals, however, restricting the agent's authority to commit is the most effective way to safeguard the internal equity goal of the principals, while allowing the agent to explore options with the outside. The desirability of granting veto power to the principal has been examined by a number of authors. Some authors have analyzed this issue as a choice made by the negotiator himself to employ a principal as a veto player.[21] From such a viewpoint, the less aligned the agent's interests are with those of the principals, the less desirable the veto is as a strategic weapon. For the same reason, however, the principals might be less inclined to grant authority to an agent with divergent interests.[22] This is especially true if the goal of internal equity is paramount. In short, principals with the least trust in an agent do not necessarily need to agree among themselves *ex ante* to ensure that the agent serves their interest. Reducing her authority to commit is a more efficient mechanism.

To be sure, lack of trust in the agent already has an independent effect on an agent's behavior. Numerous studies have shown how such lack of trust will lead her to adopt more aggressive external strategies, thus increasing the risk of no agreement. This is akin to the role of uncertainty, not surprisingly because lack of trust and transparency are corollary. In this context, the lack of authority to commit on the part of an agent who is known to have autonomous interests from his principal is likely to lead to less loss in credibility.

> *Hypothesis 3:* Decreasing agent autonomy should be used to compensate for relaxing the other two constraints.

The third hypothesis is based on the premise that imposing constraints through inflexible mandates or low authority may be overly costly. Lessening the autonomy of the agent is not a panacea, in that it may inhibit creativity, especially in cases of conflicting interests among principals. Lessening autonomy, however, can be systematically envisaged as a least costly way of attaining the same objective, as with the manipulation of the prior two attributes. I mentioned above the trade-off between initial flexibility and ongoing autonomy: With less autonomy, there is less of a requirement to update the mandate every time the agent's position must change. This trade-off has the advantage of eschewing the need for prior negotiations between principals while serving the same informational purposes. In addition, it serves to co-opt principals with outlying interests. Therefore, it is all the more useful the greater the divergence between principals themselves. Decreasing autonomy to allow for broader mandates also has a strategic advantage in that, by increasing uncertainty regarding the internal ZOPA, it may increase the initial incentive for the agent to seek greater gains externally (through framing, anchoring, etc.) while the risks of overshooting are minimized through monitoring.

Similarly, the authority of the agent to commit may be increased if a decrease in autonomy serves informational and signaling purposes. Decreasing autonomy can be seen as similar to reducing authority with less uncertainty: The agent checks with his different principals that he is in their zone of acceptable agreements. Beyond this informational function, lesser autonomy can also be construed as enhancing the capacity of the agent to influence the principals' perception of their interest in the light of information that he has obtained. Lesser autonomy can allow the agent to go "a bit beyond" his instructions.

TESTING THE HYPOTHESES

These three hypotheses lead both to possible diagnoses and to general prescriptions for better institutional design in cases such as that of trade authority delegation in the EU and the United States. To what extent does the design of mandates we can observe in the real world reflect the above hypotheses? How does the design of the U.S. and EU mandate affect the level of efficiency and equitable character of the negotiations from the viewpoint of U.S. constituents, on one hand, and EU member states, on the other? What recommendations follow from the above analysis regarding the possible reform of trade negotiation mandates in these two contexts? How could patterns of delegation be adapted across instances of trade negotiations to better reflect changing interest configurations?

The above analysis suggests that traditional principal-agent interest configuration in the United States and the EU would have led to different original institutional design. In both cases, however, the degree of conflict between the interests of the principals along the free trade-protectionism axis and the degree of conflict of interest between a significant proportion of principals and the agent on each side seem to have been increasing with time. Under the model proposed here, in the EU, the initial system reflects two assumptions. First, it assumes that the degree of interest alignment between member states was high enough to make it possible for them to agree on an initial mandate but too low to allow for a periodic renewal of the mandate without sacrificing efficiency; constraint through less flexibility might have been desirable, but decreasing autonomy instead would do. Second, it assumes that the EU formal jurisdiction over trade matters called for a greater degree of authority for the Commission, under the implicit assumption that the Commission could act as a neutral broker without pursuing an electoral mandate of its own. Analytically, the EU trade problem was conceived as a search problem left to the expertise of the Commission, under the supervision of member states.

Two current trends may call for some adaptation of the process. On one hand, the forces of globalization, while increasing centrifugal forces in the short run, are likely eventually to increase internal convergence. If pressures over competitiveness, the completion of the internal market, and the movement toward a European monetary union lead the member states to converge economically, a plausible case could be made for tightening the flexibility of the mandate through periodic reevaluation. Creating a process for periodic adaptation of the mandate would also serve as a mechanism to enhance this sense of common interest. Because EU instructions are very transparent and the mandate is known by the other side, this may also enhance EU bargaining power.

There has been a growing loss of trust in Commission negotiators, however, as they assert their own agenda on the international scene. As the EU seems to move in the direction of a trust problem, member states have been tempted to restrict its authority through the assertion of mixed competence and national veto over ratification. This would certainly be a premature move. The EU states and the Commission may be better off finally devising a workable "code of conduct" addressing not only the degree of autonomy of the Commission but also the specific ways in which this autonomy can be kept in check. For member states that have an interest in preserving Commission authority when this serves their interests but who are wary of losing control in specific instances, this approach would allow more adaptability. Most important, principal-agent interest divergence may have been perceived only temporarily, making costly attempts to reduce Commission authority unnecessary.

In contrast, the U.S. model seems to have reflected a much greater sense of conflict of interest on both axes at the outset. Traditionally, the United States has suffered from an entrepreneurship problem: The executive branch has often sought external agreements without fully taking into account internal constraints, thus running the risk of involuntary defection. U.S. negotiating partners have been acutely aware of the problem, and the fast track was introduced in part to address it by designing a formula for delegating authority that was to give Congress a greater sense of control than through the previous arrangement, while at the same time allowing the USTR to negotiate more credibly.

In recent years, a majority of lawmakers seem to have increased their suspicion of White House trade policy. The tension has increased between those in Congress who believe that the mandate of the legislative branch is to curb the executive and protect special interests and those who believe that the pursuit of trade liberalization requires giving a freer hand to the executive. In the last two debates over fast track renewal, Democratic leaders in the House have asked to enshrine a number of specific goals into the negotiation objectives, including treating the NAFTA agreements as the "floor for any future agreements." Republicans, however, insist that the authorizing mandate should reflect a "broad bipartisan consensus" and thus should not include such specific clauses. Analytically, and in view of the degree on divergence inside Congress, it is hard to see how legislators could agree on a very flexible mandate, but it might be possible to put more "teeth" in the mandate than the purely hortatory approach currently prevailing. As with the EU, a lot hangs on whether principals and their agent are able to devise a better working relationship to regulate USTR autonomy during the negotiations so as to allow lawmakers to better assess the costs and benefits of their position on the external front. Whether or not a majority in Congress finally votes to renew trade authority, the prospects for speedy ratification may, in part, depend on such arrangements.

Another option in the United States is to seek to conduct more trade negotiations as executive agreements, thus radically increasing the president's authority (as for the WTO Information Technology

Agreement, the Mutual Recognition Agreements with the EU, or the OECD Multilateral Investment Agreement). The requirement that such agreements do not involve changes in domestic law can be stretched through evolving interpretation of domestic laws. The cost of this approach is that it may encourage more free riding on the part of U.S. trading partners by decreasing the strategic advantage implied by ratification obligations. Only if the procedure could be amended to involve greater coordination between the two branches would it seem a plausible option. In the meantime, the fast track needs to be renovated to address the concerns of aggrieved principals without denying authority to the executive altogether. Some have proposed to allow greater leeway for Congress to amend "in the spirit of an agreement." It would be even better to allow for amendments prior to final agreements.

Whatever revisions are proposed, it seems increasingly hard to reassure Congress about the action of U.S. negotiators, give the latter enough flexibility to negotiate effectively, and address the fears of U.S. trading partners that any agreement they reach with one branch of the U.S. government will be renegotiated by another. The crisis of the U.S. system seems even greater than that of the European Union. Whether innovative approaches to minimizing agency costs in these increasingly complex two-level games can solve these inherent conflicts of power and interest remains to be seen.

 NOTES

1. For a comparison between patterns of delegations in the United States and the European Union, see Coglianese and Nicolaïdis (1996). For a focus on the European Union, see, for example, Pollack (1995). For an application to the external economic relations of the EU and therefore a focus on agents as negotiators, see Meunier and Nicolaïdis (1998).

2. Among international relations scholars, neoliberals are characterized by this bottom-up understanding of foreign policy making and therefore international relations. Neorealists, on the other hand, focus instead on how the distribution of power in the international system determines national policies irrespective of domestic factors.

3. See Putnam (1993). Game theorists have tested and refined this framework to capture more systematically the impact of different configurations of interest on outcomes in these games. See, for example, Mo (1995).

4. This is a core finding of the sociopsychological literature explaining the apparent irrational behavior of individuals in negotiations (as illustrated by allocation games). It is less clear whether this "fairness requirement" applies to the allocation of benefits "inside" one of the parties, but there seems to be little a priori reason why this should not be the case.

5. For more detailed discussions of the modes of delegation in each of these cases and the adjacent controversies, see VanGrasstek (1997) and Meunier and Nicolaïdis (1999).

6. Note that the Council of Ministers is the closest Europe has to a Senate, that is, an assembly representing the states, and that a two-thirds majority is required in both the Council and the Senate to approve foreign trade agreements. In Europe, however, the two thirds is a weighted majority partially reflecting the relative size of member states.

7. These include the enactment of ordinary legislation (bills or resolutions requiring only a simple majority in Congress), the enactment of implementing legislation prior to negotiation, executive agreements (agreements proclaimed by the president), and the legislative veto (agreements go into effect unless explicitly rejected by Congress). The latter has never been used.

8. The RTAA was used to negotiate 32 bilateral agreements and six rounds of General Agreement on Tariffs and Trade (GATT) tariff negotiations.

9. VanGrasstek (1997) argues that the power of the fast track to restrain Congress is often exaggerated and provides evidence to that effect. He characterizes the fast track as a hybrid between treaties and executive agreements.

10. The "preapproval" procedure predefined terms for tariff cuts or allowed only retaliatory protectionist measures. Similarly, the act allowing for the first use of executive agreements included a requirement of "reciprocal concessions." The 1934 RTAA provided that no existing rate could be reduced by more than half.

11. The Commission can be represented by either the Commissioner for External Economic Affairs (Sir Leon Brittan for the period 1995-2000) in the context of bilateral trade relations, or the head of the EU mission in the World Trade Organization (WTO) context.

12. The Senate rejected all but 5 of the 28 treaties including trade commitments submitted to it between 1789 and 1933. Traditionally, the Senate added, deleted, and modified articles in submitted treaties after the fact, a practice that should not be confused with the internationally accepted practice of lodging reservations in a treaty itself. One third of the treaties that the Senate amended between 1789 and 1934 ultimately were rejected either by the president or by negotiating partners, but this did not deter the Senate from this practice.

13. A fast track bill is not amended on the floor. Instead, trade committees in Congress (House Ways and Means and Senate Finance) process it be-

fore it is formally tabled by the president. During so-called mock markup sessions, lawmakers can introduce interpretations of their own to the agreement or can seek to have additional items appended to the draft bill. Although the president is under no obligation to base his implementation bill on these "suggestions," it would be most politically unsavvy not to do so. Although this procedure has fallen short of flatly contradicting international agreements, it has sometimes betrayed their spirit. The 1979 provisions on the injury test for countervailing duties were an early example. The NAFTA ratification debate was a more extreme one. In the latter case, after the Clinton administration imposed the addition of side deals on labor rights, the environment, and import surges, members of Congress made further demands addressed in "side letters" between the presidents of the United States and Mexico, each targeted at winning the vote of a particular legislator. See United States Congress (1993).

14. The procedure will be used for the Information Technology Agreement.

15. Under full certainty, it would correspond to the internal bargaining zone or internal ZOPA, or to Putnam's (1993) "win-set".

16. At a more micro level, we can discuss which strategies inside of each of these boxes is most conducive to the goal at hand. This implies discovering which variables control value creation and value distribution externally and feeding this information back into the internal negotiations. Strategies might consist, for instance, of the design of compensation mechanisms on either side that will relax the constraints imposed by certain "blocking" principals. For a discussion, see Mayer (1992).

17. For an early review, see, for example, Wall (1975).

18. I recognize that in practice such interest alignment can be determined only imperfectly either by the parties themselves or by neutral observers.

19. The analysis of how attributes ought to vary over the time span of a negotiation is not fully developed here because I concentrate on interest configuration as my independent variable. This question obviously warrants an analysis of its own, as done in other contributions to this volume.

20. The strategic role of uncertainty discussed earlier also speaks for a broad mandate but will be treated separately.

21. Note that Mo (1995) uses a reverse terminology from this book. He refers to the negotiator in the middle as the "principal" and to groups or agencies with potential veto power as "agents." In this model, it is the agent (in my terminology) that has the power to design a ratification procedure. In my model, the ultimate decision is the principal's even if the agent/negotiator has power of influence over such a decision.

22. Factors other than interest alignment may influence the degree to which restricting authority through principal veto power is an effective tool.

One, mentioned earlier, is the degree of transparency or information available to the other side. Uncertainty about the other side and *ex post* veto can be seen as functionally equivalent. The more information the other side holds, the greater the incentive for the agent to be constrained by veto players. Mo (1995) argues that when the other side has complete information on the principals' preferences, it is always better for the negotiator to "grant veto power" to an internal party. In this view, the veto's attractiveness results from its informational effect, in that it will induce the negotiator to reveal his true type (e.g., moderate) rather than try to bluff the other side. The threat of veto acts as a credible commitment not to bluff.

▓ REFERENCES

Arrow, K. 1985. The economics of agency. In *Principals and agents: The structure of business*, edited by J. Pratt and R. Zeckhauser. Boston: Harvard Business School Press.

Coglianese, C. and K. Nicolaïdis. 1996. *Securing subsidiarity: Mechanisms for allocating authority in tiered regimes.* Working paper, Kennedy School of Government, Cambridge, MA.

Lax, D. and J. Sebenius. 1986. *The manager as negotiator: Bargaining for cooperation and competitive gain.* New York: Free Press.

Lax, D. and J. Sebenius. 1991. Negotiating through an agent. *Journal of Conflict Resolution* 35(3):474-493.

Low, P. 1993. *Trading free: The GATT and U.S. trade policy.* New York: Twentieth Century Fund.

Mayer, F. 1992. Managing domestic differences in international negotiations: The strategic use of internal side-payments. *International Organization* 46(4):793-818.

Meunier, S. and K. Nicolaïdis. 1999, September. Who speaks for Europe? The delegation of trade authority in the European Union. *Journal of Common Market Studies.*

Mo, J. 1995. Domestic institutions and international bargaining: The role of agent veto in two-level games. *American Political Science Review* 89(4): 914-924.

Pollack, M. 1995. *Obedient servant or runaway Eurocracy? Delegation, agency and agenda setting in the European Community.* Working Paper No. 95-10. Cambridge, MA: Center for International Affairs, Harvard University.

Pratt, J. and R. Zeckhauser. 1985. Principals and agents: An overview. In *Principals and agents: The structure of business*, edited by J. Pratt and R. Zeckhauser. Boston: Harvard Business School Press.

Putnam, R. 1993. The logic of two-level games. In *Double-edged diplomacy: International bargaining and domestic politics*, edited by P. B. Evans, H. K. Jacobson, and R. D. Putnam. Berkeley: University of California Press.

Raiffa, H. 1982. *The art and science of negotiation*. Cambridge, MA: Belknap Press of Harvard University Press.

United States Congress, House of Representatives. 1993. *North American Free Trade Agreement supplemental and additional documents*. House Documents 103-160. Washington, DC: Government Printing Office.

Valley, K., S. White, M. Neale, and M. Bazerman. 1982. Agents as information brokers: The effect of information disclosure on negotiated outcomes. *Organizational Behavior and Human Decision Processes* 51(2):220-236.

VanGrasstek, C. 1997. Is the fast track really necessary? *Journal of World Trade* 31(2):97-123.

Wall, J., Jr. 1975. Effects of constituent trust and representative bargaining orientation on intergroup bargaining. *Journal of Personality and Social Psychology* 31(6):1004-1012.

Minimizing Agency Costs

Toward a Testable Theory

Gordon M. Kaufman

When an agent must negotiate for multiple principals with another agent who also represents multiple principals, what principles should guide the choice of the agents' mandates? What is the effect on agency costs? What is the probability of striking a deal acceptable to all parties? Do these principles lead to an "optimal" mandate? What lessons do we learn by "backing up" and examining the implications of a prescriptive framework of assumptions about "reasonable" criteria that a mandate must obey? For example, do we better understand conditions under which a "tight" mandate is preferred to a "loose" mandate? Do operationally meaningful "rules of thumb" emerge? In short, if I am a principal, does this sort of analysis provide practical guidelines for structuring my agent's mandate that are likely to make me better off?

Kalypso Nicolaïdis sets the stage for study of these questions with two cases: U.S. "fast track" negotiations and negotiations within the European Union (EU) about "individual competence over trade matters" (p. 87). These cases highlight the tension between slowly unfolding, richly textured, and complex negotiations between multiple parties with multiple agents and prescriptive analysis built on a parsimonious set of assumptions about the behavior of both principals and agents.

Nicolaïdis begins by identifying important differences between her model of this type of agent-principal negotiation and other principal-agent theories. For example, when an agent represents multiple parties, "mandates generally are not handed down as one-way instructions; they are negotiated with the agent" (p. 91). This sharpens possible effects of incomplete knowledge on this internal negotiation: "Agency costs occur [when] the negotiator knows more about the external negotiations (the external zone of possible agreement, or ZOPA) [and when] principals know more about their reservation price and [preferences]" (p. 90). When there are several principals, the degree of alignment or misalignment among principals' preferences influences how they negotiate a mandate with their agent. Misalignment among principals may possibly enhance an agent's ability to shape her mandate *and at the same time* allow her to influence the principals' perceptions of acceptable deals. (To divide difficulties, Nicolaïdis assumes at the outset that "the degree of alignment of interests between the agent and his principals is structurally given.") Another difference is that "contrary to the assumption prevailing in the traditional literature regarding the one-principal case, the agent may be more certain about the internal ZOPA than each of the principals separately" (p. 91). These differences lead to a rich set of hypotheses about how an agent negotiating for multiple principals *should* behave to arrive at an "optimal" agreement and about how multiple principals *should* negotiate a mandate with their agent.

Her analysis builds on the observation that "by disaggregating the notion of mandate into attributes that can presumably be traded off against one another, we can generate hypotheses as to what type of mandate better fits alternative patterns of the principal-agent relationship" (pp. 88-89). She identifies three such attributes and uses them to construct a prescriptive model expressed in words—not mathematical symbols—of multiple principals negotiating an agent's mandate so as to achieve an "optimal" outcome. A host of interesting hypotheses emerge.

What is an "optimal" mandate? Nicolaïdis defines mandate optimality as "the extent to which it maximizes the likelihood of achieving [a] negotiation outcome that will maximize the expected value of the agreement for the principals" (p. 93). (It is possible that the joint welfare function of the principals is maximized by leaving the agent out of the picture altogether!)

This definition of optimality has pitfalls. It can happen that the other side's preference structure makes it impossible to strike a deal that exactly maximizes "our" joint welfare function. At the same time, there may be lots of deals that are efficient (Pareto optimal) for us and do not maximize our joint welfare function, deals that lie well within the zone of agreement. We may a priori assign a large probability of agreement to one or more deals that maximize our joint welfare and find out later that this probability is vanishingly small. Then the reasonableness of the criterion vanishes along with this discovery. Add the proviso to "Maximize the likelihood of an agreement that, subject to constraints imposed by our (continually unfolding) perception of the ZOPA, achieves the largest possible joint welfare for us" and you have a prescriptive guide to choice that takes this scenario into account. This goal allows us to start with Nicolaïdis's definition of optimality and then modify it in the light of new evidence about feasible deals.

Nicolaïdis next proposes external efficiency (Pareto optimality) and internal equity ("some measure of fairness in allocation") as "generic criteria" for optimality of an agreement from the principals' perspective, but not as necessary ingredients of instructions to an agent. These criteria are, in practice, not separable. External efficiency comes first—most of the time. If you wish to do all that you can to create value, you may wish to resist the temptation to instruct your agent to impose binding restrictions suggested by prescriptive "standards of fairness" such as Nash until she negotiates to create value. Then act on possibilities left on the table. If you begin with active imposition of your side's version of internal equity and it does not fit well with the other side's perception of a ZOPA, you are unlikely to maximize the probability of agreement on a deal that comes close to maximizing your side's joint welfare. You may have finessed agreement on a "reasonable" but less than optimal settlement. Again, a mandate that maximizes the likelihood of satisfying these criteria may not maximize the probability of a *feasible* agreement.

This discussion slides into consideration of how to *sequence* instructions to agents. (Nicolaïdis suggests "iterated mandates," or updating your agent in the light of unfolding evidence, as one way of granting flexibility to the agent.) You may, if lucky, be able to recoup from failure to reach agreement caused by binding your agent with nonachievable "optimality" restrictions by relaxing them late in the game. What gambit works best? Typical extremes are to begin tough and then become reasonable or to begin reasonable and then become tough, with lots of possibilities in between and lots of interesting hypotheses to explore.

Following her discussion of optimality, Nicolaïdis presents a list of essential attributes of an agent's mandate "that can be manipulated to maximize the likelihood of satisfying these efficiency and equity criteria" (p. 94). These are flexibility, autonomy, and authority.

The attribute "autonomy" describes the degree to which principals appear "at the table" alongside the agent. When principals are at the table, they can *individually* influence the agent's behavior, according to Nicolaïdis. In addition, principals *and* their agent at the table send a different signal to negotiating counterparts than an agent alone at the table.

Authority, the right of the agent to make concessions and/or commitments on the part of the principals both during negotiations and at the end of negotiations, is, according to Nicolaïdis, "the most visible and quantifiable constraint" (p. 98).

We now have an objective function, a definition of an optimal agreement, that can be coupled to a mandate model composed of three operationally measurable attributes. Nicolaïdis uses this mandate model to dissect mechanisms employed to delegate trade authority in the EU and in the United States. Nicolaïdis's model strikes me, as a naïve observer of descriptively complex international negotiations of this sort, as a helpful framework for understanding who did what to whom and why. That is, this framework is useful for *ex post* analysis of real-world multiple principal–agent negotiations. It also suggests a number of testable hypotheses.

To this end, Nicolaïdis turns next to the "agency strategic dilemma": "How much flexibility or margin of maneuverability should be given to the agent to maximize the expected value of the agreements to the principals?" (p. 105). A concrete representation of trade-offs that arise from increasing or decreasing the margin of maneuverability appears in Figure 3.2. Each agent is presumed to have the twin objectives of maximizing "the likelihood of reaching a value-creating agreement, while at the same time he wants to manipulate the relative strategic advantage between the two sides in his favor (claiming value)" (p. 106). The figure is motivated by government negotiations involving trade authority. Agents here are literally government agents.

Imagine a different setting: An agent must negotiate on behalf of members of a corporate team with an agent who represents another corporate team. Each agent reports to a "boss" who may veto what she sees as an unacceptable agreement. This negotiation could take place entirely *within* an organization or *between* organizations. Does Nicolaïdis's description of the agency's strategic dilemma fit these types of negotiations as well? If, with some changes in wording, the description of the dilemma fits a wide variety of negotiation settings, then it is *robust*. We can also ask if the descriptive hypotheses she poses are robust in the same way.

Nicolaïdis suggests several reasons why the received wisdom that "the principal generally wants the agent to have less flexibility, whereas the agent would like more" may be off the mark in the multiple principal–agent setting. Leaning on early research, Nicolaïdis asserts that principals face a trade-off between "increasing the likelihood [that the agent will arrive at] value-creating agreements and decreasing [the agent's] margin of maneuverability to increase his strategic advantage. . . . An actual broad margin of maneuverability ensures that acceptable agreements are not left on the table, and a perceived narrow margin of maneuverability ensures a fair share from the value" (p. 108). This fundamental trade-off is the springboard for Nicolaïdis's classification of interest alignments among principals and between principals and agents (Figure 3.3), which in turn leads her to three (testable) hypotheses:

1. The greater the degree of interest alignment among principals, the less flexible the mandate should be.

2. The greater the degree of interest alignment between principal and agent, the more authority the agent should be granted.

3. Decreasing agent autonomy should be used to compensate for relaxing the other two constraints.

Before stating these hypotheses, Nicolaïdis declares that "Greater alignment of interest between principals makes it easier for them to collectively narrow the margin of maneuverability to increase their strategic advantage externally" (p. 111). This reasonable assertion leads naturally to the first hypothesis. Now imagine a negotiation in which principals on our side are perfectly aligned, but we and our agent are highly uncertain about the preferences of principals on the other side and so are uncertain about their degree of alignment. We are also uncertain about the degree of flexibility allowed the other side's agent. Do we really want to provide our agent with an inflexible mandate? It seems plausible that we would want to begin with a very flexible mandate and then tighten or loosen it as we learn more about the other side. This scenario is not a rare occurrence in business negotiations.

A rigorous test of the first two hypotheses requires specific *measures* of degrees of interest alignment among multiple principals and between principals and agents. Even in settings where this seems easy a priori, such measures can be elusive. Principals may *announce* preferences that differ from their *true* preferences in the belief that they will gain a strategic advantage. An agent will certainly learn an announced preference but may be highly uncertain about true preferences. Is the mandate strictly a function of announced preferences? Imagine that Michael Jordan and Scottie Pippen employ the same agent to negotiate with the Chicago Bulls management. Jordan has declared that he will not play for Chicago if Phil Jackson, the current coach, is not on board next season. If Pippen also publicly declares that he will not play for Chicago unless Jackson is reappointed coach and accepts, then the principals are publicly perfectly aligned on one key issue. They may be misaligned on other key issues such as pay and guaranteed playing time. Is public alignment of principals all that counts in shaping the mandate? Clearly not.

It would be informative to translate some version of Nicolaïdis's prescriptive model of negotiating a mandate, a model described here in words, into a well-posed mathematical model. The usual tension between accurate description of very complex real-world behavior and mathematical parsimony arises. Nevertheless, it seems possible to conduct laboratory tests of Nicolaïdis's behavioral hypotheses by *scaling down* the setting from description of complex international negotiations that unfold over long periods of time to a relatively simple framework of, say, two parties of two principals each, each party represented by an agent. This is, of course, not a new idea, but it would allow tests of the robustness of her descriptively rich hypotheses. Do experiments support these hypotheses? Are they good descriptors of behavior up and down levels of complexity of principal-agent negotiation settings? Let's see!

PART II

Agency in Context

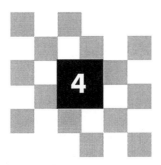

Challenges for International Diplomatic Agents

Eileen F. Babbitt

What is meant by "international negotiation?" Embedded in this phrase are three assumptions: Negotiations occur between groups or countries rather than individuals, which makes the use of agents an imperative; they often occur across cultures (racial, ethnic, religious, national); and they sometimes involve an "agent" of the international community, most often the United Nations, or a mediator from an outside country. Thus, for example, the ending of civil war in El Salvador, although not involving two or more cultures, is considered by most analysts to have been an "international" negotiation.

International negotiations encompass everything from treaty talks about climate change to the establishment of cease-fires and peace accords. They can be bilateral or multilateral; be conducted by political, military, or nongovernmental actors; and be widely covered by the media or entirely secret. In the international context, agents are ubiquitous. Official representatives are sent by their principals to formal negotiating forums; however, unofficial representatives often participate in informal "Track II" processes as well. In addition, the principals themselves can meet directly, although such summit diplomacy is often an elaborate stage from which to launch agreements that already have been hammered out by agents.

The focus of this preliminary discussion is on negotiations carried out by officials representing governments or national groups within states, in both bilateral and multilateral settings, for the purpose of settling violent inter- and intrastate disputes. The agents include ambassadors, agency officials, foreign service officers, military officers, special envoys, and designated leaders of subnational groups. Examples are drawn from situations involving the United States government as a participant or ones in which the United States has aligned with the "international community" to designate an agent.

The discussion focuses on the most salient challenges to international diplomatic agents. The traditional principal-agent issues, which provide the framework for this book, include structuring a mandate for the agent, determining the authority an agent will have to make commitments, creating incentives that align the agent's interests with those of the principal, and determining the extent of information that will be passed between the principal and the agent. The basic model from which these concerns are drawn is that of a single principal operating with a single agent. In the international context, these issues are complicated by several additional factors: multiple principals, shifting mandates, multiple agents, and role conflicts for the agent. This chapter explores each of these new permutations. It then offers several prescriptive suggestions, including the importance of training for diplomats in negotiation and mediation; the value of keeping diplomats in place for longer periods, to ensure their deep understanding of people and cultures; and the wisdom of giving such diplomats more leeway in exploring options with their counterparts in the context of negotiations—relying less on central control over negotiation processes and more on the judgment and skill of diplomats on the ground.

MULTIPLE PRINCIPALS

The most notable feature of international diplomatic negotiation is that it is carried out by agents who are working for a multiplicity of principals in a complicated web of relationships. This makes traditional principal-agent analysis quite problematic. In the classic principal-agent analysis, there is one person in each role. The concerns that arise are those identified elsewhere in this volume: potential differences between the interests of the principal and those of the agent; information asymmetry, with one of the two knowing or sharing more or less than the other; and second-order problems, building on these first two, of deciding what authority and mandate the principal should provide and the agent should seek (Pratt and Zeckhauser 1985).

These concerns are compounded enormously in the international context. There is no single point of reference for the agent, in terms of receiving instructions, gaining authority, or procuring information. For example, in the United States, the secretary of state (agent) may give instructions to an assistant secretary (agent), based on the instructions that the secretary has received from the president (principal). Those instructions may be superseded at any point by the president himself, especially if he is pressured by Congress (principal) or by adverse reactions from the American public (principal). Thus, the assistant secretary, who is at the end of this particular agent-principal chain, must pay attention to direct instructions being given by the secretary but also be ready to respond to political intervention from Congress or a backlash in public opinion.

This is a variation on the "agent-mediator-partisan" continuum described by Joel Cutcher-Gershenfeld and Michael Watkins in Chapter 1 in this volume. The problem the agent faces is not only reconciling conflicting interests within his or her constituency but also anticipating different mandates from each of several principals. The agent may not be in a position to mediate or make a choice among them but must be prepared to answer for discrepancies between the agent's actions and the expectations of various principals.

An example is provided by Chester Crocker's role as U.S. Assistant Secretary of State for African Affairs in the Reagan administration from 1981 to 1988, when he acted as an agent of the State Department in negotiating a series of peace treaties in southern Africa. His superior in the State Department was the Secretary of State (Alexander Haig and then George Shultz), but his mandate was not taken directly from either of them. It was constructed from a complex analysis of U.S. interests in southern Africa, including the administration's desire to get Cuba out of Angola, and of the possibilities of U.S. success in entering into negotiations with the southern African parties. It was also at odds with what Congress and public opinion preferred, given the pariah status of South Africa and the many United Nations resolutions calling for continued sanctions.

Crocker himself laid out the basis of his mandate in a 1980 article published in *Foreign Affairs* before his official government appointment, in which he called for "constructive engagement" with the South African government in service of a broader regional approach to problems in southern Africa. His views became part of the discussion of U.S. policy when he was tapped to join the 1980-1981 transition team in Ronald Reagan's first administration.[1] The transition team spent three months hammering out the details of the southern Africa policy, which hinged on the linkage of Cuban troop withdrawal from Angola with South African withdrawal from Namibia. Haig backed the team's assessment and took it to Reagan for his approval.

As Crocker reports, "Never mind that we had stacked the deck a little to obtain Reagan's approval, or that Reagan, as Haig would later put it, was 'not too steeped' in the issues" (Crocker 1992:66). In March 1981, Reagan agreed to the policy, even though the Senate had not yet scheduled Crocker's confirmation hearing. In Crocker's words, "The March 1981 decision provided my mandate for the next eight years" (Crocker 1992:67). Reagan, Haig, and later George Shultz would continue to support this policy, and Crocker's efforts, to the end of Crocker's two-term tenure. Crocker knew he had the backing of his immediate bosses, but he also knew, based on the close scrutiny he received at his confirmation hearings, that he had to "watch his back" vis-à-vis Congress and be sure he had "agents" of his own (i.e., his staff members) negotiating on his behalf in Washington. With enough pressure from Congress, Haig and Shultz might not have been able to defend Crocker's activities and could have been forced to remove him.

Both Congress and wider public opinion became deeply polarized over constructive engagement, especially during Reagan's second term, when the apartheid issue finally achieved a higher profile in the United States and spurred the demand for tougher economic and political sanctions against South Africa. As Crocker reports, "By the end of 1985, the free hand we had previously enjoyed became an object of nostalgia. Suddenly, we found ourselves ensnared in the polarization, hypocrisy, and purely political logic that flourished just outside our doors in Washington" (Crocker 1992:254). Activists and politicians on the left were incensed by the notion of any positive relationship with the racist South African regime. Those on the right were appalled that the State Department was negotiating with Marxists (the government of Angola). Crocker was thus required to defend his strategy and head off attempts to undermine it, with the Secretary of State and his team members (which included his counterparts at the Department of Defense) running interference as needed.

More significantly, the president (the principal who had officially approved Crocker's mandate) was not always helpful. In a 1991 speech (quoted in Crocker 1992:81), Reagan overplayed the importance of constructive engagement with South Africa as a "country that has stood beside us in every war we've ever fought, a country that strategically is essential to the free world. . . . If we're going to sit down at a table and negotiate with the Russians, surely we can keep the door open and continue to negotiate with a friendly nation like South Africa." Predictably, this created enormous problems for Crocker, both domestically and internationally, causing him to reflect, "The President's remark epitomized the insensitivity that would be the sad hallmark of his sporadic personal involvement on South Africa in the years to come" (Crocker 1992:81). In the international arena, it is a challenge for an agent to work with a principal who can cause damage with such public statements.

Contrast that with Crocker's assessment of George Shultz: "I would not have been able to sustain American policy in Africa without the leadership and unwavering support of George P. Shultz. . . . Shultz created and sustained the running room that I and others required to do our jobs" (Crocker 1992:14). Clearly, one key to effective agency in international diplomacy is the relationship not only to principals but also to the other agents farther up in the chain.

The principal-agent dynamic becomes still more complicated when the agent is acting on behalf of the "international community." This quite often means receiving a mandate from the United Nations Security Council (UNSC), a consortium of permanent and rotating members who do not always agree. Mandates in these instances are usually spelled out in UNSC resolutions, often in broad terms that the agent (often a special envoy of the UN Secretary General) has to keep clarifying as the mission proceeds because of the diverse interpretations inherent in the Security Council itself. In at least one case, that of the High Representative for Bosnia designated by the Dayton Accords of 1995, the agent was not even required to report to the UN (Neville-Jones 1996). Who, then, was the "principal" to whom this agent was responsible?

In the case of the High Representative, the disjuncture resulted from a lack of unity on the part of the international community as to how this role should be structured. The United States wanted an American in the post; the Europeans insisted on a European, because the Americans were controlling the military and Organization for Security and Cooperation (OSCE) components of the Bosnia intervention. A European was appointed, but the United States then insisted on restricting the authority given to the High Representative position, even though the mandate was extremely expansive. The High Representative would have no control over military operations, with military forces in Bosnia reporting to the U.S. military commander through their sector commanders (the British in the north, the French in the south, and the Americans in the east of the country).

Likewise, civilian agencies would not have to report to the High Representative; it was expected that they would somehow coordinate their activities through the High Representative's office, but the mechanism for such coordination was not specified, and the High Representative was not given oversight or control over their activities. The High Representative conceivably could have overcome this weak oversight authority with moral suasion, with a strong consensus-building vision, and with substantial funding and the ability to move money as needed, but this last source of leverage, too, was restricted because of the slowness with which the High Representative's office was provided funding by the donor countries.

At the same time as the authority was limited, the mandate was extensive. The expectation was that the High Representative would harmonize the civilian implementation in the same way that the military commander would blend troop activities as forces were supplied from different countries. Insufficient authority or other means of leverage, however, severely hampered the initial civilian operation, with no opportunity provided for revision of either the mandate or the authority as deficiencies were discovered. With the changeover to a second phase of the military operation and the appointment of a new High Representative in 1997, the international consortium of donors increased the authority vested in the High Representative to make decisions on the ground, but the lack of progress during the first phase of implementation continued to haunt the intervention effort.

A different example is provided by Richard Holbrooke and the agent role he played in brokering the Dayton Accords. In this case, the "principal" took yet another form, that of an alliance between the United States and Western Europe. Even though there was disagreement within the alliance about the form that a peace accord should take, there was agreement that something forceful had to be done. Holbrooke, therefore, had a lot of leeway to construct whatever he thought would work between the parties, even though certain U.S. interests (e.g., a very well-defined military commitment) and European interests (e.g., visible European leadership in the implementation) had to be satisfied.

Thus, the "principal" in an international negotiation of this kind is an alliance of actors, either within the U.S. government or among the world's major powers. The interests of each principal in the alliance are also products of nonmonolithic domestic actors. Thus, the agent must represent shifting coalitions, both within and between principals. This has profound implications for the mandate that the agent is given.

 SHIFTING MANDATES

Many of the principals in an international negotiation are elected (e.g., in the United States, the president and Congress are prime examples). Agents are not. Instructions may therefore change on short notice, depending on events on the ground that stir public opinion or shift the political winds. "Elected" principals are very susceptible to such influences, and they can, in turn, put pressure on "appointed" and "career" agents. Mandates therefore can be a moving target, and agents may get caught in the shifting currents and then become scapegoats for failed foreign policies.

One such example involves the U.S. relationship with Iraq in the period preceding the Gulf War. Covertly, the United States had been supplying arms to Iraq during the Iran-Iraq War, seeing Iraq's victory as preferable to the triumph of the mullahs of Iran. Quoting from a 1987 issue of *The New Republic*, journalist Christopher Hitchens shows Middle East analysts at the time espousing the U.S. backing of Iraq: "The fall of the existing regime in Iraq would enormously enhance Iranian influence, endanger the supply of oil, threaten pro-American regimes throughout the area, and upset the Arab-Israeli balance" (in Pipes and Mylroie 1987: 14-15).

U.S. support of Iraq continued up until the time of the Kuwaiti invasion on August 2, 1990. The U.S. ambassador to Iraq during this period, April Glaspie, was an experienced foreign service officer and well-respected diplomat. In a July 25, 1990, meeting with Saddam Hussein six days before the invasion, she is reported to have communicated continuing support for Iraq, in addition to concern about its aggressive moves toward Kuwait. In a transcript of the meeting released to the *New York Times* on September 23, 1990, Ambassador Glaspie responded to President Hussein's description of his country's economic concerns by saying:

> I have a direct instruction from the President to seek better relations with Iraq. . . . But we have no opinion on the Arab-Arab conflicts, like your border disagreement with Kuwait. I was in the American Embassy in Kuwait during the late 1960s. The instruction we had during this period was that we should express no opinion on this issue and that the issue is not associated with America. James Baker has directed our official spokesmen to emphasize this instruction. We hope you can solve this problem using any suitable methods via Klibi or via President Mubarak. All that we hope is that these issues are solved quickly. ("Excerpts From Iraqi Document" 1990:19)

After the invasion of Kuwait, the U.S. government position changed dramatically. President Bush spoke from the Oval Office on August 8, 1990, saying that "there is no justification whatsoever for this outrageous and brutal act of aggression" (quoted in Sifry and Cerf 1991:197). In editorials and articles in major newspapers and journals, Saddam Hussein was cast as the incarnation of Hitler, with any positive moves in his direction labeled "appeasement" (Krauthammer 1990; Safire 1990b; Solarz 1991; all quoted in Sifry and Cerf 1991). In that light, Ambassador Glaspie's cordial meeting with him made her appear weak and uninformed.

By all appearances, Ambassador Glaspie was left to become the scapegoat for a failed policy. In an interview with Elaine Sciolino of the *New York Times*, she said, "Obviously, I don't think, and nobody else did, that the Iraqis were going to take all of Kuwait" (Safire 1990a). She was withdrawn from Baghdad during the run-up to the war and banished to obscure posts at the State Department. James Baker, then Secretary of State, "disowned Glaspie by saying that his clear instructions to her in a difficult embassy at a crucial time were among probably 312,000 cables or so that go out under my name" (Hitchens, in Sifry and Cerf 1991:116).

International agents must therefore be very aware of the shifting winds in international politics, especially as these are affected by domestic political concerns. In Chester Crocker's case, he had anticipated a difficult reception at home and therefore had bolstered his "rear flank," as he liked to say. April Glaspie apparently did not feel the need for such protection, probably assuming her principals would back her up as long as she followed instructions. Maybe nothing can be done if one's principal decides it is better to sacrifice the agent than to admit a mistake, but it is clear that, as an international agent, complacency about support from one's principal can have serious consequences.

Another related issue is the effect of technology on diplomacy. In previous eras, ambassadors and other foreign service staff were the only source of information available to their principals. This gave them enormous power over their own mandates (and authority), as these were shaped by the perceptions of the world that they themselves formulated. With telephones, instantaneous news coverage, and now Internet access, the principals themselves have much more direct access to their counterparts abroad and to breaking news in other countries. This has diminished the role of diplomats to some degree (depending, of course, on the accessibility of a particular country via these technologies) and has certainly constrained their dominance over the information flow back home.

In addition, other sources of "ground truth" are being courted, as governments are seeking information more consistently from international humanitarian organizations about political changes on the ground in volatile parts of the world. Mandates given to official agents are therefore much more fluid, as principals may recalibrate their actions on a more frequent basis as new information becomes known.

MULTIPLE AGENTS

In addition to multiple principals manifesting multiple and mutable interests, there are often multiple agents working on the same issue as representatives of the same principal. Sometimes they are functioning as a designated team or delegation, but often they are using different points of entry from different parts of the coalition of principals. The U.S. delegations in post-Dayton Bosnia were an example, in which different messages were being conveyed by different agency representatives (i.e., State Department, Treasury, Commerce, Defense) to the European allies and to the Bosnian parties. Coordination among the agents was very difficult, and often impossible, to achieve, because coordination in their headquarters on both policy and implementation was not agreed upon (confidential source, U.S. Department of Defense 1996). The result was that others on the ground, particularly local organizations and officials, did not know who really spoke for the U.S. government. This type of situation obviously can undermine any authority or call into question the credibility of any or all of the agents, which in turn weakens the position of the principals for whom they work.

Another example may be found in central Africa. In addition to the U.S. ambassadors in the region, there are several special envoys working on various disputes. In Burundi, for example, envoys from Belgium, South Africa, Canada, the United Nations, the Organization for African Unity (OAU), and the United States are on the ground. In this case, the special envoys have established close collaboration, periodically meeting to "develop a consultative approach" so that the parties are not hearing different things from different sources (H. Wolpe, personal communication, September 1997). It is not clear how these efforts affect the credibility of the ambassadors from these countries in continuing their other diplomatic duties in Burundi, when other agents are seen to take on what traditionally would be the ambassador's responsibility.

A related issue is that agents may form their own "epistemic community," a collaboration of individuals who share a professional culture and orientation (e.g., scientists), or whose issue area of expertise is the same (e.g., arms control) (Haas 1990). In the diplomatic context, such a community could involve alliances between representatives of counterpart agencies in other countries (e.g., military commanders). Although this may enhance the negotiations that occur in each substantive sector, it can inhibit negotiations, and therefore coordination, across sectors in a multilateral operation. Without guidance and authority from their home principals, the agents may not have the capacity to set up such cross-disciplinary coordination on the ground.

ROLE CONFLICTS

Role conflicts can occur when the negotiation being conducted is about existential issues such as whether the groups in question will be able to survive in relation to each other, or if one will be eliminated by the other in war or by other means. In such negotiations, the agents walk a fine line, sometimes referred to as managing the "inside-outside" tension (i.e., working within one's group vs. with the other side) or as constructing delicate coalitions across the conflict line (Fisher 1991; Kelman 1993). If agents develop a relationship with the other side in which a "working trust" is established and negotiations can proceed, they may be seen as traitors to their own side. If they do not develop such trust, negotiations may break down and war will ensue. The problem is how to transfer their experience of the other side in such a way that the working trust (if it is built) can be brought back to one's constituency. This is not about relationships only as a means to achieving one's tangible goals; it is about a relationship as a goal in itself. How does an agent translate the trust and confidence that he or she has built back to a very scared and untrusting home community? It is the community that has to be convinced, not just the leaders (i.e., the multiple principal problem). In the international arena, this role conflict may be a difference in degree rather than in kind from other contexts.[2] The difference in degree is striking: Yitzhak Rabin and Anwar Sadat were assassinated because they could not bring their constituencies along in supporting the relationship they had built with the other side.

These examples also bring up another form of role conflict: that of being both a mediator and a negotiator. As the negotiator, an agent must represent the interests of his or her principal. Often, the agent is spanning two very different cultures, defined in the traditional sense as cutting across national boundaries but often cutting across class or professional lines as well. In doing so, the agent must mediate between the two groups, representing not only the interests of each but also the understandings and perceptions of each to the other.

Analysts have referred to this as a "network" of intermediaries, each one acting as a bridge between those on either side of them in the decision-making chain (Pruitt and Carnevale 1993:159). At either end of the chain are the stakeholders, or principals. In between are a series of "linking pins," or intermediaries, who have to face in both directions. Each of the linking agents has to articulate the views of his or her primary stakeholder but also has to interpret the messages coming from the stakeholder at the other end of the chain. According to Pruitt and Carnevale (1993), the most important activities in an arena (i.e., the interface between two adjacent persons in the chain) are information transfer, persuasion, and problem solving. It stands to reason that to fulfill these obligations successfully, agents need to have a deep understanding not only of their own principals but also of the other side's principals.

In diplomatic tradition in the United States, foreign service officers are rotated every two years, ostensibly to keep everyone a generalist but also to prevent agents from becoming too identified with any one foreign country. The difficulty, however, is that the deep understanding that comes from longevity in a posting, which can be crucial when acting as a mediator between the two cultures, is lost in such rotations. The bridging function is compromised to preserve identification with one's own group. This can have serious consequences in a negotiation, when there is a need to understand the motivations and interests of the other side, as they perceive them. Without a cultural interpreter, such understanding is distorted and can have serious consequences in the quality of agreements reached.

A third form that such role conflict may take is that of representing one's principal versus being a cooperative member of the diplomatic community. In protracted multilateral negotiations, for example, a diplomatic subculture develops in which personal relationships are forged and norms of behavior are consciously or unconsciously prescribed. Some have described the professional diplomatic community as a "guild," a group "engaged in kindred pursuits, or having common interests or aims, [or practicing] the same craft or trade" (Henrikson 1998). Such long-standing relationships and shared experience and worldview can facilitate agreements but can bring such agreements down to a lowest common denominator so as to preserve the relationships. In some international treaty provisions, for example, the final wording is left purposely vague or filled with caveats, watering down the treaty's impact and making the enforcement of such provisions very difficult. This outcome, however, is not inevitable; many ongoing international negotiations are quite contentious and founder repeatedly because the agents cannot work together. A tension could develop, especially in negotiations that take place over long periods of time, between being perceived as a "good" member of the guild versus being tough for one's own side.

PRESCRIPTIONS FOR PRACTICE

Although the role of agents in the international context is ubiquitous and necessary, their effectiveness is often diminished by long-standing ways of working in foreign affairs that might now be usefully revised. The first is in the training of diplomats. To prepare for the variety of roles that they are expected to play in crucial negotiations, they should build their skills in mediation as well as negotiation. It may be that these can be learned on the job, but it would be far better to prepare someone ahead of time and to alert that person to the need to manage perceptions, expectations, and interests not only across national boundaries but on one's own side as well.

To handle such functions effectively, agents need to be kept in place long enough to fully understand the culture of their opposite number and be able to translate it back to their principals. In the current world of diplomacy and into the foreseeable future, diplomats will be called on to understand much more about negotiating parties than their place in, for example, the relatively simple alliances of the Cold War era. Although attention must be paid to the problems inherent in keeping people in one place too long, this must be balanced with the great benefits gained from deep knowledge of a people and a culture, or of relationships forged over time in a multilateral setting.

Particularly if diplomats are to remain in place for protracted periods of time, they must have access to adequate information. It is imperative that agents operating outside their home country have their own source of information on what is happening back home. Without the calibration of domestic politics, they can be caught off guard by shifting mandates dictated by political pressures or public opinion. Conversely, agents must keep their principals informed as they develop relationships with their counterparts abroad. As powerful as information technology has become, it cannot adequately convey or transfer the essence of trust as it is being forged. Ironically, personal contact between principals and agents is even more critical as technology becomes more sophisticated.

The final, and crucial, point follows from the first two. With sufficient training and adequate grounding in a given country or negotiating forum, agents should be given more independence to explore options at the table, based on their experience and intimate knowledge. As was mentioned by Roger Fisher and Wayne Davis in Chapter 2 of this volume, such independence can be increased gradually over time and tempered with the judgments of the principals. Without the flexibility to explore options, agents will not do as well for their principals. This does not, however, have to be joined with increased authority to commit. In fact, the exploration process could be conducted more openly if such authority were not granted. Then it would be the task of the agent to "sell" the newly created ideas to his or her principals, knowing the interests of the principals and wanting to provide them with a set of options to which they could conceivably say yes.

 CONCLUSION

The basic difficulties inherent in the principal-agent relationship are exacerbated by the complexities and current realities of the international context. With an increasing number of international actors, technologies that make information available to both decision makers and average citizens that were never dreamed of even a decade ago, the growing number of international conflicts that are existential in nature, and the increasing pace at which situations on the ground change, the role of agents in international negotiations must also change. Rather than keeping control firmly at the center, back in the capital and solely in the hands of the principals, international diplomatic agents must be given more freedom to respond to negotiation challenges as they unfold, more responsibility to structure their negotiation strategy, and therefore more accountability for outcomes. This will require a rethinking of the qualifications for such agents, including their training and ongoing education.

This does not mean, necessarily, that such agents should be drawn only from the foreign service ranks; one need only look at the successful ambassadorship of the late Pamela Harriman in Paris to see how the right fit of person and assignment can be made outside the State Department career track. Appointments at both the diplomatic and agency levels, for those who will be representing the United States as a negotiating agent, should be made with a new set of criteria in mind. These agents must understand the complexities of the negotiating environment; be equipped, through language skills, cultural sensitivity, and process training, to act as both mediator and negotiator; be able to exercise sound judgment and creativity if given flexibility and responsibility; be open to, and skillful at, creating alliances with other agents on the ground; and be strategic in their reading of the domestic environment as well as the international system.

In addition, principals must be willing to cede some of their power to their agents, recognizing that being on the front line provides a level of experience and insight into negotiation dynamics that are impossible to obtain from a distance. This means that principals must be in better communication with their agents, possibly through secure video-conferencing, to allow the flexibility but also provide the oversight that the relationship requires. This would also allow better coordination as new data appear. It would also provide more ongoing information on the changing status of the relationship between the agent and the "other side," to bring the principal(s) along in the trust-building process.

In terms of theory building, scholars must adjust their theories of agency to take the sometimes extreme challenges of the international context into account. The complexity, long duration, and high stakes of many international negotiations put a unique set of pressures on the principal-agent relationship, and the recommendations offered here may well serve agents in other settings as well.

 NOTES

1. Chester Crocker recounted his experiences in his 1992 memoir *High Noon in Southern Africa: Making Peace in a Rough Neighborhood.*

2. Dean Pruitt and Peter Carnevale draw from the organizational behavior literature to discuss "Adam's Paradox," in which

> representatives who are trusted and given autonomy by constituents will feel especially free to advocate concessions to the other side. The result of this behavior is likely to be suspicion of the representatives' loyalty, leading to closer monitoring of the representative's behavior. This, in turn, may cause the representative to become rather tough with the other party, resulting in poor relations with that party, and a poor agreement. The poor agreement reinforces the constituent's monitoring and suspicion. (1993:156)

The issue of trust-building is not discussed here specifically but can be inferred from the scenario (1993:159).

▨ REFERENCES

Crocker, C. 1992. *High noon in Southern Africa: Making peace in a rough neighborhood.* New York: W. W. Norton.

Excerpts from Iraqi document on meeting with U.S. envoy. 1990. *New York Times*, September 23, p. 19.

Fisher, R. 1991. Negotiating inside out: What are the best ways to relate internal negotiations with external ones? In *Negotiation theory and practice*, edited by J. W. Breslin and J. Z. Rubin. Cambridge, MA: PON Books.

Haas, P. M. 1990. *Saving the Mediterranean: The politics of international environmental cooperation.* New York: Columbia University Press.

Henrikson, A. K. 1998. Diplomacy for the 21st century: "Recrafting the Old Guild." Occasional Paper 1. West Sussex, UK: Wilton Park.

Kelman, H. C. 1993. Coalitions across conflict lines: The interplay of conflicts within and between the Israeli and Palestinian communities. In *Conflict between people and groups*, edited by J. Simpson and S. Worchel. Chicago: Nelson-Hall.

Krauthammer, C. 1990. Nightmare from the thirties. *Washington Post*, July 27.

Neville-Jones, P. 1996. Dayton, IFOR, and alliance relations. *Survival*, Winter.

Pipes, D. and L. Mylroie. 1987. Back Iraq. *The New Republic*, April 27, pp. 14-15.

Pratt, J. W. and R. J. Zeckhauser, eds. 1985. *Principals and agents: The structure of business.* Cambridge, MA: Harvard Business School Press.

Pruitt, D. and P. Carnevale. 1993. *Negotiation in social conflict.* Buckingham, UK: Open University Press.

Safire, W. 1990a. Calling to account. *New York Times*, September 17.

Safire, W. 1990b. The Hitler analogy. *New York Times*, August 24.

Sifry, M. L. and C. Cerf. 1991. *The Gulf War reader.* New York: Random House.

Solarz, S. J. 1991. The stakes in the Gulf. *The New Republic*, January 7 and 14, pp. 18-25.

The Role of Agents in International Negotiation

Bruce M. Patton

In her chapter on international agents, Eileen Babbitt notes four challenges for such agents: multiple principals, shifting mandates, multiple agents, and role conflicts. The first challenge is that international agents often represent amorphous or multiheaded constituencies that may be incapable of offering or maintaining clear and sensible directions. The second challenge is often a consequence of the first: mandates that change with shifts in home politics. The third challenge, multiple agents, is likewise related to the complexity of the principal: Discrete interest groups among the home constituency may empower their own agents, crowding the field and often pursuing divergent and even conflicting agendas.

The fourth challenge, as Babbitt describes it, is more generic. It refers to the conflicting incentives and goals of agents who are simultaneously representing principals, pursuing their own careers or substantive ends, and operating as members of a professional community with relationships to maintain. It also applies to agents who are both members of the principal group and vulnerable to symbolic expulsion from it if they are seen to build too close a relationship with members of an opposing group in a highly polarized conflict. These kinds of complex incentives are part and parcel of agency in many conflicts, as explored throughout this book.

Babbitt illustrates these challenges with a diverse array of examples and offers four summary prescriptions for how agents can be helped to deal with them better: (1) better training in negotiation and mediation theory and skills; (2) longer tours of service to build deeper knowledge of local conditions, cultures, and counterparts; (3) better channels of communication with home constituencies; and (4) more flexible and nuanced instructions, along the lines of those recommended by Roger Fisher and Wayne Davis (Chapter 2, this volume).

Although these prescriptions should improve an international agent's ability to cope with the challenges Babbitt has enumerated, they do not address the fundamental question of how an international agent should conceptualize his or her role in the face of these challenges to help guide choices in dealing with them. To stimulate further thinking on that topic, let me offer here some thoughts derived by analogy to a proactive mediator.

The use of a mediator analogy makes some sense structurally because an agent is positioned between the principal(s) and the other side(s). One way to think of both mediators and agents is as additional parties to the situation who bring their own interests to the table. In both cases, it makes sense for a principal to choose an agent or mediator whose mix of overlapping, shared, different, and conflicting interests (as affected by whatever incentives the principal can bring to bear) seem most compatible with the principal's ends and values.

So when and how should agents or prospective agents announce their interests, and how should they weigh their interests against those of the principal in carrying out their role? These are, of course, not easy questions. Nor are answers easily implemented, because much of what a person thinks and does is automatic and not fully conscious. Again, it would help to have some general ideas on the role of an agent to guide one's thinking. Let me offer five suggestions.

1. *Ultimately, the principal should decide.* As with a mediator, the first thought is that, in the end, the important choices are the principal's to make. For the most part, this refers to *substantive* choices, leaving the agent to control process, but the distinction might not hold for a process choice that was likely to have an irrevocable effect on substance. This

guideline does not mean, however, that the principal should make all decisions up front. Negotiation inevitably involves learning. This leads to the second guideline.

2. The agent's role is to facilitate wise decisions with a minimum of subsequent regrets. The agent's role is to help the principal recognize choices and think through their consequences, to identify and weigh trade-offs between, for example, short-term victory and a longer-term loss of power or the establishment of a troublesome precedent. Or an agent with technical expertise might help a principal identify which avenues of possible effort are likely to prove more or less fruitful. The so-called Wizards were agents who served this role during the Cold War. The Wizards were a group of scientists who met privately under official auspices, but without any kind of authority to commit, to think through the technical issues involved in various possible arms control agreements and report which approaches seemed technically feasible and promising to pursue in negotiations.

The importance of this role cannot be overstated. Principals in all negotiations tend to have complex and often internally inconsistent interests, many of which come to light only in response to particular concrete proposals. Principals begin to feel what it would be like to accept a particular proposal and suddenly, through their reactions, discover new information about priorities. They also begin to see the trade-offs they face among various interests, which often necessitate difficult and painful choices. This phenomenon is only exaggerated in international negotiations, where the number and complexity of the principals tends to expand both the pool of interests to be served and the internal conflict among them.

The agent's role is to help the principal clarify interests and priorities, to invent possible solutions that necessitate the fewest painful choices, and to serve up those choices that remain in ways that help principals appreciate and weigh wisely the full spectrum of interests at stake. This leads to the third guideline.

3. Ordinarily, the agent should be the chief manager of process. One of the most important insights of negotiation research is that the process used to discuss the issues in dispute affects the kind and likelihood of outcomes. Some approaches are more conducive to creative, mutual-gain solutions, others less so. Some are more likely to produce sensible precedents, others more arbitrary ones. Consistent with Babbitt's emphasis on training, international agents, as a rule, should be process professionals with the skill and insight to structure and manage the process of negotiation to help principals (their own and others), as well as the group of agents, explore the issues at stake to best achieve the goal of sophisticated, informed choice.

Although occasionally a principal might have more process expertise than an agent, the principal lacks the detailed information available to the agent on the scene and should be wary of exerting control at too fine a level. More often, agents are likely to have the time and expertise to be much more focused and farsighted in understanding the terrain of issues and interests and thinking about how to help principals explore that terrain effectively.

Agents also may find it easier to distance psychologically from short-term emotional hot-button issues and give due weight to longer-term considerations. To the extent they can do so, agents can then design communication processes at the table and with their constituents that help principals gain a similar sense of perspective.

The danger of process control, of course, much like information control, is that it can serve to manipulate principals and dictate outcomes. This suggests the fourth guideline.

4. *The agent should be as transparent as possible, consistent with the first three guidelines.* Complete agent transparency is not appropriate. If an agent suggests a process, thinking that it may help a principal unfreeze psychologically from a position that seems emotionally driven and shortsighted, the principal might well refuse or participate less fully if this purpose were trumpeted up front. In other situations, however, there is no such bar to an agent sharing his or her thinking, if a principal is or perhaps should be interested.

The check on less transparent moves should be a willingness on the part of the agent to become transparent post hoc. That is, if the agent were to record his or her honest thinking at the time of a less than fully transparent move, the thinking should be such that a principal reviewing the record later would not be troubled. In the end, the principal should feel that the chosen process helped him or her understand and weigh all relevant factors in a balanced and appropriate way.

To the extent that an agent has strong substantive interests or process preferences that a reasonable principal might want to consider in choosing an agent, transparency would suggest that the agent make these biases generally known. This leads to the final guideline.

5. *The agent should advertise key values and beliefs up front.* This helps a potential principal weigh what interests prospective agents are likely to serve on their own behalf. Because agents, as human beings, cannot divorce themselves or their behavior from influence by their own interests, principals should be able to make their own *ex ante* judgment about whether they are comfortable working with someone with a particular conceptual frame, skill set, or core values. On the agent's side, such an approach eases somewhat the challenge of serving one's own interests along with a principal's by moving discussion and negotiation over how that will work up front, prior to representation. In a domestic context, many divorce mediators take such an approach routinely, printing information for potential clients about the standard approach to property and custody issues. Many well-known international agents do much the same by making speeches and publishing articles.

Certainly these guidelines are far from all-inclusive and do not yet paint a robust or succinct statement of the generic role of an international agent. If, however, they serve only to stimulate further discussion, whether critique or elaboration, it will be to the good.

Law and Power in
Agency Relationships

Jeswald W. Salacuse

The complexity of modern transactions and organizations makes the use of agents in negotiation the rule, rather than the exception, in virtually all areas of life. Diplomats in treaty negotiations are agents for their governments, executives in merger discussions are agents for their corporations, and labor leaders in wage talks are agents for their unions. Although commentators often speak of the agency relationship as though it were a single type, different kinds of relationships between agent and principal exist both in fact and in law.

The specific nature of the relationship between principal and agent can profoundly affect the negotiation that the agent conducts. Two important contextual variables shaping agency relationships are law and the power dynamics between agent and principal. Often, these two factors are in tension. While law seeks to structure the agency relationship in accordance with a particular model, the power dynamics between agent and principal may counter or even thwart the elements of the legal model. The purpose of this chapter is to explore the role of law and power in agency relationships and to suggest their implications for the conduct of negotiations themselves.

▓ THE LEGAL MODEL OF AGENCY

Law is a fundamental factor shaping relationships between agent and principal. Whatever else it may be, agency is fundamentally a legal relationship in the sense that the law creates it and specifies its consequences. In common law countries, the courts, rather than legislatures, have created the law of agency through their decisions in countless cases over the years. Drawing on those decisions, the *Restatement (Second) of Agency* (1958), s.1., defines agency as "the fiduciary relationship which results from the manifestation of consent by one person to another that the other shall act on his behalf and subject to his control, and consent by the other so to act." From this definition, four key elements emerge to form the legal model of the agency relationship:

1 A fiduciary relationship between agent and principal,

2. Control by the principal over the agent,

3. Action by the agent on behalf of the principal, and

4. Consent by both principal and agent to the agency relationship.

Let us consider briefly each element of the legal model.

Fiduciary Relationship

The agency relationship exists for the benefit of the principal; consequently, the law considers the agent's interests to be subordinate to those of the principal. To achieve that subordination of interests, the law declares all agents to be fiduciaries. As a fiduciary, an agent has a duty of loyalty to the principal—a legal duty to act, within the scope of the agency, only in the best interests of the principal, rather than in the agent's own interests. Thus, the law imposes obligations on the agent in his or her relationship with the principal that are different from those that exist between a buyer and a seller in the marketplace. Accordingly, an agent must inform the principal of all relevant information about the negotiation, such as the receipt of any offers, and may not have a personal interest in the transaction without the principal's consent (see Reuschlein and Gregory 1979). A fiduciary relationship, in the words of the common law, is a "relationship of trust and confidence," and the courts impose a variety of sanctions to enforce the duties of that relationship and to punish any agent who violates them. Accordingly, a court can force an agent who makes an unauthorized profit from his or her agency to "disgorge" it and turn it over to the principal. For example, a corporate officer who learned of a business opportunity during the course of a negotiation for the corporation and invested in it personally instead of informing his employer could be forced to transfer the investment to his corporate principal.

The fiduciary duty seems to run counter to human nature in that it seeks to constrain the self-interest of the agent. It is perhaps for this reason that the courts are given to lofty rhetoric in describing and applying the fiduciary duty owed by the agent to the principal. Thus, Justice Benjamin Cardozo, in one of the most often cited cases on the subject, wrote:

> Many forms of conduct permissible in a workaday world for those acting at arm's length, are forbidden to those bound by fiduciary ties. A trustee is held to something stricter than the morals of the market place. Not honesty alone, but the punctilio of an honor the most sensitive, is then the standard. (*Meinhard v. Salmon* 1928)

It is interesting to note that a principal has no corresponding duty of loyalty to the agent. A principal, unless he has specifically agreed otherwise, therefore is free to engage two agents, unknown to each other, to negotiate for the same objective. For example, the United States government, after designating an official diplomatic representative to specific negotiations, such as arms control talks, has in some cases also appointed other agents secretly to conduct "back channel discussions" on the same subject with the same negotiating counterpart.

Control

A second element in the legal model of agency is the principal's control over the agent. Because the purpose of the relationship is to conduct the business of the principal, the courts have concluded that the principal should be able to determine how those business interests are advanced. Accordingly, the agent has a duty to follow the orders of the principal and, where no specific instructions have been given, "to act only in accordance with what he reasonably believes the principal has directed or, if he knew the facts, would direct the agent to do at the time and place of action" (Seavey 1964:239).

Agent's Actions on Behalf of the Principal

The third element in the legal model is that the agent has the power to act on behalf of the principal, which, in legal terms, means that the agent in appropriate circumstances has the power to create legal relationships between the principal and third persons with whom the agent deals. It is in this area that the courts and legal commentators have devoted major efforts in the development of agency law. Indeed, their principal preoccupation has been finding a basis to hold the principal legally responsible to third parties for the agent's actions in respect of that third party. The fundamental question they have addressed is this: How, and under what circumstances, does the agent create legal obligations between the principal and third party as a result of a transaction (or negotiation) in which the principal was not directly involved? To explain and justify such a result, which in theory seems to conflict with the notion of individual responsibility that is basic to Western law, the courts and commentators developed a variety of concepts. They have held that the acts of the agent will obligate the principal to a third party where the principal has given specific instructions so to act ("authority"); where authorization for the agent's acts might reasonably be inferred from the principal's direction ("implied authority"); where the principal did or said something to lead a third party to believe that an agent had authority to act, although no such authority existed ("apparent authority"); or where subsequent to the agent's unauthorized act, the principal did or said something to indicate approval of that act ("ratification").

Consent

The final element in the legal model is consent. Agency is fundamentally a consensual relationship. Despite the existence of an agreement to the contrary, an agent may stop acting as agent at any time, and the principal may withdraw or modify consent at any time and thus terminate the agent's power to act on the principal's behalf immediately. Implicit in the idea of consent is the notion that agency is also a personal relationship, that the principal is appointing a specific person to act as agent and the agent is agreeing to act on behalf of a specific person as principal. The implication of the consensual nature of the relationship is that the relationship automatically dissolves upon the death of either party and that neither party can, without agreement of the other, substitute another person to act as principal or agent.

The purpose of the legal model is to create a structure to ensure that the principal's work is done as the principal directs and in his or her best interests alone. It has been designed primarily with the principal's interest in mind. Through the legal devices of the principal's *right of control* and the agent's *fiduciary duty and duty of obedience*, the law seeks to counter the human tendency of all individuals, left to their own devices, to give priority to their own interests and to pursue their activities in the way they think best.

The legal model, in demanding the agent's obedience and commitment to the principal and in imposing sanctions for the failure to carry out those duties, is fundamentally coercive in nature. It relies on the *coercive* power of the law to achieve the principal's goals. It thus stands in sharp contrast to the organizational model of agency found in the management, economics, and behavioral science literature (e.g., Milgrom and Roberts 1992; Williamson 1985), which focuses primarily (though not exclusively) on incentive structures as fundamental to inducing agent behavior that is desired by the principal. Unlike the judicial cases and doctrinal scholarship on the law of agency, this literature rarely mentions the agent's legal obligations of loyalty and obedience, to say nothing of "the punctilio of an honor the most sensitive" that concerned Justice Cardozo. On the other hand, the legal model leaves matters of incentives and internal governance largely to private ordering between agent and principal.

THE LEGAL FORMS OF AGENCY: CONTRACTORS, EMPLOYEES, AND PARTNERS

Although the law establishes a basic agency model, it also provides differing forms of agency within that model for structuring the relationship between principal and agent. Each form carries with it different legal consequences. An agent who negotiates on behalf of a principal may do so in one of three legal forms: as an independent contractor, as an employee, or as a partner.

An important distinction in agency law is between agents who are *employees* ("servants" in the language of the common law) and agents who are not employees (commonly called "independent contractors"). The distinction between an agent as an employee and an agent as independent contractor resides in the degree of control that the principal exercises over the "physical conduct" of the agent's activities. According to sections 2 and 220 of the *Restatement (Second) of Agency* (1958), an employee (a "servant") is an agent whose employer ("master") controls or has the right to control the "physical conduct" of the employee in the performance of the services rendered; however, a principal who engages an independent contractor as an agent, although entitled to general control of the agent, has no such right to control the physical performance of the agent's undertaking. Whether or not a principal has sufficient control of the agent's physical conduct to make the latter an employee as opposed to an independent contractor has been the subject of much litigation, and the distinction between these two legal forms of agency has not been readily apparent in all cases. Indeed, because the distinction is often so difficult to determine, the *Restatement (Second) of Agency* (1958), rather than specifying a precise differentiation, merely lists 10 factors to be considered, among others, in distinguishing between the two. (Five of the most important are the extent of control that the principal by agreement exercises over the details of the work, whether or not the agent is employed in a distinct occupation or profession, the length of time that the agent is employed, the degree of skill required of the agent, and whether the principal or the agent supplies the instrumentalities, tools, and place of work.)

The distinction between employee agents and independent contractor agents has application in negotiations. For example, a vice president of a multinational corporation negotiating a joint venture is an employee, but a lawyer from the corporation's outside law firm engaged in that same activity would be considered an independent contractor because, in theory, the corporation does not have the same degree of control over the physical conduct of the lawyer's activity that it does over its own executive. In the case of the vice president, the corporation, by hiring him as an employee, has contracted for the right to direct the details of his performance of a specific activity (i.e., his activities as vice president of marketing), but in the case of the outside lawyer—an independent contractor—the corporation has contracted for the performance of a specified activity (i.e., the negotiation of a joint venture) (see Posner 1972).

The law also recognizes a third type of agent—the partner. A partnership is an association of two or more persons to carry on, as co-owners, a business for profit (Uniform Partnership Act s.6[1]), and every partner is an agent of the partnership for purposes of its business (Uniform Partnership Act s.9[1]). The act of every partner in apparently carrying on the business of the partnership obligates the other partners. As a partner, a person is liable for partnership debts and is entitled to share, according to the partnership agreement, in the firm's profits and assets. In negotiations pertaining to the business, a partner is an agent of the partnership and is also a principal at the same time. Decisions on ordinary partnership business are made by a majority of the partners; however, no act that violates the partnership agreement may be performed without the consent of all the partners (Uniform Partnership Act s.18[h]).

The law thus offers principals three possible legal structures for organizing a relationship with a negotiating agent: independent contractor, employee, or partner. For example, a small toy manufacturer seeking to expand sales through an agent has basically three legal structures to bring about that result: an independent sales representative, an employee salesperson, or a new partner with an ownership interest in the firm. In fact, within the small-scale manufacturing sector, one can find numerous examples of all three agency arrangements. The parties are free to determine details of their relationship by contract within the limits of the specific legal form they have chosen or that a court may judge them to have chosen. For example, the agent's compensation in all three cases might include some percentage of sales made by the agent. In judging which particular form exists, the courts look to the substance of the relationship rather than merely to the name the parties give it. For example, if a company engaged a "consultant" to negotiate a transaction as an independent contractor but exerted significant control over the physical conduct of the negotiation, a court might hold the relationship to be that of employee rather than of independent contractor.

CONTRACTORS, EMPLOYEES, AND PARTNERS AS NEGOTIATORS

The existence of these three legal structures of agency raises questions as to when and under what circumstances a principal—whether an

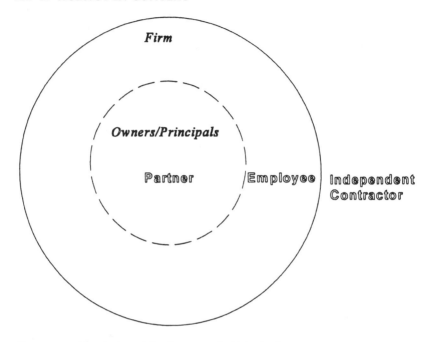

Figure 5.1. Proximity of the Agent to the Principal

individual, a company, a government, or an international organization—should use one type or another to conduct a given negotiation. A further question is what impact a particular form may have on a given negotiation. Does the legal form have any effect on the behavior of the agent, or is the fact that an agent is an independent contractor, employee, or partner fundamentally irrelevant to the conduct of a negotiation? This section seeks to explore those questions.

At the outset, one should note that the chosen agency form gives a basic structure to the relationship between agent and principal and that each of the three structures are fundamentally different from one another. The independent contractor as negotiator works outside the principal's firm or organization, the employee as negotiator works within the firm, and the partner as negotiator is a co-owner of the firm and thus both principal and agent at the same time. Thus, one difference among the three agency structures resides in the degree of organizational proximity that the agent has with the principal on whose behalf he or she negotiates. That proximity is illustrated in Figure 5.1.

Although an agent and principal, through the device of contract, can determine the precise attributes of their relationship within each of these forms, the forms themselves limit the parties' contractual freedom to a certain extent. For example, regardless of the parties' stated intentions, the law will consider a declared "independent contractor" to be an employee if the principal exercises too great a degree of control over his activities, and it will also find that an alleged "employee" is a partner if he or she has what amounts to an ownership interest in the principal's business. Once a court has made such a determination, a variety of legal consequences will follow in the relationship of principal and agent, consequences that the parties may not desire or even have contemplated.

In *The Economic Institutions of Capitalism*, Oliver Williamson (1985) reminds us that organizational choice has significant consequences for economic activity, particularly with regard to transaction costs, and that the choice of a particular organization form always involves trade-offs. "Improvements in one or more performance measures," he writes, "are realized only at the sacrifice of others" (Williamson 1985:402-408). Similarly, in the case of negotiations on behalf of others, the selection of a particular legal form of the agency can have an important effect on the relationship between agent and principal, at least with respect to four vital elements: (1) costs and benefits of using an agent, (2) control of the agent by the principal, (3) alignment of principal and agent interests, and (4) negotiating effectiveness of the agent. Moreover, the design of a given agency relationship through the use of law and private ordering also involves trade-offs among these elements.

Relative Costs and Benefits

An evaluation of the relative costs and benefits to the principal and the agent of a particular structure is an important threshold consideration. Costs to the principal include not only the compensation to be paid to the agent but also the transaction costs of planning, adapting, and monitoring the execution of the desired tasks under each of the three organizational structures (Williamson 1985). In addition, the cost of terminating an agency relationship may also vary depending on whether the agent is an independent contractor, employee, or partner.

The small-scale toy manufacturer who has identified a dynamic and skilled salesperson must decide which structure will yield the greatest amount of revenue from new sales contracts at the least cost. The independent sales representative may cost the company little in terms of cash outlay or potential liabilities because he or she will be paid on the basis of a commission only and will have little or no power to obligate the principal; however, the independent sales representative as negotiator may bring the company little revenue because he or she will devote only a portion of time and effort to the toy manufacturer's business and may see little point in investing significant time and effort in expanding sales if he or she represents better-known and more popular toy manufacturers. In short, despite the existence of a legal right of control and a fiduciary duty in this particular type of agency, an independent sales representative in a given context may not yield the kind of results desired by the principal.

Compared to an independent contractor, having a full-time employee as a negotiating agent assures the principal greater control over the agent's activity and increased effort by the agent in the principal's business to the exclusion of any other manufacturer; however, in this situation the toy manufacturer faces increased costs not only in terms of compensation to the agent but also through increased expenses incidental to employee status (e.g., Social Security contributions), as well as the principal's increased management costs and potential liability for an employee's civil wrongs committed in the course of employment. Moreover, by virtue of being an employee and gaining the associated incidents of that status, an agent may, in the eyes of the law, have apparent authority to obligate the principal to certain types of unauthorized transactions.

The toy manufacturer might choose to make the salesperson a partner in the business and thereby give him or her a significant incentive for intensified activity that will increase revenues to the firm. The costs to the toy manufacturer of a partnership relation, however, may be substantial because a partner, as a co-owner, has a claim on an agreed-upon portion of business profits and assets and is also in a position to incur debts and liabilities that will bind the partnership.

An evaluation of costs and benefits can influence the decision on agency forms in many contexts. Invariably, the agent and principal are faced with a host of trade-offs in seeking to structure their relationship, and the precise nature of those trade-offs and how they are valued will differ from context to context. For example, a company that contemplates the negotiation of a single joint venture may decide that the most cost-effective agency structure is to engage an outside law firm or consulting group (i.e., an independent contractor) as its negotiating agent; however, a company that plans a series of such joint ventures may find it more profitable and less costly to hire a negotiator as an employee of the company.

Similarly, a government might use a member of its foreign service (an employee) to conduct one kind of negotiation but might ask an outside consultant or volunteer (an independent contractor) to conduct another type. For example, a U.S. president would certainly designate an employee, such as the U.S. trade representative, to conduct negotiations in formal trade talks such as the Uruguay Round of the General Agreement on Tariffs and Trade (GATT) but might entrust politically sensitive discussions, such as overtures to an adversary like Fidel Castro or Saddam Hussein, to an independent contractor—a friend or volunteer whose actions can more easily be disavowed than can those taken by a U.S. diplomat in his or her official capacity.

In the early 1990s, one of the approaches to downsizing American corporations was to shift large numbers of workers from the status of being employees to that of being independent contractors—a shift that brought cost savings to the companies but also reduced their ability to manage those workers because of diminished control. More recently, in an era of heightened competition and business consolidation, some companies are exploring the creation of partnership arrangements with persons and organizations with which they traditionally had independent contractual arrangements (Henderson 1997).

An agent also weighs relative costs and benefits in deciding on which agency relationship to accept. For example, the independent sales representative who is offered employment or partnership arrangement with the toy manufacturer must weigh the advantages of a proposed salary against the opportunity costs of forgone income that would result if he or she were free to negotiate on behalf other principals, as well as the increased responsibilities and risks of liability that an employee or partnership relationship may entail. Moreover, such a change in status also subjects the agent to increasing control of his activities by the firm, a change that many independent contractors find unacceptable.

Principal's Control of the Agent

As indicated above, every agency relationship gives the principal control over the agent and, through the imposition of the fiduciary duty, seeks to ensure that the agent will work in the best interests of the principal. Nevertheless, the degree to which the principal is able to exercise control over the agent varies among the three agency forms. Whereas principals have a general right to control agents who are independent contractors, they have a right to a higher degree of control over employees because that right extends to "the physical conduct" of the employee's activities. Controlling a partner, on the other hand, is more difficult than controlling an employee or independent contractor. In legal terms, partners can control one another only by majority vote of the partners; however, regardless of a majority vote, partners by virtue of their status have apparent authority to bind the partnership for matters apparently relating to the business of the partnership (DeMott 1995). In practical terms, a partner's ownership interest in the partnership gives him or her power in relationships and negotiations with other partners that an employee or independent contractor would not have.

In theory, the agent's fiduciary duty also acts as an element of control because it places basic limits on what an agent may or may not do. For example, an employee must not appropriate a business opportunity that he or she uncovers while working on behalf of an employer, and partnership status prevents a partner from engaging in any activities that may compete with the partnership business.

The effectiveness of the legal right of control and the fiduciary duty in securing desired agent behavior is, of course, highly problematic. Despite the coercive structures of the law, agents are self-serving, lazy, disobedient, and inattentive. Although the existence of legal sanctions does have some impact on agent behavior, their use by the principal normally involves high costs, not only with respect to judicial enforcement but also with respect to monitoring the relationship to determine whether in fact an agent has been disobedient or disloyal.

Interest Alignment

More important than control in securing desired agent behavior are incentives. A major problem in any agency relationship is to align the interests of principal and agent so that the principal can be assured that the agent will in fact exert maximum efforts on the principal's behalf. To the extent that the principal's and agent's interests are aligned, the agent has an increased incentive to act in the interests of the principal. One can view the legal relationships of independent contractor, employee, and partner as three legal structures on a spectrum that increasingly aligns the interests of principal and agent. As one moves along the spectrum from independent contractor to partner, the agent's interests become increasingly aligned with those of the principal; however, the principal purchases that increasing alignment at an increased price. Thus, in the absence of some special contractual arrangement, an independent sales representative's interests are less aligned with those of the small toy manufacturer than are those of a partner in the business; consequently, the partner has much greater incentive to exert efforts on behalf of his or her principal than does an independent sales representative.

Negotiating Effectiveness

The particular agency form selected may also influence the negotiator's effectiveness at the table. For example, an independent contractor, being neither an employee nor a partner, may have less knowledge about the principal's interests, strategies, and capabilities than would an employee or a partner, both of whom work within the firm. Moreover, in a specific negotiation, the other side may view a partner, and in some cases an employee, as a negotiator more seriously than an independent contractor because a partner and some types of employees, by virtue of their position, speak more authoritatively for the firm and may be more likely than an independent contractor to deliver on commitments made at the table. On the other hand, an independent contractor, less subject to the control of the firm and less influenced by its prevailing culture, may feel freer to propose new ideas and approaches to his principal than would an employee. Partners may also feel free to propose new ideas, and they are also able, by virtue of their apparent authority, to implement them despite opposition from their partners.

POWER IN AGENCY RELATIONSHIPS

The Legal Model in Practice

Agency in practice does not always correspond to the legal model. The most significant divergence between law and practice concerns the principal's power over the agent. The legal model assumes that the principal in an agency relationship is the more powerful, if not the all-powerful, party. After all, the principal "controls" the agent, who acts on behalf on the principal subject to the principal's consent. To bind the principal to any obligation toward a third party, the agent must have authority, and the principal—and the principal alone—is the source of that authority. An examination of many agent-principal relationships indicates that reality does not always conform to the legal model.

Two areas where practice and law often are in tension concern the ability of the principal to control the agent and the obligation of the agent to work exclusively in the principal's best interests. Agents are driven primarily by their own interests, not their principal's, and to pursue their interests they often seek to avoid or attenuate the principal's control. Principals on their part seek to ensure control of the agent through a variety of devices, not only to be sure that their interests are advanced but also to be certain that they are advanced in acceptable ways. On the other hand, there may be times when an agent honestly (and perhaps correctly) believes that he or she will be most effective in a negotiation if he or she can reduce the control by the principal over the agent's activities. For example, a negotiating agent who has received instructions from a principal to adhere to rigid positions in a negotiations may feel that such controls prevent an exploration of mutual interests with a negotiating counterpart so as to arrive at the optimal deal for both parties.

In short, although the legal model may view the principal-agent relationship as a feudal hierarchy in which the principal directs and the agent obeys, in practice relationships between principal and agent may be very much a continuing negotiation. Two important factors affecting this continuing negotiation are the organizational structure in which the agent-principal relationship is embedded and the power dynamics between principal and agent.

Structure: A Chain of Agents

If it is true that most negotiations are conducted through agents, it is also true that in most cases the persons directing and controlling agent negotiators are themselves agents. The legal model, of course, assumes that the principal directly controls the agent. In most cases, however, although agents negotiate for a distant principal, they are at the same time negotiating for other agents. For example, the assistant U.S. trade representative in auto talks with Japan negotiates under the control of the U.S. trade representative, who is herself an agent of the president of the United States. The director of international development in a multinational corporation negotiates a joint venture under the direction of the corporation's international vice president, who is an agent of the company's CEO, who in turn is an agent of the board of directors. Thus, principals often use a chain of agents to conduct negotiations.

What is the effect on the negotiation of the fact that a negotiating agent reports to and follows the directions of persons who are themselves agents? For one thing, the longer the chain of agents between the principal and the negotiating agent, the greater the risk that the negotiator is not receiving optimal information about the principal's interests, goals, and needs. For example, the director of international development, because of his midlevel position, might have less information about the company's goals and interests than would the international vice president. The lack of such information can inhibit the negotiator's effectiveness at the table. Conversely, a long chain of agents may reduce flows of information about the negotiation to the principal. Second, the longer the chain of agents, the greater the risk that agreements negotiated at the table, although conforming to the instructions of the negotiator's direct supervisor, will not be approved or ratified by the ultimate principal. For example, even though the director of international development has negotiated a deal according to the instructions of the international vice president, the CEO may ultimately reject the negotiated agreement or demand revision of its terms not only because it may not conform to his original instructions to the vice president but also because his distance from the actual negotiations makes him feel less invested in the process. Finally, the longer the chain of agents, the more the various agents' interests may intervene to complicate the negotiation process.

Because of the complexity of transactions and organizations, the use of a chain of agents in conducting negotiations is a necessity in most cases. The above-mentioned factors, however, suggest several principles that should guide the design of agency relationships in cases of multiple agents. First, the chain of agents should normally be kept as short as possible. Second, the parties should seek to ensure maximum flow of information along the chain in both directions. Third, mechanisms and incentive systems may need to be put in place throughout the chain to inhibit self-serving behavior by all the agents concerned.

Power Dynamics Between Principal and Agent

Although the law gives the principal authority over the agent, the context may give the agent power over the principal. For example, the position of Henry Kissinger, as an agent of President Nixon in the disengagement negotiations between Egyptian and Israeli forces after the 1973 October war, was one of exceptional power vis-à-vis the president. Nixon, distracted and politically weakened by the Watergate scandal, was not in significant control of his negotiating agent. On the other hand, U.S. negotiators at the arms control talks in Helsinki in 1969 were tightly controlled and directed by Washington and felt they had little power in their agency relationship with National Security Advisor Henry Kissinger.

Power in an agency relationship can be defined as the ability of principal and agent to influence the each other's decisions in a desired way. In the Israeli-Egyptian disengagement talks, Kissinger, in the context of the times, had significant influence over Nixon, whereas the arms control negotiators at Geneva had virtually no influence with Kissinger, their ostensible principal.

The power relationship between agent and principal can have a direct effect on the conduct of the negotiations themselves. Certainly one of the first elements in assessing a counterpart in a negotiation is to determine whether the counterpart has "clout" with his or her principal. Clout in this context does not mean the legal authority to make commitments binding the principal, for in most significant negotiations the parties at the table know that any agreements they make are subject to the approval of their principals. Rather, clout refers to the ability of negotiators to persuade their principals—their bureau-cracies, governments, or corporate organizations—to accept deals made at the negotiating table. Without power, a negotiator may not be able to deliver on commitments and understandings made in the ne-gotiations.

Although a lawyer may analyze a negotiator's power in terms of her legal authority (i.e., the legal ability to bind the principal in the latter's absence), a negotiating agent, without any authority to bind at all, may nevertheless possess a great deal of power because of her abil-ity to influence the decisions of the principal. Indeed, it may be pref-erable to negotiate with an agent without authority but with power, rather than with an agent who has authority and little power with the principal, because the former may have the flexibility to deliver agree-ments that the principal and agent may never have considered prior to the negotiation. Moreover, negotiations with a powerful agent are likely to proceed more quickly than they will with a less powerful agent who must constantly check back with the principal during negotiations.

If, then, the agent's power with the principal is an important ele-ment in the agency relationship, what factors will strengthen or weaken an agent in the agency relationship? What factors should a negotiator look for to determine whether a counterpart across the ne-gotiating table has clout with his or her principal? Although an agent's power is a matter of influence, few agents rely only on the quality of their arguments to influence their principals. Several other factors can affect the power dynamics in an agency relationship.

First, of course, is the nature of the personal relationship between agent and principal. With close political ties to their presidents and direct access to the Oval Office, Robert Strauss and Mickey Kantor were particularly powerful agents as U.S. trade representatives. Strauss's relationship with Carter and Kantor's relationship with Clinton gave them power as negotiating agents that technocrats in similar negotiating roles, regardless of negotiating skills and knowl-edge of international trade, could not hope to have. A close personal relationship gives a principal confidence that an agent is working in the principal's best interests, confidence that the most highly skilled technocrat may not be able to give.

A second factor that affects the power relationship between agent and principal is the adequacy and availability of alternative agents to act as negotiators on behalf of the principal. During the Watergate scandal, Nixon had few alternatives to Henry Kissinger as Secretary of State, a fact that increased Kissinger's power with his principal. Similarly, a corporate executive with knowledge of the Chinese language, years of business experience in China, and broad contacts within the Chinese government will by virtue of these facts have influence with his or her principal; however, that influence will be even greater to the extent that the corporation has no other executive with similar abilities and experience.

A third power factor, not contemplated by the legal model, is the network of alliances that the agent has with other persons who can influence the principal in a desired way. Thus, negotiating agents cultivate their relationships not only with the principal but also with appropriate departments and bureaucracies that can be mobilized to influence the principal's decisions on matters affecting the negotiation. An agent's power may also stem from his relationships with the principal's adversary in the negotiation. For example, the toy manufacturer who has selected a sales representative with close contacts to purchasing managers at Toys-R-Us would normally be reluctant to terminate that relationship, even in the case of unsatisfactory performance by the agent, for fear that the disgruntled former agent would injure the manufacturer's future sales prospects with the giant retailer.

Finally, although the legal model contemplates a principal who is autonomous and an agent who is dependent on the principal, in fact agents seek to create a situation in which the principal is dependent on the agent. In many cases, when a principal must decide on a course of action in a negotiation or approve agreements made at the table, he or she will turn first to the negotiating agent for advice and guidance. Although the legal model requires the agent, as a fiduciary, to convey to the principal all relevant information concerning the negotiation, agents may in fact be selective in the information they convey so as to create and maintain their principal's dependence on them and thereby preserve their power in the agency relationship.

CONCLUSION

Persons who negotiate on behalf of others do so within a framework of relationships created by law, contract, and power. These three factors can have important consequences on the performance of agents at the negotiating table. Consequently, in seeking optimum agent performance, principals should be aware of the interplay of these elements in selecting an agent and designing an appropriate agency relationship. A single ideal agency relationship does not exist. Rather, the appropriate agency relationship for a given task is highly context specific. Its design depends on a host of trade-offs and an evaluation of costs and benefits. Once having created an agency relationship through negotiation, both principal and agent need to remember that, regardless of law and contract, events may intervene to change the power dynamic between the parties and thereby alter the agency relationship itself.

 REFERENCES

DeMott, D. A. 1995. Our partners' keepers? Agency dimensions of partnership relationships. *Law and Contemporary Problems* 58:109-134.

Henderson, A. B. 1997. Ford explores idea of joining dealers. *Wall Street Journal*, May 12, p. A2.

Meinhard v. Salmon, 249 N.Y. 458, 164 N.E. 545 (1928).

Milgrom, P. and J. Roberts. 1992. *Economics, organization and management.* Englewood Cliffs, NJ: Prentice Hall.

Posner, R. 1972. *Economic analysis of the law.* Boston: Little, Brown.

Restatement (second) of agency. 1958. Philadelphia: The American Law Institute.

Reuschlein, H. G. and W. A. Gregory. 1979. *Handbook on the law of agency and partnership.* St. Paul, MN: West.

Seavey, W. A. 1964. *Handbook of the law of agency.* St. Paul, MN: West.

Uniform Partnership Act (National Conference of Commissioners on Uniform Laws, approved 1914). 1978. Reprinted in R. T. Steffen, *Agency-partnership in a nutshell.* St. Paul, MN: West.

Williamson, O. E. 1985. *The economic institutions of capitalism.* New York: Free Press.

Law and Power in
Agency Relationships

Janet Martinez

A ppoint a lawyer to manage the sale of a business, an interior designer to decorate a home, a labor leader to represent workers, or a former president to facilitate a diplomatic mission: The ubiquitous use of agents represents a demand for division of labor in negotiating a range of commitments between individuals, groups, and states in the world at large. The extensive social and economic externalities generated by agency compel a public interest in circumscribing the role of agents, and thus the intervention of legal institutions—the public contract, if you will—to govern the principal-agent relationship.

Salacuse's chapter outlines a legal lens through which to glimpse this agency relationship. The basic legal forms of agency—independent contractor, employee, and partner—represent an increasing colinearity between the interests of the principal and the agent. This legal lens is necessary but insufficient to understand the implications for negotiation. Salacuse notes that although the law creates the agency relationship and specifies its consequences, in fact this legal structure is seemingly irrelevant. Salacuse's second-level analysis suggests that agency in law and in fact can be explained by examining a principal's and agent's respective power.

The law grants a presumption of power to the principal to determine a level of control over the agent's actions, although specific contextual and personal attributes of the principal and agent may shift that power balance. Sebenius (1996) has described negotiation in terms of structure, people, and context. Structure denotes the architecture of parties, interests, alternatives, and processes that establishes the negotiation baseline, but that is further defined by the individual and social behavior of the people involved, as well as the organizational and cultural norms of the context in which the negotiation proceeds. Salacuse's analysis of agency explores how personal and contextual power shape the legal structure of a principal's relationship with his agent, whether categorized as an employee, independent contractor, or partner. The legal parameters established for different types of agents is the public contract between society and its citizens. The chapters in this volume try to organize our thinking for negotiating the private contract between the principal and agent in defining their relationship, specificity of instructions for action, authority, incentives, and information exchange. The legal structure serves as a tool for designing that relationship—working forward and backward to calibrate an optimal balance of costs and benefits for both the principal and the agent.

 PRINCIPAL-AGENT: THE PUBLIC CONTRACT

The principal-agency literature carefully outlines the advantages and disadvantages presented by use of an agent. The potential value of drawing on an agent's expert substantive and procedural knowledge, extensive experience, special resources, and skills is balanced against the potential costs of an agent's interests being obliquely aligned with those of the principal. Each factor in the cost-benefit analysis is tempered by whether there is a long-term relationship between the principal and agent, reputational costs or benefits to either, incentives to align the agent's interests with the principal's, information asymmetries between the principal and agent, and the costs to the principal of monitoring the agent's actions. Salacuse's chapter clarifies this analysis through both elucidating the legal options and providing examples in private and public arenas. Table 5.1 summarizes the legal forms of agency as applied to a sample case: a toy manufacturer seeking to

TABLE 5.1 Comparative Cost-Benefit Analysis of Agent Types From the Principal's Point of View

Legally Defined Agent Type	Interest Alignment	Economic Cost	Control of Agent's Actions	Knowledge of Enterprise	Flexibility in Thinking
Employee	**High** The employee's interests are aligned with those of the employer-principal	**High** The principal is responsible for the employee's full compensation and is liable for the employee's actions within the scope of his employment	**High** The employer-principal is able to prescribe the employee's activities	**Fair** The employee will have a high level of inside knowledge but limited knowledge of information outside the enterprise	**Minimal** The employee-agent may well be constrained by the expectations and the authority of the employer
Independent contractor	**Low** The contractor has outside interests and limited commitment to the firm	**Low** The contractor is compensated only for value given the firm and has little or no power to obligate the firm	**Medium** The principal has general control over the contractor	**Low** The contractor will have limited inside information about the firm	**High** The contractor is free to be flexible and visionary in options to meet the principal's interests
Partner	**High** The partners' interests are likely to be highly aligned with one another	**Mixed** Partners share in both the profits and the costs of the enterprise	**Low** Partners have limited control over one another, because each has apparent authority to bind the enterprise	**High** Partners will have full inside information	**Medium** Partners may be flexible and think freely in developing options for the enterprise

178

expand sales through an employee salesperson, an independent sales representative, or a new partner with an ownership interest in the firm.

Salacuse points out, however, the prevalence of multiple agent relationships—or complex agency—that attenuate issues of information, ratification, and interest misalignment. A longer chain of agents increases the risk of information and signaling disconnects, the risk that the principal will not ratify the agent's commitments or recommendations, and the risk that the agent's interests will intervene.

 ## PRINCIPAL-AGENT: DESIGNING THE CONTRACTUAL RELATIONSHIP

The legal structure options merely provide a starting point for a principal and agent to design a contract within the institutional context that maximizes the value surplus and minimizes the costs to be shared. Given the relative costs and benefits derived from the legal forms—partner, employee, or contractor—and any agency complexity, a power assessment establishes any shift in the relative presumption of control between the principal and agent.

The principal's power stems from its legal status: power to control and ratify the agent's acts, access to information, and ability to monitor the agent and structure incentives. The agent's power stems from its authority—whether explicit, implied, or apparent—to act on behalf of the principal, plus its ability to influence the decision of the principal, based on its personal relationship, the adequacy and availability of alternative agents, the agent's network of alliance (both personal and organizational), and the principal's dependence on the agent.

Negotiating the optimal contractual arrangement is, in the most important case, an iterative rather than a linear process. Assessing the composite of legal form, organizational context, and relative personal clout of a particular principal and agent is a complex variant of multistakeholder, multi-issue negotiation analysis: Who are the parties and their respective interests, and what are the options that will maximize those respective interests in a sustainable fashion? The analysis calls for working the parameters forward and backward to achieve the best balance—an effort that may be abbreviated based on experience or parsed into successive stages of the agency relationship as the balance of the principal's and agent's interests and power shift over time.

 ## PRINCIPAL-AGENT: INTEGRATED ANALYSIS

Salacuse reminds us of the legal structure that underlies agency relationships but cautions that the reality of an agent's unconditional fiduciary duty to the principal and the principal's control over the agent is at least tempered, if not countered, by the power dynamic between them. As outlined in Table 5.1, the choice of *legal form*—employee, independent contractor, or partner—establishes the basic parameters for the relationship and authority granted to the agent. These include (1) the principal's level of control over the agent's activities and (2) the agent's legal fiduciary duty to act within his scope of authority, only in the best interests of the principal.

The general allocation of authority and power as indicated in each cell of the figure is qualified by contextual norms and the individual and organizational *power* granted under law to the principal to set the form of the relationship and derive from the agent's ability to influence the principal by virtue of their personal relationship, the availability of alternative agents, the agent's network of alliances (personal and organizational), and the principal's dependence on the agent.

Once the specific attributes and preferences of the principal and agent are determined, the contractual relationship can be designed to take advantage of the legal forms available to capture their respective contributions and minimize their relative risks. Thus, Salacuse's approach usefully reminds us of the legal tools available and articulates the subjective dimension for structuring effective principal-agent relationships.

 ## REFERENCE

Sebenius, J. 1996. *Introduction to negotiation analysis: Structure, people, context.* Harvard Business School Case #2-896-034. Cambridge, MA: Harvard Business School Press.

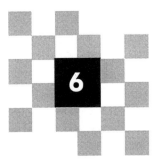

Agency in the Context of Labor Negotiations

Robert B. McKersie

The earliest writings about collective bargaining recognized the important fact that agency was a key part of the system. Embedded in the actions of organizing workers came the reality that the union would serve as a representative for the workers that it sought to enroll and speak for in dealing with management. Correspondingly, on the management side of the equation, although the agency role has not been as explicit, it has been just as real. The chief negotiator for the employer is a representative or agent for the interests that management brings to the employment relationship.

I see my assignment in this chapter as elucidating the dilemmas and presenting some examples of best practice in labor-management relations. My hope is that this material will have applicability to other settings where agency is an important dimension of the negotiation process.

Author's Note: I would like to thank my colleagues Richard Walton and Joel Cutcher-Gershenfeld, the participants in the Conference on Agency and Negotiation, and many unnamed practitioners for their counsel and suggestions.

HOW WE THINK ABOUT THE SUBJECT OF AGENCY IN LABOR NEGOTIATIONS

In *A Behavioral Theory of Labor and Negotiations* (Walton and McKersie 1994), first published in 1965, Richard Walton and I reasoned that the interaction between a chief negotiator and his/her organization was so important that it was necessary to frame a specific subprocess to capture these dynamics. We labeled it "intraorganizational" bargaining. In this subprocess, we sought to capture the reality that a representative or agent must negotiate in two directions, achieving alignment and agreement both within his or her organization as well as with the negotiator representing the other organization. In this chapter, I focus primarily on the interactions between the agent and his or her organization and deal with actions (strategy and tactics) only at the "main table" as they relate to this first assignment, namely, bringing about a settlement that is acceptable to the clients and principals.

THE HIGH STAKES THAT ARE INVOLVED

Unlike many settings in which an agent is hired only for a specific negotiation, in the labor-management sphere, an agent typically is elected or hired on a long-term basis. Accordingly, the agent is motivated to perform effectively so as not to engender displeasure and face the resulting possibility of being replaced.

Union and management negotiators (i.e., agents) frequently talk about the hazards inherent in their roles. Union leaders can be removed at the next election. Similarly, chief negotiators on the company side may be removed when the outcomes are not in line with the expectations of top management, specifically, when the negotiators have not been able to produce cost-effective settlements and the other changes that management feels the competitive environment requires. One management negotiator we talked with in our research revealed that this can occur if the chief negotiator misgauges the resolve of senior management and/or agrees to unattainable contract objectives.

▓ THE IMPACT OF A SHIFTING LABOR-MANAGEMENT RELATIONSHIP ON THE ROLE OF THE AGENT

The challenge that all agents face in performing their roles changes dramatically as the tenor of the labor-management relationship shifts over time. Typically, during the early phases of collective bargaining, representatives on each side experience little, if any, role conflict. On the union side, the labor leader concentrates on developing solidarity and presenting a united front to management in pursuit of concessions and an acceptable agreement. Often, the labor leader's agenda may be more ambitious than that of his membership. (A first contract that "goes out in front" can be used by the union leadership as a strong selling point in its organizing campaigns.)

On the employer side of the table, the representative will be vigilant in protecting management's rights and flexibility to run the operations efficiently. Again, the agent's interests are aligned with those of the organization that he or she represents.

The dilemmas and role conflicts for the agents develop as the labor-management relationship matures. In most labor-management relationships, the agents interact intensively and regularly over an extended period of time—not just during contract negotiations but also during the contract administration phase. Increasingly, they come to see their roles as negotiating and implementing the succession of labor contracts in an efficient and constructive manner. They may even describe the overall relationship as cooperative.

Chief negotiators place considerable importance on the development of rapport with their counterparts. Trust serves as the mechanism for understanding the interests of the other side and working collaboratively to fashion agreements that satisfy the needs of the respective organizations.

The role conflict that develops is a product of two vectors. On one hand, the chief negotiator carries a portfolio of objectives and an agenda that has been shaped by the constituents who either have elected or selected him or her. On the other hand, a working relationship, complete with expectations and norms, has been developed with the counterpart from the other organization.

When an agent views the messages received along these two axes as equally important, then the role conflict is especially intense, particularly when the respective "demands" on the agent are in conflict. This state of affairs is most likely to exist when the labor-management relationship falls in the middle range between very adversarial (when the agent only needs to be responsive to the wishes of the principals) and very cooperative (when the interests of labor and management converge). Today, most relationships fall in this middle range.

THE AGENT ACTING AS PRINCIPAL

Narrowly construed, the chief union and management negotiators are strictly agents for their respective constituencies, the rank-and-file and stockholders. Other agenda items emerge, however, in the interactions between these constituencies and their agents. Union leaders often bring into collective bargaining the interests of the institution as much as they do those of a particular set of members. For example, they often oppose granting concessions in wages for a high-cost plant, even though such action might save jobs for these members, out of fear that such a change would create a pattern that other employers would insist be adopted, thereby weakening the wage standard across the industry.

Similarly, on the management side of the table, the representatives of stockholder interests often bring their own "baggage" into negotiations. For example, the reluctance of management to share information with employees and union representatives concerning executive salaries can be understood more as a means of maintaining status and power than as representing stockholder interests.

Given this reality that agents are often acting on their own behalf, what difference does this make for understanding the labor-management process? There are several implications. Clearly, this dimension adds considerable complexity to labor negotiations. Also, because these institutional or organizational interests are shaped by particular individuals, a very dynamic element is added to the equation as different leaders come and go in the key roles of the labor-management relationship.

▓ THE MAJOR CHALLENGES AND DILEMMAS FACED BY UNION AND MANAGEMENT NEGOTIATORS

The key challenge faced by all agents arises from the negative range that often develops between the expectations of the clients[1] and those of the other organization. This divergence can occur over both the substantive agenda and the social contract—the latter referring to expectations regarding the bargaining style of the agent as well as the desired relationship between the two organizations. How these gaps develop and their amenability to resolution depends on several factors, including the orientation of the principal to the agent, time horizons, the nature of the issues, and anti-union lobbying by management.

Orientation of Principal to Agent

To start with, the principals often hold orientations very different from those of their agents. Top management generally is more concerned about cost and changes in the contract that have a bearing on productivity than in the relationship between the two organizations. Correspondingly, rank-and-file members usually hold strong views about the appropriate behavior that their agents should exhibit in negotiations with management. Often, they feel that unless their agents behave very vigorously and use coercive forms of power, then the best possible settlement will not be realized. Moreover, rank-and-file members will judge the "fairness" of the proposed contract against settlements that they know exist in other employment relationships.

Time Horizons

The time horizons of the various parties (both principals and chief negotiators) also affect expectations. Chief negotiators (who may have held their positions for some time) are more inclined to think about the long-term relationship and the tenor of future dealings with their opposites than are their clients. By contrast, top management today tends to bring a short-run orientation to the negotiation process.

In our first book on labor negotiations, we attempted to explain the bonding that often occurs between respective lead negotiators, as follows:

> There are several reasons why negotiators for the two parties have a relationship with each other not shared or valued by their respective principals. The relationship develops naturally out of the interaction between the two men and their joint responsibility for hammering out an agreement. They also sometimes have unique responsibilities for administering that agreement. These factors may lead to positive sentiments toward each other. The relationship also grows out of a need that they feel for some limits to the contest and for some predictability of the outcome. Since the two chief negotiators have to live together during the course of the ensuing contract, they both desire some predictability in the behavior of the other person. Often the result is a sense of mutual obligation in certain areas. (Walton and McKersie 1994:284)

Nature of the Issues

The nature of the issues that are in contention will certainly shape the outlook of the various parties. If the overriding objective is to increase productivity and add value (with emphasis on quality and timely delivery), attitudinal factors will be especially important. Correspondingly, if the focus is on short-term efforts to reduce costs—for example, via staff reductions—then substantive issues will be much more dominant, and the reaction on the union side is likely to be a source for considerable divergence, with members resisting the proposals of management to become "more competitive."

Emerging Anti-union Lobbying by Management

Another development that exacerbates the role conflict experienced by the chief spokespersons in labor relations is the emerging conviction within employer circles that management should fight vigorously to limit the expansion of unions and collective bargaining. As a result, management, almost without exception, now will go all out to convince employees that they do not need to join a union to achieve fair wages and working conditions or to realize fair settlement of complaints.

I would like to expand on this point. Consider a typical manufacturing plant where the hourly or blue-collar workers have been organized for decades and a very mature and stable labor management relationship is in place. In addition, the lead negotiators have held their positions for some time and have developed a good working rapport. Suppose that at this point the union decides to organize the white-collar workers at this plant, possibly because some of these workers have expressed interest in joining a union as a result of downsizing (and given the decline in membership, the union, for its part, is very eager to add members to its ranks).

On first consideration, some observers might expect that a company that has enjoyed a constructive relationship with its union might remain neutral during such an organizing campaign.[2] Typically, in the face of an organizing campaign, management hires consultants, who are experts in developing a strategy and the associated communications, to persuade the target employee group that they do not need a union, and the reaction on the union side is often one of outrage. This is especially the case when the union negotiator sees his counterpart with whom he has worked cooperatively orchestrating the campaign to keep the union out of the white-collar ranks. Union leaders able to see the irony in the situation point out to their management counterparts that if it had not been for the arrival of the union, there would not be any need for labor relations professionals, and now these same individuals are leading the campaigns against the need for a union.

For most union leaders, the reaction to this "double breasted" posture of management goes far beyond irony and involves bitterness and a reevaluation of the working relationship that they may have developed with their counterparts in management. As a result, in a number of labor-management situations in the telephone, auto, and steel industries, where partnerships have developed (with the result that many of the dilemmas normally experienced by bargaining representatives have been resolved in the process of enhancing corporate viability and employment security), the conflict over organizing campaigns has moved the relationship back to arm's length dealings, with the result that the role of the agent has become substantially more complicated.

THE STAGES OF THE PROCESS FOR MANAGING INTERNAL NEGOTIATIONS

It is useful to segment the coping activities of the agent into a time continuum, starting with the initial phase when negotiations take place within each organization over expectations, followed by the negotiations at the "main table" with the other side, and finally ending with the phase during which the agent works for understanding and acceptance of the proposed settlement on the part of the clients.

Negotiating the Instructions

Certainly, an experienced negotiator desires to retain as much flexibility as possible. On the other hand, given the concern that clients have that their needs may not be met, there will be efforts on their part to "put some stakes in the ground" so that the agent has specific "marching orders."

Most labor negotiators have a fairly good idea of the prospective settlement range, and they will spend time in initial sessions with their principals shaping expectations so that there is a reasonable chance that they can be fulfilled. Important exceptions exist, however, and they often occur on the union side. Recently, I attended a town meeting type of event. The union negotiating team sat on the stage in the union hall and encouraged rank-and-file members to sound off and express their concerns and their needs for the new contract that was soon to be negotiated. In this case, the union leaders found it difficult to "shape" the aspirations of their members in a more realistic direction for fear they would be told, in effect, "We elected you to represent us. Don't tell us what is feasible. Go and achieve what we feel is desirable."

Historically, this initial phase of the process might not have been as difficult for the lead negotiator on the employer side. Today, however, given all the emphasis on downsizing and responding to competitive pressures, company negotiators also find themselves increasingly holding instructions to bring back a contract that they know will be very difficult to achieve—short of some type of showdown, possibly involving a long strike.

The Negotiation Process at the Main Table

Given the common challenge that each chief negotiator faces in dealing with the divergence of expectations on the part of his or her principals and the prospects for realizing them, and given the fact that chief negotiators often interact regularly, the bonding or natural alliance mentioned earlier motivates the agents to help each other with their respective internal negotiations. One such technique is for the concession schedule or the convergence profile to be managed in such a way that the constituents are convinced that it is necessary for them to revise their aspirations.

Another technique is for the negotiator to present proposals in such a way that the main purpose is not to change the position of the other side but to convince the constituents that the agent is doing the best possible job. I do not want to demean the integrity of chief negotiators—indeed, integrity is one of the most prized attributes of successful negotiators. There can, however, from time to time be a type of "winking of the eye" across the table between the two chief negotiators as they "put on a show" for their principals.

When, as is usually the case, negotiations at the main table cannot be observed by constituents, then the chief negotiators need to report back and provide a picture of how negotiations are unfolding. This has to be done in a way that helps the constituents revise their expectations. On the union side, the chief negotiator may actually go into some detail about how the company was "given hell"—all of this being done to convince the rank and file that the best possible agreement was negotiated:

> We sold a contract that the membership of this local did not want by telling the members how I—an outsider representing them—"told off" the vice president of the company during negotiations. . . . My highly dramatic description of how I rubbed these executives' noses in the dirt gave the membership the vicarious thrill of talking back to management, something all of them had wanted but none dared to do. . . . So pleased were they that, without any discussion, they unanimously voted acceptance of the contract. (Walton and McKersie 1994:238)

Another technique for chief negotiators in their quest for internal alignment is to bring individuals who are most likely to object to the expected outcome directly into the bargaining process. For example, militants on the union side and guardians of the game plan on the management side, perhaps financial types, can be brought to the table to experience the realities at first hand.

Recalling one mediation, Peters (in Walton and McKersie 1994:322) provides an excellent illustration in which an experienced union negotiator says:

> Finally, we brought back a package I didn't hesitate to recommend. . . . Some guys with more mouth . . . raised the roof about the things we conceded, and got the membership so stirred up that in spite of my recommendations the package was rejected. Do you think I folded? Not me. I just asked the membership to put the two super dupers on the committee so they could try their luck.

The negotiator chuckled at his recollection:

> Yup, I just leaned back and let them go under the gun for a change. Hah! It was something to watch. When the management sailed into them at the next session, they found out: speeches in union halls are one thing; being on the firing line is something else. They had it! And from then on I had no more trouble from that bunch—not since then.

The most effective technique at the main table for solving their dilemma is for the negotiators to be effective in creating new value via problem solving. By utilizing all the potential of integrative bargaining, the parties can fashion a settlement that meets the expectations of all stakeholders. To the extent that this is not possible, then the negotiators at the main table fashion a settlement that is viewed as fair by all concerned when judged against data that have been assembled during negotiations. The agents may not be successful in getting everything their clients wanted, but they can help them rationalize their misgivings and come to the conclusion that "this was the best that could be gotten under the circumstances."

The process by which the agent convinces his or her constituents that the proposed settlement is the best settlement under the circumstances is not one of "smoke and mirrors," as may have been implied. The use of comparisons—what is called in the current lexicon "benchmarks"—can be very helpful to the agent in selling the package as a "good deal."

The chief negotiators have considerable information about contract settlements in comparable situations. In fact, each side will have used such information at the main table to argue its case. When it comes time for each agent to face inward and complete the internal negotiation, the information will be used for a new purpose: helping the constituents rationalize the discrepancy between their "going-in" expectations and the reality now in front of them. For example, the union negotiation may have ignored the company's assertion that its offer was better than certain other labor agreements, when this information was presented at the main table. When it comes time to confront the rank and file, the union negotiator may very well use this information to establish the superiority of the proposed contract.

Achieving Acceptance of the Proposed Settlement

Various techniques are used to bridge the gap that often remains between what has been agreed to tentatively at the main table and what the clients hope will be in the final package. The availability of a deadline and the associated costs that arise from not reaching settlement become important levers for the negotiators. In effect, the principals on both sides have to make choices between getting less than they hoped for in the proposed contract and the anticipated losses of not reaching agreement at the deadline. Chief negotiators are in a very strategic position to manage this equation so that clients perceive greater costs in not settling and as a result reluctantly go along and accept the proposed settlement.

Professors who teach labor relations often show a film titled *Final Offer* that presents Bob White, president of the Canadian Auto Workers, vigorously defending a tentative agreement by showing in detail how much better it was than the agreement reached in the United States with General Motors. Several dissidents on his bargaining committee are on the receiving end of a blistering attack in which White pulls out all the stops in an ultimate test of his leadership—but the foundation for his use of personal power is the hard reality that the Canadian agreement did surpass the U.S. agreement in some very important respects.

In other instances, chief negotiators—again drawing on their shared objective of bringing about internal alignment—may obscure the discrepancy between the terms of the actual settlement and assumptions that the principals hold about what is in the agreement. This is not as easily done when the agenda involves money items but can more readily be the "escape hatch" for complicated programmatic issues. In the latter case, by the time a particular interest group realizes that a key item on its wish list has not been obtained in the settlement, it is too late—the window has closed, and the only course of action is to accept the terms as a *fait accompli*. One delegate spoke of the technique in this way: "We never sign a contract until 4 o'clock in the morning. Things happen so quickly that we do not know what we are agreeing to." In the last-minute rush to achieve agreement, things are dropped or lost sight of, and none of the delegates really knows what is happening to his special needs (Walton and McKersie 1994:334).

Of course, there are situations in which the chief negotiators are surprised by principals on one side or the other rejecting the proposed agreement. This happens more often on the union side and represents as much a setback for the management negotiator as for the union negotiator.[3] In early 1997, for example, the pilots at American Airlines rejected a recommended settlement. This rejection set in motion a whole series of moves, countermoves, and acrimonious accusations. In such a situation, the lead negotiators faced a challenging situation. Their jobs were on the line, and they very much needed to produce a revised agreement that would be acceptable to their respective organizations. In this particular case, union members desired larger increases in pay and more slots in the expanding regional carrier business, while on the management side, the main concern was to keep the cost structure in line, especially for the American Eagle subsidiary.

Ultimately, a settlement was reached only after the White House intervened and appointed an emergency board to avert a strike. The company improved its offer in some small but significant ways, and the new proposal then ran the gauntlet of the union council and the full membership. The respective votes were positive.

How do we explain this story in terms of agency concepts? Basically, the lead union negotiators were convinced of the merits of the company's case for cost control in the face of the rapid expansion of low-cost regional carriers and consequently recommended acceptance of the first package. The pilots saw the situation differently. They viewed the growth of American Eagle, where the pilots are represented by a different union, as a real threat to their long-term employment opportunities, and as a result, they rejected the agreement. Alignment between the pilots' outlook and the company's position occurred only after intervention of the federal government, the passage of time, and a face-saving improvement in the package.

 CONCLUSION

The ground on which agents in the collective bargaining process stand is constantly shifting. Consider the high-drama negotiations during the summer of 1997 between the United Parcel Service (UPS) and the Teamsters Union. A nationwide strike commenced over the big issues of subcontracting and part-time work.

It is clear that the lead negotiators certainly were representing the interests of their respective organizations. On the union side, the objective was to stop the shrinkage of full-time jobs vis-à-vis part-time employment. In turn, the company negotiator was under instructions from top management to maintain the flexibility that it needs to use sources of labor other than full-time drivers, especially at times of peak loads, to remain cost-effective in competition with other carriers, some of which are nonunion.

At the outset of the strike, each side made strong statements. Management urged the union leadership to take the company's last proposal to the membership, implying that the union leadership was out of touch with its constituents. Clearly, such statements and tactics served to undermine rapport at the main table. Even in the most contentious negotiations, experienced bargainers have their eyes on the future: A new contract eventually was signed, and the parties have to work together as constructively as possible; this perspective serves to restrain highly adversarial moves such as impugning the integrity of the other negotiators. This is the central characteristic of agency in the context of collective bargaining; namely, the parties have a continuing relationship to manage and to preserve.

To end the discourse on a more forward-looking note, I turn to the subject of the role played by agents in restructuring processes that have become increasingly pervasive. In some recent research work that I have done with Joel Cutcher-Gershenfeld and Richard Walton, two change strategies were identified: forcing and fostering (Cutcher-Gershenfeld, McKersie, and Walton 1996).

Elements of both strategies inevitably are present in major change initiatives, and agents play key roles in the skillful execution of these strategies. For example, a forcing strategy is often needed to launch a change program. Management may take the initiative and frame the necessity for change in a way that says to the rank and file, "Change or accept the consequences" (such as a plant shutdown). Assuming that the economic imperatives are real, then it is quite likely that the representatives on the union side are well aware of the pressures, and they may quietly advise management to present the story as graphically as possible to get the attention of members who may not be aware of the new economic environment. At the same time, the story has to be presented in as constructive a manner as possible to avoid a confrontation that would make the lives of agents on both sides of the table exceedingly difficult.

Similarly, when the parties are pursuing a fostering strategy and using problem-solving tactics to generate solutions to the many issues involved in designing and implementing fundamental change, representatives of the two sides have to manage the process so that results of the collaborative process are accepted within their respective organizations. For example, on the employer side of the table, it may be necessary to involve line managers and finance types to achieve their input and ownership for the outcomes of integrative bargaining.

The point in citing these examples of coordinated behaviors that are required for forcing and fostering strategies to be successful is to underscore the proposition that in the labor-management context, agents in varying degrees also play partner roles.

▨ NOTES

1. I use several terms interchangeably. The agent is often referred to as the negotiator (chief) or as the representative. In turn, those who are being represented are referred to as clients, principals, or constituents.

2. Increasingly, unions have attempted to secure clauses that require employers to remain neutral, although for reasons relating to the strongly held conviction within the management community that they should be able to speak out against the need for unorganized workers to be represented, unions have not been successful in this regard.

3. In many cases, the rejection of a proposed contract, especially on the union side, comes about as a result of the "news blackout" and the round-the-clock bargaining that often takes place just before the deadline. Within this "space capsule," the agents hammer out what they feel is the best settlement under the circumstances. Constituents well removed from the pressures and trade-offs may not accept the proposed package as the best attainable, at least without another round of negotiations. With this possibility in mind, one experienced management negotiator does not shake hands with his union counterpart until he gets a favorable answer to the question "Can you sell this?"

 REFERENCES

Cutcher-Gershenfeld, J., R. B. McKersie, and R. E. Walton. 1996. *Pathways to change.* Kalamazoo, MI: Upjohn.
Walton, R. E. and R. B. McKersie. 1994. *A behavioral theory of labor negotiations.* Ithaca, NY: ILR Press.

Agency in the Context of Labor Management

Kathleen Valley

In his chapter, "Agency in the Context of Labor Negotiations," McKersie provides some useful examples of agency issues and best practices in labor management relations. Through this presentation, he hopes to provide useful insights for other agency-assisted negotiations. In my response to his chapter, I outline what I see as the most valuable contributions he provides and suggest areas in which the study of agency in labor-management contexts could provide further understanding and direction for negotiations in general. McKersie presents a number of important features of the agent role in labor management negotiations. Below, I highlight five of the features introduced by McKersie and present further questions and challenges in each area.

Both management negotiators and union agents are hired on a relatively long-term basis. This has a number of consequences for incentives. McKersie argues that the desire to avoid the sanction of removal provides "potent incentives" for agents to work in the best interests of the principal. In contrast, I assert that this long-term role will increase the agents' manipulation of the perceptions of the principals but will not necessarily forward the interests of the principals in the negotiations. As McKersie states, "When, as is usually the case, negotiations at the main table cannot be observed by constituents, then the chief negotiators need to report back and provide a picture of how negotiations are unfolding" (p. 189). Because the principals are not present in the bulk of the negotiations, the agent wanting to keep his or her position must become adept at "spin," choosing comparisons and process stories so that the principals *believe* the agent is working in their best interest. This works not to align incentives but rather to give the perception of aligned incentives.

The agents are negotiating both a labor contract (i.e., the substantive issues of management rights vs. union and/or employee rights) and a social contract (i.e., the day-to-day working relationship between represented employees and management. Getting a good deal on one may not be synonymous with getting a good deal on the other. In positional bargaining, the two may even be negatively correlated, such that the better the substantive deal, the worse the relations will be in practice. McKersie argues that changing to interest-based bargaining will bring the labor contract and the social contract more in line with one another. This seems to evade the reality of contract negotiations specifically and many other agent-agent negotiations more generally: Regardless of the negotiation approach, there is inevitably a tension between a short-term, contract orientation and a long-term, relational orientation. It is the agents who play out this tension in their negotiations at and away from the bargaining table, and the principals are only peripherally involved in the decision regarding the balance between these orientations.

Often, there is no positive bargaining zone at the onset of the negotiation. The job of the agent then becomes a dual one of managing the agent-agent negotiation process to increase the likelihood that some agreement is possible and managing the agent-principal negotiation process to lower the expectations of the principal. Although McKersie does not mention it, a critical companion to a negative bargaining zone is the absence of viable alternatives. Unlike many other agent-assisted negotiations, in labor-management negotiations the alternative of walking away from the table and moving easily into a better deal with another partner is almost never available. Some labor-management negotiations do result in management essentially choosing another partner through lockouts and replacement workers. Two prominent examples are the Detroit newspaper strikes in the mid-1990s and the Hormel strike in the mid-1980s. Even in these situations, management's choice to go with the alternative was made long after the negotiation began and was not seen as an immediate alternative to a negotiated settlement with the union. The alternatives in practice are essentially to settle now or keep on negotiating. In a context in which the parties *must* eventually settle, a negative bargaining zone is something of a fiction.

The cultural orientations of the two agents differ greatly. How different are they, really? "Management" and "labor" differ, but it does not necessarily follow that the cultural orientation of the two agents will differ in the same degree. In many cases, the perception of difference may be the result of partisanship rather than fact. Although local union representatives may be newly off the line and inexperienced in business and negotiations, high-level union representatives are as business-oriented as their counterparts on the management side. One of the surprises that always awaits me when I teach at Harvard's Trade Union Program, an executive education program for union representatives, is how similar those students are to my Harvard MBAs—savvy regarding economic issues, interested in adaptation in a rapidly changing technological environment, and up to date on the latest management fads and practices. This is not to say that the perception of differences isn't a powerful force in the negotiations—McKersie argues cogently that it is—but it is critical to understand that these are *perceived* rather than *actual* differences. These perceptions are likely to be held more strongly by the principals who are removed from the negotiation process than by the agents who are regularly interacting with one another.

*The agents **are** the principals in a real sense.* The chief negotiator often acts as an agent for management at the bargaining table, and the labor relations manager acts as the principal working out the day-to-day implementation of and adherence to the contract. Similarly, the union representative must negotiate the agreement and then live by it. This ties closely with the fact that these agents are negotiating both a substantive contract and a social contract. McKersie presents the paradox of agents as principals but does not consider the effects of this unique aspect of labor-management negotiations. To gain some insights into the effects of the dual agent/principal role played by labor relations manager and union reps, consider the following scenario. L. Paulsen negotiates contracts for management once every four years. In the intervening periods, it is Paulsen's job to ensure that relations between management and workers "on the line" are sufficiently harmonious that the work of the organization gets done without major or frequent upset. Grievances by represented employees and difficulties or complaints of supervisors or managers make Paulsen's job tougher and more negatively visible to those at the top of the organization. F. Hernandez is in a similar position with represented employees—the more harmonious the relationships between workers and their direct supervisors, the easier is Hernandez's job.

This is not to say that both of them will not conjure up grievances as the time for renegotiation grows closer, but that is the beginning step of the actual negotiation, and it is disconnected from the day-to-day management of the contract. When, in this scenario, the principals prefer clauses in the contract that will make day-to-day management more difficult, there is great disutility to both agents. Given the long term of the agent's placement in the position, the lack of transparency in the negotiation process itself, and the possibility for the agents to present their own versions of the outcome and the comparisons, agents are unlikely to bargain in a way that benefits the other principals at a high cost to themselves as principals.

Incentives of principals and agents are imperfectly aligned in most agent negotiations, but this is exacerbated in labor-management negotiations because the incentives for the agents are largely disconnected from those of their principals. It is this point, one that McKersie leaves unmentioned, that I turn to next.

A CRITICAL ISSUE: ALIGNMENT OF INCENTIVES

McKersie provides some useful insights into the use of agents in the labor-management process, but he is fairly silent on one issue that I see as critical in defining the roles of agents in this context: The incentives of the agents and the principals are largely not aligned. McKersie talks briefly of the role conflict experienced by the agents, but this conflict is portrayed at an elusive, psychological level. The crux of the problem is not ambiguous role conflict but explicit discrepancies between the incentives of the agents and those of the principals. This is a critical issue in labor-management contexts and one that ties study in this area to the study of agency in a broader arena.

McKersie explains that the agents are often negotiating within a long-term relationship with the other agent and with their managers and employees. Their incentives lie in (1) making sure they keep their jobs, (2) making sure their jobs are not too onerous, (3) maintaining a positive working relationship with the other agent, and (4) maintaining a positive reputation as a skilled and principled negotiator. Of these, only (1) is closely associated with the preferences of the principal. In the long run, (3) and (4) may also be in the best interest of the principal, but this is seldom the perspective taken by management in any single contract negotiation.

Integrally connected with the issue of incentives is the relationship between the agents. McKersie writes of "the labor-management relationship" and states that top management is generally more concerned with costs and productivity, while the agents are more concerned with relational issues. This relationship is only one part of a parallel set of ties—that between labor and management, and that between the agents on the two sides. Whereas the former is a formal relationship between organizational entities, the latter is an informal relationship between two people. When McKersie speaks of trust, rapport, and mutual understanding, he is speaking of mechanisms that occur at the interpersonal, rather than the interorganizational, level. It is the personal relationship that strongly affects the incentives of the agents, but this relationship is largely neglected in the research on labor-management negotiation. This is an obvious area for future research, for it is from this level that we can begin to draw generalizable lessons from agency in the labor-management arena to that in other arenas.

The issue of incentives based on relational issues has a number of interesting aspects. First, these incentives affect the entire process of negotiations. For example, consider the difference between the current norms for negotiations in the private sector and those in the public sector. The incentives of the agents do not differ dramatically across public and private sectors, but the alignment between the incentives of the agents and those of the principals does. In the public sector, the incentives of the agent and the principal are much more closely aligned, in that long-term relations with employees are critical. In the private sector, the short-term profit incentive of management creates a disjunction between the long-term, relational and reputational incentives of the agent and the short-term, monetary incentives of the principals. It is not surprising, given these differences, that the public sector is the clear leader in interest-based bargaining, whereas the majority of contract negotiations in the private sector continue in the mode of positional bargaining. This suggests that we could fruitfully look at the alignment of principal-agent incentives when making predictions about the type of negotiation and outcome that will occur. Similarly, understanding the alignment may allow us to make prescriptions for how to move effectively to a more interest-based approach in the private sector.

Second, the presence of varying relationships between agents of management and labor makes the labor-management sector an ideal one in which to study the effects of long-term relationships in bargaining. The age and tenor of the relationship between the negotiating agents can be treated as a variable predicting the match between management's initial stated preferences and clauses in the final contract, controlling for industry and company specifics. Rapport and trust can be measured as procedural variables arising out of the relationship and influencing the final outcome.

Studying the effects of personal relationships in the context of labor-management negotiations would allow us to overcome the shortcomings of nearly all existing studies investigating the effects of personal relationships on bargaining processes and outcomes. The weakest of these studies manipulate the relationship, telling people to *imagine* they are friends or colleagues, or have some sort of relationship, with the other party. The best of them use a subject with prior actual personal relationships and take some measure of this relationship as the independent variable. These studies usually fall short on three dimensions: (1) The negotiation is completely outside the normal experience of the related dyad (e.g., two classmates are negotiating the sale of a fictitious house); (2) even if the scenario is a reasonable one for the dyad to engage in (e.g., splitting $20), there is no expectation that a similar negotiation or problem will arise for the dyad to solve in the future; and (3) the only actual incentive is relational—the monetary or reputational stakes are relatively inconsequential when compared to maintenance of an actual relationship. It is difficult to assess how to generalize the findings from these studies to real-world negotiations between people with personal relationships. Exploring the impact of personal relationships between agents in the labor-management context would present other questions of generalizability that would need to be addressed but would allow us to study the phenomenon in an arena where the issues are real and repeated, and the monetary and reputational incentives are as weighty as the relational incentives.

Legislators as Negotiators

David C. King
Richard J. Zeckhauser

A ll laws are born of negotiations. Politicians are the negotiators, yet they also act as agents, with constituents and other politicians as their principals. The settings and contexts for these negotiations, however, contrast sharply with those for lawyers, business executives, and sports agents, who are usually blessed with unified principals, quiet negotiation rooms, and the task of completing a single deal. Politicians often negotiate in a bubble, with interest groups, and with the media watching. Their constituents rarely speak with a single clear voice. Negotiations on dozens of issues happen simultaneously, some failing and some succeeding. This chapter introduces the interesting and distinctive world of legislative negotiations within the principal-agent framework. We discuss the role, mission, and authority of political negotiators, and we present a model of the negotiation process that helps us understand why legislators select relatively extreme leaders to negotiate on their behalf.

Politicians are the "human embodiments of a bargaining society," and their careers depend on successful negotiations to shape laws (Dahl and Lindblom 1953, quoted in Jones 1995). Bargains are struck to pass legislation (about 300 congressional bills become laws every year), and bargains are struck to block legislation (more than

5,000 bills are introduced in a typical year). In almost every instance, legislative entrepreneurs fashion laws to satisfy a multitude of interest groups, committees signal what is likely to happen with a bill, and temporary coalitions are formed. This rhythm is repeated over and over within the country's 50 state governments, 3,043 county governments, 14,422 elected school boards, and 35,935 city councils (Ornstein, Mann, and Malbin 1996:158, 160, 165).

Legislative negotiations touch nearly every aspect of modern society, from the amount of pollution in our air to the quantities of pesticides on our produce, from the strength of the national defense to the shape of the country's income distribution. The consequences of legislative bargaining can be profound, although we should not lose sight of the fact that politicians negotiate on behalf of principals— voters and moneyed interests—who can punish wayward agents directly or indirectly at the ballot box. Much of the literature applying principal-agent models to politics explores when and why principals take self-interested actions at the expense of their principals (Bianco 1994; Ferejohn 1986a, 1990; Kalt and Zupan 1990; Kau and Rubin 1979). This is an interesting monitoring and reward problem for voters, and it is typically studied only with respect to how legislators vote. Politicians, however, are held accountable only every few years at the ballot box, which weakens the power position of citizen principals. (Presumably, errant-voting legislators can at some point be removed from office.) Voting, however, is merely the final—and usually anticlimactic—act in a long negotiation over a piece of legislation (Hall 1996). Votes are visible and easily monitored by principals, but the shaping of legislation is the art of negotiation, and that is our focus here.

Contrast the negotiating task of politicians with that of business executives bargaining on behalf of stockholders. Stockholders have easily imputed and homogeneous preferences; they all want stock prices to increase. Business executives also want stock prices to increase, regardless of anyone else's wishes. The principals and agents have convergent preferences, and the principals' preferences are substantially homogeneous. The same is true of sports and literary agents, in that their paychecks are maximized by getting clients the most remunerative contracts possible. Agency losses in such situations are minimal.

Politicians, by contrast, are agents for voters with heterogeneous preferences, and a politician's interests may readily diverge from those of the voters. Political agents often run for office because they have deeply held views; such views are never aligned perfectly with those of most of their constituents. Ambitious and sometimes seized by political causes, office seekers are much more likely than voters to view the world from within an ideological framework (Converse 1967). Thus, whereas most agent negotiators have relatively aligned preferences with relatively homogeneous principals, political negotiators may have divergent preferences from most of their heterogeneous principals. The more heterogeneous one's electoral district, the greater the expected agency loss (Fiorina 1974; King 1997a).

Take the case of the 16th California Congressional District, stretching from urban San Jose to the agricultural Santa Clara Valley and represented by Democrat Zoe Lofgren. The principals are ethnically heterogeneous, with a population that is 37% Hispanic, 37% white, and 21% Asian, including the largest concentration of Vietnamese in the United States (Barone and Ujifusa 1995). When Lofgren negotiates on issues that could pit the Hispanic and Asian communities against each other, on whose behalf is she working? At the other extreme is Republican Harold Roger's 5th Congressional District in Kentucky, which includes Middlesboro and Pikeville. Uniformly white and rural, the district is highly homogeneous. This makes Roger's district easier to represent than Lofgren's district, though ethnic diversity is only a proxy for heterogeneity.

The kind of heterogeneity that matters most to agents can be thought of as the variance around a point estimate of public opinion in a district. On a few motherhood and apple pie issues, there is little variance; principals have homogeneous preferences. Few public policy issues, however, yield such a clear signal to politicians. Electoral districts are becoming more diverse, and special interest groups are proliferating. How, representing this mixed and changing constellation of preferences, and given their own preferences, do political agents negotiate?

THE POLITICS OF LEGISLATIVE NEGOTIATIONS

Consider two aphorisms: (1) Politics makes strange bedfellows, and (2) in politics, one has no permanent friends and no permanent enemies, just permanent interests. Both imply fluid coalitions supporting various policy proposals. The fluidity of issue-by-issue coalitions is partly the result of a society comprising many small factions or interest groups, and legislatures are designed for factions to coalesce in the pursuit of voting majorities (Weingast and Marshall 1988). Agriculture bills in Congress, for instance, combine the interests of dairy producers, cotton farmers, peanut growers, and cattle ranchers. The dairymen—on their own—could never hope to gain a legislative majority. Cotton, peanut, and cattle interests are likewise permanent minorities. In collaboration, however, minority interests can constitute a majority through logrolling votes and creating committees that institutionalize their cooperation (Ferejohn 1986b).

Such is the nature of legislative coalition building in Western-style legislatures. Strange bedfellows fashion temporary voting majorities as one-bill stands, and enemies on one vote may be needed as friends for a subsequent skirmish (Riker 1962). Fashioning these temporary coalitions is often done through staff. Staff are omnipresent in the U.S. Congress. The average House member has 17 personal staff members at his or her disposal, which adds another layer of agents on top of agents, though most are loyal to their bosses because their fortunes rise or fall with them. Staff, however, play a much less central role in school boards, city councils, and state legislatures. Accordingly, we limit our discussion to three crucial elements of legislative negotiations that virtually all these institutions have in common: They are subject to open meetings laws, meaning that negotiations are done "in a bubble"; most proposed laws die; and there are strong pressures to pass legislation before elections, making it seem as if there is a big "sell by" date looming over the bargaining table.[1]

Politicians Negotiate in a Bubble

Negotiations are usually private affairs, held behind closed doors while the news media and interested observers wait outside for shards of information about prospects for a settlement. Consider how the news media cover labor talks during a strike, with cameras poised for sweaty negotiators to emerge from a hotel room after hours of give-and-take to issue some code words, which are then read like tea leaves. In contrast, much legislative negotiating is done in a bubble, with all the world able to watch. (Because few people do watch, the media stand guard and tell the public when something important happens.) Beginning in the late 1960s, sunshine laws opened political deliberations to public view. Before 1970, most votes in Congress were not recorded, television and radio coverage of committee hearings was prohibited, and citizens were barred from learning how their representatives voted in committees. By the end of that decade, all committee hearings and votes—including conference committees between the House and Senate—were opened to the public (Rieselbach 1994).

Two arguments were used in support of opening political negotiations to public scrutiny. First, open negotiating was intended to educate citizens about the merits and demerits of public policies.[2] Second, public negotiating was intended to ease the monitoring of legislators so that constituents would have a better sense of whether their representatives should be rewarded or punished at the next election (Bianco 1994).

Openness comes with costs, some trivial and others severe. For legislators, the trivial cost is having to endure the public grandstanding of one's colleagues. The presence of C-SPAN cameras in a hearing or conference committee promotes puffery and posturing.[3] This stretches out the proceedings and makes them somewhat more difficult to interpret. The more serious cost, however, may be in limiting the kinds of solutions that are possible. If politics is the art of crafting temporary coalitions of strange bedfellows, those awkward embraces may be more difficult when the public is watching. It is important to compromise, but it is also politically risky to be seen compromising.

To the extent that negotiators can choose where they are along the principal-agent continuum, negotiating in a bubble likely drives them toward the agent end. This is because as voters learn more about what their legislators are doing, voters are more likely to reward them for being pure agents. In an illuminating experimental study, a group of political scientists led by Lee Sigelman presented voters with descriptions of two types of legislators: delegates and trustees, sometimes called "puppets" and "pied pipers" (Sigelman, Sigelman, and Walkosz 1992). This is a crucial distinction employed by political theorists, with delegates (puppets) behaving as perfect agents, doing their constituents' bidding moment to moment (Pitkin 1967).

Trustees, on the other hand, seek to do what they think best for their constituents in the long run, sometimes ignoring the vocal preferences of their constituents. This is the type of representation that

John F. Kennedy praised in *Profiles in Courage* (1956). Sigelman and his colleagues found voters saying that they want their own lawmakers to look after long-term concerns, yet when the same respondents voted—in an experimental simulation—they rewarded delegates, not trustees.[4] The implication for political negotiations is that the more public bargains become, and the easier they are to monitor, the more likely agents will remain faithful to their principals on an issue-by-issue basis. The downside is that negotiations in a bubble may take longer, may be harder to conclude, and probably limit chances for politicians to act as trustees.[5]

Most Proposed Laws Die

Lawmakers, from school board and city council members to U.S. senators, have ample opportunities to kill legislation. Laws are like frogs: Out of dozens of tadpoles, only a few survive. In the House of Representatives, for instance, the average member submits 8 bills per year, yet only 7 out of every 100 bills become law. What happens to the other 93 bills? It is difficult to say precisely, but a significant number of bills never have a chance; they are introduced for purely political purposes. A number of additional bills become the subject of negotiations but perish because negotiators fail to reach compromises.

In *Strategic Disagreement*, John Gilmour (1995) identifies three reasons for failures to compromise in political negotiations. First, politicians need to be distinct from their competitors in the next election; they need to differentiate their product in the political marketplace.[6] Negotiations that resolve political differences between political parties can make it much more difficult for some players to get elected. Second, the kinds of voters who follow political negotiations most closely are ideologically concerned, least in favor of compromise, and most likely to cast stones. The most politically interested observers would, in general, rather be "right" than win (McCann 1996), and that enthusiastic supporters of an idea may regard compromise as a display of weakness (Gilmour 1995). Third, despite the dictum "half a loaf is better than none," taking half a loaf today may preclude getting the whole loaf in a future negotiation. Momentum is crucial in politics, and ameliorating problems by compromise may lose an issue its moment on the agenda.

What one could casually observe as failure by political negotiators—the high death rate of bills, for example—may be a calculated loss by political agents. This creates a dilemma for legislators who have to give occasional reports to their principals. Although "no deal" may be better for the principals in the long run, "any deal" is often more politically expedient.

Elections as a "Sell By" Date

The political need for a victory, even a symbolic one, is keenly felt by lawmakers the closer they come to an election. For a typical election, more than a third of all voters—and the majority of the independent "swing" voters—decide whether and how to vote in the final two weeks of a campaign. News coverage and campaign literature will focus on recent legislative victories and defeats; this places a premium on concluding last-minute bargains.

Compounding the electoral incentive to negotiate before elections is the rule in most legislatures that all bills automatically expire when elections are held. A bill could make it 99% of the way through the legislative process, past public hearings, through the committees, beyond passionate debate in the chamber, and yet still die if not signed by the mayor, governor, or president before the legislature adjourns for an election. After an election, negotiations must begin anew, with a new bill, new public hearings, new committee votes, and new passionate debates in the chamber.

Negotiators of all stripes set deadlines, such as strike deadlines and target dates. These may be good disciplining devices for focusing the attention of bargainers, yet if a business agreement is not settled by some deadline, the deadline often can be pushed back if some progress has been made. This cannot happen in legislatures if an election is coming. Every negotiation is stamped with an indelible "sell by" date.

In Congress, the final days are sometimes called "crazy time," with Capitol halls labeled the "bargain basement." The trade-off between advantageous outcomes and getting something done often tips toward the latter; bargains are much more likely to be struck. Deliberation presumably suffers in this last rush of negotiating, but it can also be a moment of great creativity as nongermane bills are linked together and deals are concluded (Connor and Oppenheimer 1993).

Typically, an omnibus package—a collection of largely unrelated bills—passes as one of the last congressional acts. "Christmas tree" bills tend to proliferate, so called because there are presents under the tree for virtually everyone, and these omnibus bills provide the most likely hiding places for special tax breaks, new bridges and federal buildings, and other spoils of patronage.

THE ROLE, AUTHORITY, AND MISSION OF LEGISLATIVE NEGOTIATORS

Being a legislator is a do-it-yourself type of business. The legislator is supposed to be a jack of all trades. Although he can have advisers or implementers, he is supposedly the one who weighs the evidence, makes his decisions, and casts his votes. Visible delegation of responsibilities is discouraged.

The legislator's role as negotiator may also be multifaceted. Different legislative negotiators have different situations and talents. Moreover, different circumstances call for different negotiation strategies. Thus, the same legislative negotiator may sometimes locate at one point, sometimes at another, even within the same legislative session. We find it helpful to classify negotiating representatives in general on the three dimensions of role, authority, and mission, as shown in Figure 7.1.[7] Where legislators will locate themselves in role-authority-mission (RAM) space will depend on the their personal qualities, the issue at hand, and the security of their position. Thus, agents from secure districts will have more freedom to be visionaries, to work as principals, and to make their preferences (not those of constituents) those that matter. Congressman Rogers, from Kentucky's homogeneous 5th district, might capitalize on such a job description.

Within legislatures, the role and authority of a negotiator often trade off against one another. In Figure 7.1, we have drawn the possibility frontier for role-authority combinations for a legislator of modest vision—m on the Mission scale—as curve RA. When negotiating on behalf of a large group of fellow legislators, a frequent task for a majority or minority leader, she would need authority if the negotiation is to be conducted fruitfully. To be ceded such authority, however, she would have to constrain her role and act more in the role of agent than of principal, and thus locate at point 1 in the figure. By contrast,

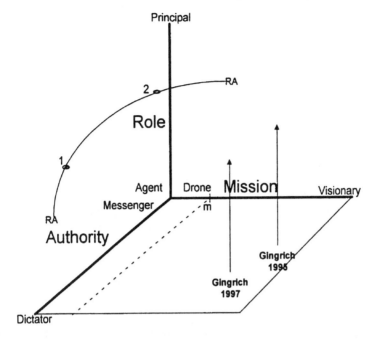

Figure 7.1. The Role, Authority, and Mission of Negotiators

when the coalition is small, as it might be among party members on a committee, the legislator leading a party's negotiations on an issue—though having less authority—may be able to push her own interests, to act more like a principal. This role is illustrated by point 2.

Although a legislator can easily respond to circumstances in selecting his authority and role, mission—particularly at the visionary end—may be less subject to choice. The potential to be a visionary is given to few and depends very much on a legislator's personal capabilities. Representative Harold Rogers (D-KY), for example, is not known as a visionary leader in any field of legislation. Senator Paul Wellstone (D-MN), by contrast, despite being elected by a razor-thin margin in his first term, set forth an innovative, extremely liberal agenda. The more conservative citizens of Minnesota, despite the gap between their preferences and his, reelected him by a comfortable margin in 1996, presumably rewarding his vision.

Whatever the consequences back home, being a visionary has severe consequences for one's negotiation potential. We distinguish heavenly from earthbound visionaries. A visionary whose wisdom derives from the heavens may be perceived as being less likely to modify her position and is indeed less likely to do so. She is less likely to strike a deal, but if she does, it probably will be on more favorable terms to her. A down-to-earth visionary, by contrast, may be hurt in her bargaining position because she is capable of convincing those behind her to compromise and may feel that she should be persuasive in this fashion. Such visionaries mix the moral and the practical in the spirit of Mahatma Gandhi. By foreseeing the consequences of compromise arrangements for their constituents, these practical visionaries may prove to be great leaders and may well serve their constituents.

We placed Speaker Newt Gingrich (R-GA) twice on Figure 7.1, once for 1995 and once for 1997. Readers may disagree with how we place him in RAM space, and we welcome the dialogue. We simply want to observe that there are trade-offs across the dimensions, and different circumstances may call for different roles. In 1995, when he first became Speaker of the House, Newt Gingrich was widely hailed as a "visionary," and he took to the speaker's rostrum like a missionary trying to convert the natives. He delegated the day-to-day running of the House to Richard Armey (R-TX), the majority leader. The strategy was not very successful, as measured by legislation passed, by public opinion ratings of the speaker, or by the vote total for Robert Dole in the 1996 presidential election. By early 1997, Gingrich tried to reinvent himself as a new kind of leader. In the fall of 1997 until after his resignation after the midterm elections in 1998, Gingrich—having survived a summer purge—showed himself willing to sacrifice on both role and mission, to garner authority, and concomitantly to pass important legislation.

The RAM model stresses the richness in the potential negotiating roles of legislators. Legislation, as we stated at the outset, is born of negotiations. Given the complexities of those negotiations, the multitude of issues, and the heterogeneity of constituents, effective negotiating representatives are needed. The rules of the legislative game—legislators do the work—do not permit fancy lawyers or specialized agents, who play such a strong role in business-related bargaining, to conduct the negotiations. Each legislator must play for himself; hence, the negotiating legislator may be messenger or dictator, agent or principal, drone or visionary. No less than a Kabuki actor, legislator/negotiators need to play multiple roles, all within the public spotlight. Such versatility is an extraordinary challenge.

THE IDEOLOGY OF LEGISLATIVE NEGOTIATORS

Every few years, one or another political theorist proposes that legislatures be composed of a random sample of citizens, plucked from every occupation, race, gender, and sexual preference group (Fishkin 1995). Such a legislature would maximize "descriptive representation," recognizing that elections are imperfect methods for sending a cross section of citizens to city councils, state legislatures, and so on. Indeed, in 1995, 171 of the 435 House members listed "law" as their previous occupation, 162 listed business or banking, 75 education, 20 agriculture, and 15 journalism. (Ornstein et al. 1996:23). At least in terms of its descriptive makeup, the Congress underrepresents nonlawyers and nonbusinessmen significantly, to say nothing of women and minorities.

There is more to representation than fostering legislatures that "look like" their constituencies. Economists and political theorists are especially fond of assessing representation in terms of the preferences of the median citizen. Imagine a single policy dimension, from 0 to 1, over which a legislature chooses how much money to spend. With public policies designed to reflect the median citizen's preferences, half the population would want the legislature to spend more, half less. The median is a stable political (and philosophical) solution because any move away from it will make a majority worse off and will be voted down (Downs 1957). As we noted earlier, however, candidates for office tend to have fiercely held and more ideologically consistent views than most citizens. Their views may be nonmedian, even though the median position is what political theorists might desire, or what the field of positive political economy might predict.

We mention only in passing agency problems raised by the self-nomination of political candidates. Political parties do not dictate which candidates may run in their primaries, and the parties have little influence over which citizens become activists. Empirically, we know that the more extreme one's views, the more likely one is to become a political activist, to give money to candidates, and to run for public office (Aldrich 1983). The more distant the nominees of both parties are from one's ideal position—say, from the median American voter—the less likely one is to trust the government to do the right thing, and the more willing one is to vote for third-party candidates (Hetherington 1997; King 1997b). The problem for citizen principals is to select faithful agents from a menu of biased candidates. The challenge is to find qualified and willing candidates who reasonably represent the median voter's preferences within a district.

Once elected, legislators confront a similar dilemma in selecting the leadership of their parties. Party caucuses—exclusive clubs for Democrats or Republicans—play an important role in legislatures (Cox and McCubbins 1993; Kiewiet and McCubbins 1991; Rohde 1991). The House of Representatives' Republican caucus assigns members to committees, punishes some members who stray too far from the party, and drafts bills through its policy committees. Likewise for the Democratic caucus. The presiding officers of the House and Senate (the Speaker of the House and the Senate Majority Leader) are selected by their party caucuses. Likewise for every state legislature—except, trivially, the Arkansas House and the nonpartisan Nebraska legislature (American Society of Legislative Clerks and Secretaries 1991). Party caucuses influence much about how legislatures run and who runs them.

In the House of Representatives, the critical party leaders are the speaker, the majority and minority leaders, and the majority and minority whips. The Senate leadership structure is the same, except that the majority leader also assumes a role similar to the Speaker of the House. Although one's image of a party leader may be someone like Robert Dole (R-KS), who served 16 years in various leadership positions, or Sam Rayburn (D-TX), who was speaker for 17 years, in practice legislatures select leaders nearly every year. From 1901 to 1990, 94 individuals served in one or more of the nine House and Senate leadership positions. These jobs come under the general heading "leadership," but little of the work falls under any conventional leadership category. Marches are not in their repertory, and their major speeches are more often directed to the public than to their supposed followers in the legislature.

A primary task of these major party figures is to negotiate. They negotiate with the other party, but also within their party, and at times with the president. Obviously, a party wants its stalwarts to be negotiating wizards, serving as agent or principal, messenger or dictator, as the particular legislative situation requires. To be a visionary as well, should the appropriate occasion arise, would be a lagniappe. Most great legislative leaders have superb negotiating skills, which include the capability to move about in RAM space. Party leaders play their most important roles in controlling the legislature's agenda, in laying out the broad outlines of initial agreements with the other party, and in overseeing all major negotiated policy settlements.

Party Leaders and the Caucus Median

In selecting legislative negotiators, should we expect the party caucuses to choose leaders whose preferences align closely with the caucus median, or should we expect the party caucuses to select someone "off center?" If the latter, should they be more extreme or moderate than the caucus median? Tim Groseclose (1995) examines this through the lens of a "blame game" model in which party leaders stake out positions that are more extreme than their own party's median so as to embarrass the other party's leaders. This approach hints at a bargaining model, which we develop more fully in this chapter. Naïve extrapolation of standard economic theory—as an extension of Harold Hotelling's work on the spatial location of firms (Downs 1957; Hotelling 1929/1952)—would have us expect leaders reflecting median caucus members' preferences.

Similarly, pluralism scholar David Truman argued that "the likelihood of getting elected and of performing effectively as an agent of the party both [hinge] on being a 'middleman' " (quoted in Kiewiet and McCubbins 1991:49). According to Truman (1959), a leader would be a middleman "not only in the sense of a negotiator but also in a literal structural sense. One would not expect that he could attract the support necessary for election unless his voting record placed him somewhere near the center in an evenly divided party" (quoted in Kiewiet and McCubbins 1991:49). Prophecy failed Truman. He wrote those words in 1959, about the time Everett Dirksen (R-IL)—a staunch conservative—was elevated to Senate Republican whip. Senate Democrats countered with liberal whip Mike Mansfield (D-MT). Future Democratic Senate whips included Hubert Humphrey (D-MN) and Edward Kennedy (D-MA). Both, like Mansfield, were considerably to the left of their party caucuses.

Regardless of Dirksen, Mansfield, Humphrey, and Kennedy, the intuitive plausibility of the "median leader" hypothesis has been persuasive to most scholars. It is the received wisdom among political scientists, and it has been formulated within a principal-agent framework by Kiewiet and McCubbins:

> To the extent that party leaders are able to move legislative outcomes closer to their own ideal points, potential agency losses are greatest when leaders' preferences are extreme or idiosyncratic. In order to minimize such losses, congressional members should select leaders whose preferences are as representative as possible of the caucus as a whole. (1991:48)

Kiewiet and McCubbins briefly examined the ideology of congressional leaders (excluding whips), finding mixed support for the median leader hypothesis. After acknowledging that the data are not consistently supportive of the median leader hypothesis, they concluded that "most leaders of both parties, however, have clearly tended toward the caucus median" (1991:51).

We take issue with the median leader theory and evidence marshaled in its support. Indeed, by Kiewiet and McCubbin's own data examining the ideology of Senate majority and minority leaders from 1947 through 1984, four of seven Democrats were more liberal than the Democratic caucus median, and seven of eight Republicans were more conservative than their party's median. In some cases—Howard Baker (R-TN), for example—leaders were more extreme than their party median, but just barely. Perhaps Howard Baker should count as a party leader who "tended toward the caucus median." A more appropriate test would be to see whether the set of party leaders—taken as a group—is more extreme, through a difference of means test.

Party Leaders as Negotiation Anchors

Established research traditions treat leaders as within-party representatives, influencing committee assignments, party agendas, and the like. The negotiation role has been forgotten. The theory of the median leader—whether stemming from the pluralist, Downsian, or principal-agent tradition—must recognize the critical role of leaders as negotiators. Our model of agent negotiators is fully consistent with leaders being more extreme than their party caucuses.

We view party leaders as the primary negotiators for their parties, interacting with leaders of the other party (in a two-party setting, such as the United States). Accordingly, the negotiation game between leaders of different parties is similar to the "dance of negotiation" described by Howard Raiffa (1992:chap. 4). In a negotiation dance, such as bargaining over the price of a rug at an open air market, the buyer starts with a low bid and the seller starts with a high bid. After tugging and hauling, they dance closer together and end up near the middle of the original offer range.

Similarly, imagine a legislature composed of lawmakers who can be arrayed along an ideological dimension from 0 to 1, with a chamber median of 0.5. Assume both parties elect leaders who represent their party's median—0.4 for the left party and 0.6 for the right party. If the parties have equal agenda-setting powers and equal voting strengths, one would expect the results of negotiations to settle on the chamber median. If the party of the right knew that the left party's negotiator would bargain beginning at 0.4, however, the right party would elect a negotiator at 0.8. The midpoint between 0.4 and 0.8 is 0.6—or the right party's median. Likewise, anticipating that the party of the right's negotiator would begin at 0.8, the left party should elect a negotiator at 0—the most extreme person in the party—yielding a midpoint of 0.4. The centrifugal force of this dance leads to electing the two most extreme members of the party caucuses.

There is a countervailing centripetal pull that keeps the parties from settling on their most extreme negotiator. An extreme negotiator does not achieve a better outcome by magic. He simply refuses or prevents deals that other leaders might accept. Hence, the more extreme a negotiator, the less likely a deal is to be secured. Thus, a caucus would be unwise to select its most extreme member; probably nothing would get done.

Figure 7.2 displays the calculus of a conservative caucus. The caucus median (0.65) lies to the right of the chamber median and the other party's median. The calculus involves two curves and a horizontal line. One curve, judged from the standpoint of the median caucus member, shows the expected quality of a deal conditional on a deal being consummated with the other party. Denote this value as q, where $q = Q(x/\text{deal})$, hereafter abbreviated as $Q(x)$. It is constructed assuming some location for the negotiator in the other party and a negotiat-

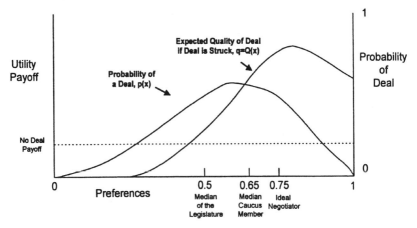

Figure 7.2. The Ideal Negotiator for a Conservative Caucus

ing process of the type described by Raiffa. Its payoff is in measured in "utiles," or more technically as a von Neumann-Morgenstern utility.

The second curve gives the probability of a deal, $P(x)$, which falls over the relevant range for x as the conservative negotiator moves to the right. Its probability values are shown at the right of the diagram. (This curve rises at the far left because the conservative would not support such a moderate leader.)

The dashed horizontal line represents the status quo, No Deal. It represents the expected value in utiles of doing nothing. Possibly nothing will happen in the future, or a new deal may be struck.

In choosing among candidates for negotiator, a caucus member will compute the expected value his ideology will bring. With a negotiator at x, the expected payoff will be

$$P(x)Q(x) + (1 - P(x))ND. \qquad [1]$$

Rearranging terms, we get

$$P(x)[Q(x) - ND] + ND. \qquad [2]$$

To maximize this, the member effectively maximizes the probability of a deal times the gain in the deal over the status quo. In the diagram, for the median voter at 0.65, the ideal negotiator is at 0.75.

Taking derivatives and maximizing Equation 2, we get

$$P'(x)/P(x) = -Q'(x)[Q(x) - ND].$$

At the optimum, the elasticity of the probability with respect to the negotiator's location must equal the negative of the gain from a deal with respect to the negotiator's location. The implication is that a caucus will choose a more extreme leader/negotiator the less this affects the probability of a deal, the more it affects the quality of a deal, and the better is the no deal outcome. What the example illustrates is that it often will be desirable for a caucus to select a legislative negotiator who is substantially more extreme than its median member.

Empirical Evidence on Leader Ideology

We are confronted with several possibilities. Perhaps legislative negotiators—defined here as elected party leaders negotiating on behalf of their party coalitions—reflect the median member of their party. This is the conventional wisdom among most scholars. None of the theories predicting median party leaders, however, explicitly accounts for how legislators negotiate. Neither party exists in a vacuum, and laws are passed by holding onto one's own party base while attracting as many members of the opposing party as possible. Temporary coalitions are built bill by bill, but party leaders anchor the negotiations. Accordingly, we suspect that partisans elect negotiators who are more extreme than their caucus medians—yet not so extreme that no credible deals can be completed.

Evidence consistent with this explanation is found in the ideology of the 94 lawmakers elected as party leaders in Congress from 1901 through 1990, or from the 56th to 102nd Congresses. The data were compiled by Tim Groseclose (1995), and we reanalyze them here within the negotiation framework.

A legislator's ideology is measured using Poole-Rosenthal NOMINATE scores. These scores come from factor loadings from a factor analysis of all recorded House and Senate votes in a given Congress. Although dependent on the magic of a factor analysis machine, NOMINATE scores are widely used and accepted as indicators of legislators' ideology, and the scores correlate highly with other measures—such as interest group ratings by the Americans for Democratic Action (Poole and Rosenthal 1997). For example, by their NOMINATE scores, the most liberal House members in the 104th Congress (1995-1996) were John Conyers (D-MI) and Ron Dellums (D-CA), and the most conservative were Mel Hancock (R-MO) and John Shadagg (R-AZ). Owen Pickett (D-VA) was the purest ideological centrist.

Following Groseclose's approach, we measure the ideological extremity of a leader relative to the party caucus by reporting the percentage of the leader's caucus who have NOMINATE scores more extreme than the leader. We use NOMINATE scores from the year prior to when a member was elected leader. This is done to get a measure that is not confounded by the leader's votes on behalf of—or in opposition to—the president. Accordingly, we only report the member's ideology before he is elected to the position of whip, leader, or Speaker of the House. We do not report a member's extremity when moving between leadership positions (as, say, from minority whip to minority leader, as Newt Gingrich did in 1993, or from minority leader to Speaker of the House, as he did in 1995). Furthermore, by tradition the speaker rarely votes on the House floor, undermining any measures of ideology based on floor votes after he has been elevated to speaker.[8]

To illustrate our measure of extremity, consider the ideology of three recent House Republican leaders when they were first elevated to the party whip position. When Trent Lott (R-MS) reached that status in 1981, just 20.5% of his party's caucus was to the ideological right of him. Lott was elected to the Senate in 1988 and was replaced as House minority whip by Richard Chaney (R-WY). Just 6% of the Republican caucus was more ideologically extreme than Chaney. After Chaney resigned to become President George Bush's Secretary of Defense, Newt Gingrich (R-GA) was elected as the new whip. Gingrich was more moderate than Chaney, although he was still more extreme than the median, with 33% of the caucus on Gingrich's right.

Lott, Chaney, and Gingrich provide three cases, although one could select anecdotes showing the opposite tendency. George Mitchell (D-ME), the Senate Majority Leader in the early 1990s, reflected his party's median almost precisely (.490 as opposed to .500), and Speaker Thomas Foley (D-WA) was even closer to his party's median (.494). Mitchell's and Foley's scores mark them as slightly more ideologically moderate than their party's median, although not by much. Across all 94 leaders in our sample, however, 70 scored more

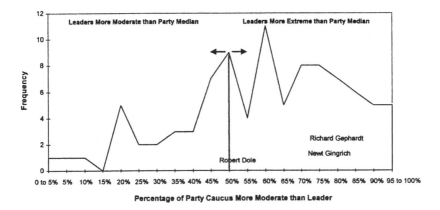

Figure 7.3. Ideological Extremity of Elected Party Leaders in Congress, 1901-1990

extreme than their party's median. The average ideological gap between the party's median and the leader (62.4% compared to the 50% base) strikes us as large, and we can safely reject the hypothesis ($p < 4.9 \times 10^{-6}$) that leaders reflect the median.

Our results are shown in Figure 7.3. Leaders on and to the right of the solid line at 50%, were more extreme than the median of the party caucus that elected them. At the time that Robert Dole was elected Senate Majority Leader in 1981, he was virtually at his party's median (52.6% of his party was more moderate than he). The present House leaders, Richard Gephardt (D-MO) and Newt Gingrich (R-GA), are more extreme than their party medians.

The evidence reported in Figure 7.3 is consistent with our model of legislative negotiators. On average, legislative negotiators are—definitively—more extreme than their party medians. The median party member may be willing to support more extreme leaders, and experience the presumed agency loss of having them represent the party in multiple arenas, because party members anticipate the "dance of negotiation" and the importance of anchoring initial positions.

Party leaders have been, about 25% of the time, more moderate than their party medians. Although this is outside the predictions of our model, we notice that parties tend to elect moderate leaders following the tenure of especially extreme leaders. Perhaps these occasional retreats to moderation reflect the trade-off between the probability of concluding a deal (which declines with the most extreme leaders) and the quality of a deal.

 ## SUMMARY AND CONCLUSION

Legislative leaders are the prime negotiators shaping our laws—on a daily basis and at every level of government. As negotiators, they are agents for themselves, their constituents, and their fellow party members.

The negotiation of legislation is a do-it-yourself job, in part because it is conducted beneath the public eye. Public attention rewards grandstanding and puffery, and it punishes concessionary compromise, which makes serious legislative action more challenging. Many bills are not serious; they are products of conspicuous introduction to impress constituents. Elections for legislative negotiations, like contract expiration dates for labor negotiations, serve as deadlines and spur deal making. The responsibilities of the effective legislative negotiator meander in what we label RAM (role, authority, mission) space, depending on circumstance.

We focus particular attention on the ideology of legislative negotiators. Conventional wisdom suggests that a party leader's ideology will align well with that of a median member. If leaders are negotiators, however, their personal ideologies will serve to anchor negotiations, implying that parties will have incentives to appoint extreme leaders. In effect, presumed agency loss actually secures more favorable outcomes. The need to reach legislative agreements, however, constrains tugs to the outside. Empirical analysis of 20th-century legislative leaders finds them to be more extreme than their parties, presumably to tug legislation in a favorable direction.

Legislation is born of negotiations. Thus, it is no surprise that arm twisting and staking out positions are as much the repertoire of great legislative leaders as managing agendas and crafting legislation.

Geometry underlies median voter models and RAM-space strategies. Negotiation underlies legislation. Political scientists and politicians could work a beneficial exchange: more negotiation analysis for the former, more geometry for the latter. Both the description and the performance of legislation would be improved.

NOTES

1. There are similarities to the strike date in a labor negotiation. With most business negotiations, by contrast, "do or die" dates have to be manufactured.

2. Woodrow Wilson, a political scientist long before he went to the White House, argued the point in the 1880s. "The chief, and unquestionably the most essential, object of all discussion of public business," wrote Wilson, "is the enlightenment of public opinion; and of course, since it cannot hear the debates of the Committees, the nation is not apt to be much instructed by them" (Wilson 1885/1981).

3. For example, the average number of hours per day that the Senate spent in session in the 10 years before TV cameras were allowed on the Senate floor was 6.6; in the 10 years afterward, it increased to 7.3 (Frantzich 1996).

4. Respondents also indicated that they wanted their legislators to consider national interests, but they rewarded those who voted parochially for the district.

5. Because legislators only get voted on periodically, however effective monitoring is, any dynamic equilibrium will engender some self-interested behavior—for example, catering to friends and overweighting personal reelection probabilities. Demonstrably faithful individuals are rarely available to challenge incumbents.

6. For example, in fall 1997, the Clinton administration negotiated what it thought was a final compromise with Congress on Internal Revenue Service reform. The lack of reform, Republicans anticipated, could be a good issue to distinguish the party from Democratic opponents. Two weeks after the compromise was fashioned, Republicans moved to a more hard-line position, putting the White House in an "awkward spot" (see Schlesinger 1997).

7. This framework is presented as a commentary on the predecessor paper to the chapter by Joel Cutcher-Gershenfeld and Michael Watkins in this volume. That paper offers a two-dimensional framework.

8. Example: 32 roll call votes were made in the House of Representatives between October 23 and October 30, 1997. Speaker Gingrich voted on just three. Most rank-and-file members vote on every measure.

REFERENCES

Aldrich, J. H. 1983. A spatial model with party activists: Implications for electoral dynamics. *Public Choice* 41:63-100.
American Society of Legislative Clerks and Secretaries. 1991. *Inside the legislative process.* Denver: National Conference of State Legislatures.

Barone, M. and G. Ujifusa. 1995. *The almanac of American politics, 1996.* Washington, DC: National Journal.

Bianco, W. T. 1994. *Trust: Representatives and constituents.* Ann Arbor: University of Michigan Press.

Connor, G. E. and B. I. Oppenheimer. 1993. Deliberation: An untimed value in a timed game. In *Congress reconsidered,* edited by L. C. Dodd and B. I. Oppenheimer. 5th ed. Washington, DC: Congressional Quarterly.

Converse, P. 1967. The nature of belief systems in mass publics. In *Ideology and discontent,* edited by D. Apter. New York: Free Press.

Cox, G. and M. D. McCubbins. 1993. *Legislative leviathan: Party government in the house.* Berkeley: University of California Press.

Dahl, R. A. and C. E. Lindblom. 1953. *Politics, economics, and welfare.* New York: Harper & Row.

Downs, A. 1957. *An economic theory of democracy.* New York: Harper & Row.

Ferejohn, J. A. 1986a. Incumbent performance and electoral control. *Public Choice* 5:5-25.

Ferejohn, J. A. 1986b. Logrolling in an institutional context: A case study of food stamp legislation. In *Congress and policy change,* edited by G. C. Wright, L. N. Rieselbach, and L. C. Dodd. New York: Agathon.

Ferejohn, J. A. 1990. Information and elections. In *Information and democratic processes,* edited by J. A. Ferejohn and J. H. Kuklinski. Urbana: University of Illinois Press.

Fiorina, M. P. 1974. *Representatives, roll calls, and constituencies.* Lexington, MA: Lexington Books.

Fishkin, J. S. 1995. *The voice of the people: Public opinion and democracy.* New Haven, CT: Yale University Press.

Frantzich, S. E. 1996. *The C-SPAN revolution.* Norman: University of Oklahoma Press.

Gilmour, J. B. 1995. *Strategic disagreement: Stalemate in American politics.* Pittsburgh: University of Pittsburgh Press.

Groseclose, T. 1995. *Blame-game politics.* Mimeo. Department of Political Science, Massachusetts Institute of Technology.

Hall, R. L. 1996. *Participation in Congress.* New Haven, CT: Yale University Press.

Hetherington, M. J. 1997. *Political trust's effect on the presidential vote: 1968-1992.* Presented at the annual meeting of the Midwest Political Science Association, April, Chicago.

Hotelling, H. 1952. Stability in competition. In *Readings in price theory,* edited by G. Sticler and K. Boulding. Homewood, IL: Irwin. (Original work published 1929)

Jones, C. O. 1995. *Separate but equal branches: Congress and the presidency.* Chatham, NJ: Chatham House.

Kalt, J. P. and M. A. Zupan. 1990. The apparent ideological behavior of legislators: Testing the principal-agent slack in political institutions. *Journal of Political Economy* 33:103-131.

Kau, J. B. and P. H. Rubin. 1979. Self-interest, ideology, and logrolling in congressional voting. *Journal of Law and Economics* 22:365-384.

Kennedy, J. F. 1956. *Profiles in courage.* New York: Harper.

Kiewiet, D. R. and M. D. McCubbins. 1991. *The logic of delegation: Congressional parties and the appropriations process.* Chicago: University of Chicago Press.

King, D. C. 1997a. *Extreme politics: Causes and consequences of polarization in American politics.* Mimeo. John F. Kennedy School of Government, Harvard University.

King, D. C. 1997b. The polarization of American parties and mistrust of government. In *Why people don't trust government,* edited by J. S. Nye, Jr., P. D. Zelikow, and D. C. King. Cambridge, MA: Harvard University Press.

McCann, J. A. 1996. Presidential nomination activists and political representation: A view from the active minority studies. In *In pursuit of the White House: How we choose our presidential nominees,* edited by W. G. Mayer. Chatham, NJ: Chatham House.

Ornstein, N. J., T. E. Mann, and M. J. Malbin. 1996. *Vital statistics on Congress, 1995-1996.* Washington, DC: Congressional Quarterly.

Pitkin, H. F. 1967. *The concept of representation.* Berkeley: University of California Press.

Poole, K. and H. Rosenthal. 1997. *Congress: A political-economic history of roll call voting.* New York: Oxford University Press.

Raiffa, H. 1992. *The art and science of negotiation.* Cambridge, MA: Harvard University Press.

Rieselbach, L. N. 1994. *Congressional reform: The changing modern Congress.* Washington, DC: Congressional Quarterly.

Riker, W. H. 1962. *The theory of political coalitions.* New Haven, CT: Yale University Press.

Rohde, D. 1991. *Parties and leaders in the post-reform House.* Chicago: University of Chicago Press.

Schlesinger, J. M. 1997. GOP may seek to toughen IRS bill, putting White House in awkward spot. *The Wall Street Journal,* November 3, p. A3.

Sigelman, L., C. K. Sigelman, and B. J. Walkosz. 1992. The public and the paradox of leadership: An experimental analysis. *American Journal of Political Science* 36(May):366-385.

Truman, D. 1959. *The congressional party.* New York: John Wiley.

Weingast, B. R. and W. Marshall. 1988. The industrial organization of Congress. *Journal of Political Economy* 96:132-163.

Wilson, W. 1981. *Congressional government.* Baltimore: Johns Hopkins University Press. (Original work published 1885)

Turning the Tables

Negotiation as the Exogenous Variable

Jonathan R. Cohen

M ost analytical negotiation research begins, implicitly or explicitly, with two basic questions: (1) What are we seeking to explain, and (2) How are we seeking to explain it?[1] In the main, such research has sought to explain the outcome of a negotiation (i.e., the agreement that the parties reached or failed to reach) in terms of variables such as the parties' interests, personal characteristics, relationship, or best alternatives to negotiated agreements (BATNAs). Methodologically, the result of the negotiation is the endogenous variable to be explained in terms of exogenous factors.[2] In "Legislators as Negotiators," David King and Richard Zeckhauser begin by following this standard approach but then depart from it. After exploring how external phenomena shape legislative negotiations, they ask how the fact of negotiation shapes an external phenomenon, namely the selection of legislative leaders. Through this ingenious reversal, they obtain pioneering results. In this comment, I suggest that their methodological

Author's Note: I thank Richard J. Zeckhauser for his helpful suggestions. All errors are mine alone.

twist can be fruitfully applied to other domains in which negotiation plays significant roles. I offer the judicial interpretation of legislation as an illustrative example. In addition to asking how external phenomena influence negotiations, we can also ask how the fact of negotiation influences external phenomena.

Exogeneity and endogeneity comprise a central methodological concern in social sciences, especially economics (see Judge, Griffith, Lütkepohl, and Lee 1985:564-565, 667-669; Kmenta 1971:531-532; or Wonnacott and Wonnacott 1970:155-156). Suppose in a given week one observes that (1) Bob always carries an umbrella on rainy days and (2) whenever Bob carries an umbrella, it rains. Despite the perfect coincidence between Bob's carrying an umbrella and the day being rainy, the causality is obvious: Bob carries an umbrella because the day is rainy; the day is not rainy because Bob carries an umbrella. The weather is the independent or exogenous variable, and Bob's carrying an umbrella is the dependent or endogenous variable. In more complex systems, causality can run in both directions, making the question of which variables are endogenous and which exogenous trickier. Does the teenager Samantha have a poor relationship with her parents because of her internal anger, or does she have internal anger because she has a poor relationship with her parents? Sometimes "both" is the best answer.

King and Zeckhauser begin by following the standard methodology of explaining the results of negotiations in terms of external factors. The more legislative negotiations are open to public scrutiny, the more difficult it is for legislators to compromise or to act as trustees rather than delegates. Because most "swing" voters decide how to vote in the last two weeks of a campaign, and because most legislatures have rules providing that bills automatically expire when elections are held, the last few weeks before an election are a negotiating free-for-all, commonly resulting in a flurry of hodgepodge, "Christmas tree" bills. Although their insights are brilliant, their methodology is standard.

The methodological twist comes in their analysis of the selection of congressional leadership. Rather than asking how the selected party leaders influence Congressional negotiations, King and Zeckhauser ask how the fact that negotiating with opposing party leaders is a primary task of a party leader influences which leaders get selected. The fact of negotiation is now used to explain who gets selected; negotiation is the exogenous variable.

Prior to their study, the conventional wisdom had been that, on average, political parties selected leaders whose ideological preferences aligned with those of the median member in that party. King and Zeckhauser offer a different model. Recognizing the centrality of negotiation to a party leader's job, they posit that parties select leaders from their extreme wings so as to "anchor" negotiations with the opposing party in their favor (e.g., if you're a Republican and you know that your leader will be negotiating against a Democrat, it is best to pick a very conservative Republican to be your leader, for he or she will be a stronger bargainer for your side than would a moderate Republican). Analyzing House and Senate leadership data from 1901 to 1990, King and Zeckhauser find, "On average, legislative negotiators are—definitively—more extreme than their party medians" (p. 221). More specifically, the average (mean) party leader was more ideologically extreme (i.e., conservative if a Republican and liberal if a Democrat) than 62.4% of his or her party. The median voter model predicts that the average party leader should be more extreme than only 50% of his or her party.

Before continuing the methodological discussion, let me make four comments on this specific finding.

1. This finding is clearly significant. It strongly refutes what had been the "conventional wisdom" of a simple median voter model. There is no doubt that "conventional wisdom" must now be revisited.

2. One suspects that the pattern to which King and Zeckhauser point—entities choosing leaders from their extreme wings so as to anchor negotiations with opposing parties—is widespread. Such posturing undoubtedly extends beyond American borders. For example, in Benjamin Netanyahu's election victory over Shimon Peres, an important element in Netanyahu's selection may have been the belief among segments of the Israeli public that he would be a tougher negotiator with the Palestinians than Shimon Peres (see, e.g., Katz 1996). Such posturing undoubtedly also extends beyond legislative negotiations. For example, if a main role of union presidents is to negotiate with management, unions might tend to do better by electing presidents from their extreme wings, again so as to anchor negotiations in their direction.[3]

3. Strictly speaking, their study does not (nor do King and Zeckhauser claim that it does) "prove" that political parties select leaders from their extreme wings *so as to do better in negotiations with the opposing political party*. Their study rejects the null hypothesis of the median voter model. Furthermore, their study demonstrates that parties tend to select leaders from their extreme wings. However, *to what extent* parties select leaders from their extreme wings *because of external negotiations* remains an issue. Put differently, how much of the 12.4% ideological gap between their results and the median voter model is fairly attributable to posturing for external negotiations?

It is conceivable that parties select leaders from their extreme wings for reasons other than posturing in external negotiations. Suppose that bashing the opposing party were effective in garnering support within one's own party, and suppose further that persons from extreme wings found bashing easier to do than ideologically moderate candidates. Could this in part explain why parties tend to select their leaders from their extreme wings? Or might extremists be more motivated to seek leadership positions than moderates: More extreme in their ideology, might they also tend to be more passionate in their desire to effectuate that ideology? King and Zeckhauser make a highly plausible case, including providing a formal model with predictive implications, that posturing for external negotiations plays a significant role in the selection of party leaders. Determining more precisely the extent of that influence awaits future research.

4. It would be interesting to know whether King and Zeckhauser are offering an account of intentional behavior by political parties or of unintentional "as if" behavior.[4] Put differently, do members of political parties intentionally choose leaders from their more extreme wings so as to anchor negotiations, or do they do so unwittingly, perhaps led by something akin to an evolutionary process involving trial and error?[5] Apart from intrinsic interest, exploring this issue could be helpful as we look at institutions less stable than the U.S. Congress. Throughout the world, new legislative bodies are forming at a remarkable rate. Should we expect the members of these legislative bodies to exhibit posturing of the same kind and magnitude as seen in the U.S. Congress? Would such behavior change over time?

It is on the methodological level that their study illustrates an important general lesson for negotiation research: In addition to using external phenomena to explain negotiation, we can use negotiation to explain external phenomena. To illustrate, consider a topic closely tied to the formation of legislation: legislative interpretation. If, as King and Zeckhauser argue, negotiation is critical to how legislators make laws, might negotiation also influence how judges interpret laws?

Although generally removed from the public's view (Greenhouse 1989:1643 n. 53), one of a judge's central tasks is to persuade other judges to accept his or her opinion. For an appellate court that sits *en banc*, such as the U.S. Supreme Court, this means getting a majority of the justices to concur with one's opinion. For a lower court judge who sits alone, this means writing an opinion that will not be overturned on appeal. Each is a form of negotiation. How does the fact that judicial opinions must be negotiated influence those opinions? (See Greenhouse 1989:1643 n. 53.)

One basic ramification is that judges who are good negotiators are likely to be more influential in shaping the law than judges who are poor negotiators. A wonderful account of interactions between the late Justice William Brennan and his law clerks illustrates this well:

> [Justice Brennan's] law clerks report an annual event: At some point early in their clerkships, Brennan asked his clerks to name the most important rule in constitutional law. Typically they fumbled, offering *Marbury v. Madison* or *Brown v. Board of Education* as their answers. Brennan would reject each answer, in the end providing his own by holding up his hand with the fingers wide apart. This, he would say, is the most important rule in constitutional law. Some clerks understood Brennan to mean that it takes five votes to do anything, others that with five [out of nine] votes you could do anything. In either version, though, Brennan's "rule of five" . . . was about the meaning of five votes on the Court. It was not a substantive rule of constitutional law. (Tushnet 1995:763)

Is it happenstance that Justice Brennan, so aware of coalition building in authoring opinions that his fellow justices called him the "playmaker" and that he began by teaching his new law clerks the "rule of five," authored the second highest number of opinions (1,360) in the Court's history?[6] Conversely, justices who are poor negotiators, despite intellectual brilliance, may be unable to gain the support needed to form a majority. Persuasiveness, rather than rightness, is the linchpin between whether or not an opinion will become law.

A second ramification may be a tendency toward centrism in judicial opinions. Consider again the U.S. Supreme Court.[7] On that Court, five votes are needed to form a majority. Suppose that, on a given case, each justice were to write one "candidate" opinion. Which "candidate" would command the requisite five votes? If opinions are viewed along an ideological spectrum, a median voter model would suggest that centrist opinions should be chosen more often than extreme ones. Furthermore, centrist opinions should stand less chance of reversal upon appeal.

A third ramification is that tactics that work well in negotiations generally may play an important role in adjudication as well. Let me highlight one in particular. Fisher, Ury, and Patton (1991) observed that *principled* argument that looks to objective standards and independent criteria is a highly persuasive form of argument. Judicial opinions follow this path. Judicial opinions invariably refer to precedent, in part with the hope that this "objective" standard will persuade the reader of the correctness of the author's view. (The same is true for other legal writing, such as lawyers' briefs.) This is *not* to say that such references to precedent are merely negotiation tactics. No doubt, judges also refer to precedent to reassure themselves that their opinions are in keeping with established law. The high frequency of such references, however, may be indicative of the importance of negotiation, by route of persuasiveness, to legal writing.[8]

In short, we can ask not only how external phenomena affect negotiation, but also how the fact of negotiation affects external phenomena. Through this methodological twist, King and Zeckhauser find pioneering results concerning the selection of legislative leaders. As we explore other areas in which negotiation is central, we should look to their example.

NOTES

1. Raiffa (1982:20-25) contrasts two, often interwoven approaches to negotiation research: analytical description of negotiation and prescriptive advice on how to negotiate effectively. Sebenius (1992) characterizes the devel-

opment of the negotiation literature. I discuss here analytical, rather than prescriptive, negotiation research.

2. Much negotiation research has also examined the role of "process" with negotiation. When process is used to explain the outcome, process may be seen as an exogenous variable. For example, Valley, Moag, and Bazerman (1996) report how different modes of communication—written, telephone, or face to face—affect negotiation. When the focus is on why the process of a negotiation occurred the way it did, however, process is then an endogenous variable. Accordingly, process is difficult to classify generally as strictly exogenous or endogenous. Such classification depends on the aims of the particular study.

3. As King and Zeckhauser observe, the impulse to select an extreme leader so as to anchor negotiations in one's favor is offset by the risk that selecting an extreme leader will result in no agreement being reached in external negotiations.

4. Friedman (1953:16) suggests that utility maximization models are useful even if agents do not consciously maximize their utilities but merely behave "as if" they do; McCloskey (1985:3) criticizes this view. See also Sen (1982:435).

5. Note King and Zeckhauser's statement, "Although this is outside the predictions of our model, we notice that parties tend to elect moderate leaders following the tenure of especially extreme leaders" (p. 221).

6. Lazarus and Sheler (1997:13) quote this exceptional figure, which is explained in part, though certainly not entirely, by Brennan's 33-year tenure on the Court, the sixth longest of any justice.

7. For analyses of the power of the centrist members of the U.S. Supreme Court, see Simon (1995) and Denniston (1996). Compare Smith (1994). For vivid accounts of the negotiations that occur within that Court over opinions, see Simon (1995) and Schwartz (1996). For studies of that Court's behavior generally, see Spaeth and Brenner (1990).

8. On persuasiveness in legal argument generally, see Singer (1989).

▨ REFERENCES

Denniston, L. 1996. The center moves, the center remains. *New York Law School Law Review* 40:887.

Fisher, R., W. Ury, and B. Patton. 1991. *Getting to YES: Negotiating agreement without giving in.* 2d ed. Boston: Houghton Mifflin.

Friedman, M. 1953. The methodology of positive economics. In *Essays in positive economics.* Chicago: University of Chicago Press.

Greenhouse, C. 1989. Just in time: Temporality and the cultural legitimation of law. *Yale Law Journal* 98:1631-1649.

Judge, G., W. Griffith, R. Hill, H. Lütkepohl, and T. Lee. 1985. *The theory and practice of econometrics.* New York: John Wiley & Sons.

Katz, N. L. 1996. Netanyahu's "persecution" tactic effectively swayed Israeli voters. *Houston Chronicle*, July 2, p. A1.

Kmenta, J. 1971. *Elements of econometrics.* New York: Macmillan.

Lazarus, E, and J. L. Sheler. 1997. Making the nation fairer. *US News & World Report*, August 4, p. 13.

McCloskey, D. 1985. The poverty of economic modernism. In *The rhetoric of economics.* Madison: University of Wisconsin Press.

Raiffa, H. 1982. *The art and science of negotiation.* Cambridge, MA: Harvard University Press.

Schwartz, B. 1996. *Decision: How the Supreme Court decides cases.* New York: Oxford University Press.

Sebenius, J. 1992. Negotiation analysis: A characterization and review. *Management Science* 38(1):18-38.

Sen, A. 1982. Description as choice. In *Choice, welfare and measurement.* Cambridge: MIT Press.

Simon, J. 1995. *The center holds: The power struggle inside the Rehnquist Court.* New York: Simon & Schuster.

Singer, J. 1989. Legal storytelling: Persuasion. *Michigan Law Review* 87:2442-2455.

Smith, R. 1994. Uncoupling the "centrist bloc": An empirical analysis of the thesis of a dominant, moderate bloc on the United States Supreme Court. *Tennessee Law Review* 62:1-36.

Spaeth, H. and S. Brenner. 1990. *Studies in U.S. Supreme Court behavior.* New York: Garland.

Tushnet, M. 1995. Members of the Warren Court in judicial biography: Themes in Warren Court biographies. *New York University Law Review* 70:748-772.

Valley, K., J. Moag, and M. Bazerman. 1996. *"A matter of trust": Effects of communication on the efficiency and distribution of outcomes.* Working Paper 96-059. Cambridge, MA: Harvard Business School.

Wonnacott, R., and T. Wonnacott. 1970. *Econometrics.* New York: John Wiley.

First, Let's Kill All the Agents!

Michael Wheeler

As negotiating has become an increasingly popular business subject, I have read and heard over and over again that the actual amount of money involved in a negotiation is only one of the crucial items that needs discussion and may indeed not even be among the most important items. As a general rule, this is absolute hogwash![1] (Donald Dell, quoted in Yasser, McCurdy, and Copelrud 1988)

[Howard Slusher] would put an offer on the table and he would not budge. He would hold a player out if the team did not capitulate. He would really go to the mat for his client. He is a very intelligent man and a good negotiator, and everyone in sports knew if you drafted a Slusher client, you were in for a long, tough, bruising battle because he was going to play hard-ball.[2] (Falk 1995)

I wanted the manager to sweat when I came into the room. When I represented players, I wanted the general manager to think this is one prepared, bright, tough son-of-a-gun, and I never wanted to think that the first question would be "how my kids are." I wanted the first question to be, "How much is this going to cost us?" From my perspective, this advice applies whether you are on my side of the table or the other.[3] (Burke, 1993)

Hard bargaining is alive and well in professional sports. Win-win, mutual gains, principled negotiation may be in vogue in other business settings, but when it comes to negotiating player contracts, it seems much more the exception than the rule. Sports agents are almost universally blamed for the phenomenon (Burke 1993).

Franchise owners detest agents, of course, believing that they goad athletes into making outrageous demands. Fans vilify them for creating auctions that lead a favorite player to abandon the hometown team for greener pastures. Even the players themselves sometimes turn on the agents they hire, suing them for embezzlement, conflict of interest, or just plain incompetence.[4] Agents are held in such popular contempt that the late Robert Woolf (who represented Larry Bird, Doug Flutie, and a host of other celebrity athletes) constantly insisted on being called *Attorney* Bob Woolf—as being at least one step up in the professional food chain.

For all the carping and ridicule, sports agents have prospered in recent years, at least a small cadre of them. Their emergence on the scene coincides with fundamental changes in the industry, not the least of which has been yearly double-digit inflation in professional athletes' salaries. That agents have found a place at the bargaining table also reflects a great deal about the nature of these kinds of negotiations. That is the focus of this chapter. Examining their role prompts reconsideration of our familiar model of negotiation as a matter of creating and claiming value within zones of possible agreement. Specifically, in many sports contract negotiations, there may be no zone of agreement, at least at the outset. An interest-based approach, no matter how sincere, may not work very well in such situations.

Sports agency may be a special case, of course, distinguishable from other situations in which one party negotiates on behalf of another. For one thing, the high visibility of these bargains certainly gives them a garish quality. On the other hand, these contextual and structural differences may be merely ones of degree. If we care to listen, we might hear subtle echoes of the same dynamics in many other lawyer-client, employer-employee, and principal-agent relationships.

Context matters, so this chapter begins with a brief survey of important developments in professional sports in recent decades. Particular emphasis is given to the increased bargaining power of players, as well as the key contractual provisions that typically are negotiated. Although salary is always a key item, trades on other issues potentially might create joint gain. Next comes a conventional negotiation analysis of these transactions. That straw man is knocked down in the section that follows. In its place, I offer a no-agreement model more appropriate to this kind of negotiation. This model is supported by analysis of the results of a recent experiment with general managers in the National Hockey League (NHL). The chapter concludes with a brief comparison of sports agents to representatives of other highly paid celebrities.[5]

AGENTS AND PROFESSIONAL SPORTS

Agents are relative newcomers to the sports scene. Until 1968, National Football League (NFL) rules expressly prohibited agents from accompanying their clients to the bargaining table. That the NFL could dictate that policy speaks volumes about its clout at that time. (The existence of the ban also reflects the teams' belief that they could strike more advantageous deals with a player on his own.) How things have changed: Now the typical contract negotiation is between the agent and the team's general manager, while the athlete sits on the sidelines.

The emergence of agents was triggered by fundamental changes in professional sports. First came the rapid expansion of television in the 1950s and 1960s. Advertising and broadcasting fees became an important revenue stream, and that meant more money was on the table to be divided among players and team owners. Second, as sports became lucrative, rival leagues sprang up in football, basketball, and hockey. New leagues and expansion teams engaged in bidding wars over players to gain instant credibility with fans and networks.[6] Third, in the 1970s, courts invalidated baseball's "reserve clause" that had previously tied players to one team and thus created free agency for veteran players. All these factors, in turn, strengthened the unionization movement among players. Strikes (and lockouts) in all the major sports have resulted in collective bargaining agreements in all the major professional leagues. Players in certain sports have won more rights than others, but today's athletes have much more leverage negotiating their individual contracts than ever before.[7]

This is not to say, of course, that negotiation of sports contracts is an entirely new phenomenon. Even when the teams had most of the bargaining chips, players always had the option of "holding out," that is, refusing to play unless their contract was sweetened.[8] Holding out is the functional equivalent of a strike with a bargaining unit of one, in which the player's sole power lies in denying his services to the team. The team loses, but so does the player who forgoes his own salary (and perhaps sows dissension among his teammates). The playing time withheld constitutes an unrecoverable cost for both sides, particularly given the relatively brief professional lifespans of players. Holding out is sometimes effective,[9] but the tactic can corner the antagonists into irreconcilable positions. The glare of television lights can spark escalating volleys of threats, ultimatums, and personal attacks.

No special skill is needed for this kind of bargaining. Indeed, before the sweeping changes in professional sports, contract negotiation was straightforward. Most agreements typically ran for just one season, with a self-perpetuating renewal option held by the team. General managers would put take-it-or-leave-it offers on the table. Unhappy players might threaten to hold out, but few actually did. At best, negotiation was a matter of haggling in a market controlled by the buyers of athletic talent.

Agents were able to justify their role—and their fees—only after the stakes got higher and the process became more complex. Now, in the new order, agents can boast of the following advantages over self-representation:

1. *Experience in the market.* Although unions and leagues publish salary summaries, well-informed agents have a much more nuanced understanding of the agreements that are struck. Agents may also better understand the needs and internal workings of various teams.

2. *Technical knowledge of the negotiation process.* The collective bargaining agreements in the various sports specify impasse alternatives; these typically vary with a player's seniority. Understanding arbitration rights may be key to determining a player's value; if negotiations fail, agents represent their players in these hearings.

3. *Negotiation skill and reputation.* Skill in this industry is usually taken to be of the hard-bargaining variety. Rightly or wrongly, an earned reputation for being tough is assumed to produce favorable results.

4. *Distance.* Substituting the agent for the player at the table may offer strategic advantage (in a Schellingesque sense) and may also protect

the player's reputation with the team and the public if the agent fills the role as the heavy. (In some respects, teams that separate the coaching function from general management similarly insulate the working relationship between the player and his bench coach.)[10]

The first three items benefit both the client and the agent himself, as they also function as barriers to entry to the agents' informal guild; it is hard to crack into the business of representing professional athletes. An agent's expertise represents intellectual capital of sorts that is enriched by having more players. Reputation, in turn, can only be made with visible experience. Agents claim that they earn their money by negotiating bigger contracts for their clients, even after their fees are deducted.[11] How often this is true and how much more they actually get may be debated, but the judgment of the marketplace is manifestly clear: The vast majority of professional athletes rely on agents to negotiate their contracts rather than doing it themselves.

How much a given player earns depends in part on his skill and the demand for people who play his particular position, but the amount is also significantly influenced by legal factors. Whatever is negotiated for the future is shaped by both a player's existing agreement and his league's broader collective bargaining agreement with the players' union.[12] The collective bargaining agreements impose constraints on both buyer and seller, so that very few of these transactions are really conducted at arm's length. Unlike disgruntled customers in an automobile showroom, most players cannot simply walk away from an unsatisfactory offer and take their business to someone else down the street. Teams likewise are bound in varying degrees to their players.

The singular exception are so-called pure free agent players who, by virtue of their seniority, can sell their services to the highest bidder, leaving their previous team empty-handed. Standards for true free agency vary from sport to sport, but only a small fraction of veteran players qualifies.[13] These cases—and perhaps these cases only—resemble the dynamics of familiar negotiation simulations, where failure to reach agreement will mean the parties will go their utterly separate ways.[14]

In virtually all other instances, the no-agreement alternative still involves some kind of continuing rights or relationship, the contractual definition of which bears heavily on the balance of power between team and player. For example, the bargaining power of an unsigned amateur or collegiate player is severely constrained by the rules governing professional drafts. If a draftee does not like the offer of the team that selected him (or does not like the team itself),[15] he can hold out, of course, but at the cost of having no sports income. Hockey and basketball players have the option of playing in Europe, and football players can flee to the Canadian league, but salaries elsewhere are much lower than those in the United States. A young athlete has real leverage only if he plays two sports[16] or if he is lucky enough to turn pro when an upstart league is offering competitive wages.

If anything, however, a player has even less bargaining power once he has signed a professional contract. Collective bargaining agreements typically require several years of major league service before a player qualifies even for arbitration rights. Before that time, the only power of a young player—no matter how productive—is to threaten to hold out, and the expense of doing so is acutely felt early in one's career.

More senior players may earn arbitration rights, although these vary significantly from sport to sport.[17] This option changes the player's best alternative to negotiated agreement (BATNA) and provides some cushion against unreasonable offers. Rather than sitting out and forgoing his pay, the player can go to a third party who, at the worst, will probably not impose a salary that is less than what the team has offered. The respective expectations of team and player shape to some degree their demands at the bargaining table. Nevertheless, the team and the player remain tied together in an asymmetrical relationship; the player has nothing equivalent to the team's right to trade his contract to another team.

Salary is usually at the heart of contract negotiations, whatever the player's status and non-agreement alternatives, but other issues can have monetary, precedence-setting, and symbolic importance. These include the following:

1. *Duration.* Until free agency and the end of the reserve clause, almost all sports contracts were year-to-year, with the team having a unilateral right to renew. Multiyear contracts are now quite common, as players have come to value security, and teams find it in their interest to lock in talent.[18]

2. *Guarantees.* Most professional football contracts are not guaranteed; that is, the player will earn his stipulated salary only if he makes the team.[19] By contrast, hockey contracts are fully guaranteed but can set two levels of salaries: full rate for playing in the NHL and a much lower level if the player is demoted to the minors. Baseball and basketball contracts are usually paid regardless of performance.

3. *Options.* Teams and players may also stipulate provisions that will extend the contract at the option of one party or the other, perhaps depending on certain contingencies.

4. *No-trade promises and other operating constraints.* Players can sometimes insist on language that prevents them from being traded or, more commonly, traded to a particular set of undesirable teams. There also can be assurances—written and otherwise—about playing time and the like.

5. *Incentives.* Prior to free agency, performance clauses were not allowed in major league baseball.[20] The rule was unilaterally imposed by the teams, of course, a policy that reflects an attitude that such clauses favor the players and undercut team performance.[21]

6. *Deferred payment and other structuring.* In the early years of free agency, when marginal tax rates were high, significant savings could be realized by extending payments long after a player retired. When such arrangements nowadays are seen in basketball and football, they usually are driven by a team's need to operate within the league-imposed salary cap.

7. *Other sweeteners and conditions.* Teams will sometimes agree to specialized provisions, such as paying tuition for a player who returns to school in the off-season to complete his degree. Players who have had substance abuse problems may agree to more rigorous drug testing than is required by the league itself.

8. *Agents' fees.* The new collective bargaining agreement in hockey ostensibly bars teams from paying such fees. Under any rules, of course, the cost of the agent is probably shared, although the proportion may be hard to trace.

Contracts incorporate provisions of the collective bargaining agreement and also include boilerplate rules obliging players to be in condition, make their best effort, and lead moral lives[22]—a requirement that increasingly seems more hope than reality.

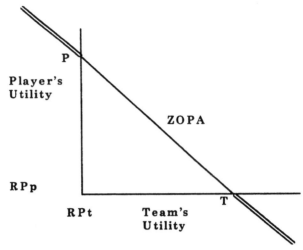

Figure 8.1. Negotiation of One-Year, Guaranteed Contract With No Incentives or Special Provisions

STANDARD NEGOTIATION ANALYSIS

The conventional way of understanding these negotiations would be to depict them as bargains within a zone of possible agreement (ZOPA) lying between the respective values that each party places on its perceived BATNA. The simplest case—a one-year, guaranteed contract, with no incentives or special provisions—would appear to be a distributive negotiation over salary, as represented in Figure 8.1.

The horizontal axis represents the utility scale of the team, and the vertical, that of the player. RP_p and RP_t represent, respectively, the reservation prices of the player and the team. Point P represents the respective utilities for the player and the team of the maximum salary that the team will pay. Point T likewise represents the corresponding valuations of the lowest figure that the player would accept.[23]

Strictly speaking, even with price the sole issue, this is not a zero-sum transaction. Instead, the amount represented by the difference between P and T is a surplus that is jointly generated if—and only if—the parties can come to an agreement. The resulting negotiation over how that surplus should be divided, however, is purely distributive. One side can gain only at the expense of the other.

Some might quarrel with characterizing sports contract negotiation as fundamentally distributive. The introduction of other issues

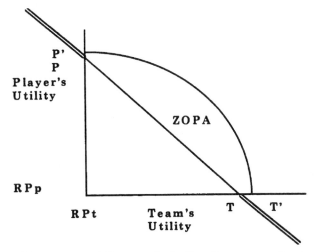

Figure 8.2. Negotiation of Contract Including Guarantees, Contract Extensions, and Other Issues

(guarantees, contract extensions, etc.) supposedly should allow value-creating trades, at least if the parties' preferences, expectations, and risk profiles differ. By this view, the contract curve might instead look something like the P'T' curve in Figure 8.2.

The ZOPA (bounded by points P, P', T', and T) might be expanded by crafting a longer-term deal, spreading payments efficiently, or building in some contingencies. The question, however, is how much weight players and teams give these other factors, relative to the salary issue, and whether their preferences differ in such a way as to significantly expand the zone of possible agreement. There apparently has not been any rigorous analysis of this question, but there is little anecdotal evidence to support belief in the possibility of tremendous mutual gains. After all, we do not hear stories of players and teams who were miles apart on salary yet managed to salvage agreement through ingenious deal structuring.

If anything, there is ample reason to conclude that opportunities for value creation are relatively limited in this domain. As a thought experiment, imagine an attempt to engage in post-settlement (Raiffa 1985) once a team and its player have provisionally agreed on a straight salary contract. A deal doctor might see if the player would take less in the way of guaranteed income in return for rich performance bonuses; value conceivably could be created if the player was more optimistic than the team about reaching the targets.

244 ■ AGENCY IN CONTEXT

In practice, however, incentive clauses are sometimes used, but they usually make up a small portion of the economic value of a contract. Thus, a player earning several million dollars in salary might be eligible for bonuses of 5% or 10% of that for being named most valuable player in the league. That teams and players do not make these a bigger element of their agreements likely says much about their relative preferences.[24] Ancillary clauses likewise appear in contracts but typically as deal closers, face-saving devices to bridge relatively small salary gaps. A player can walk away from the table believing that he has reached an important threshold (a "million dollar contract," for example), while the team can take the position that it has stayed under an important ceiling.

In short, the persistence of hard bargaining over salary testifies to the relatively low importance of other common provisions. Sports contract negotiation appears to be fundamentally dollar-driven, hence largely distributive in both theory and execution. At first blush, it would seem easy to capture this dynamic in the familiar ZOPA model reflected in Figure 8.1, yet this may misrepresent the actual process. (In fact, a closer look at bargaining in sports may argue for a revision of conventional negotiation analysis in other contexts as well.)

The concept of a zone of possible agreement is crisp and familiar, so much so that we seldom consider the assumptions on which it is based. Implicitly, the ZOPA model posits negotiation as a voluntary process in which settlement occurs when both parties jointly see a deal as preferable to the respective consequences of nonagreement. In turn, the values attached to their nonagreement alternatives (be they delicious or dreadful) serve as standards by which the parties say yes or no to a particular proposal.

Accordingly, any actual agreement would seem to imply a preexisting ZOPA, at least a very small one, as both parties have actively expressed a preference for settlement over the consequences of failure to reach a deal. If the parties are close to indifference, the ZOPA is correspondingly small; where the preference for settlement is strong, then the room for agreement is correspondingly larger.

This is a compelling model, to be sure, but it can trap us into examining only what occurs within the zone of possible agreement. In the case of sports agents, this framework might lead us to ask how agents influence outcomes within the ZOPA, for example, if they produce deals that tend to capture a larger share for their clients. We also might ask if sports agents are value enhancers who are better able to find efficiencies that otherwise would be unrealized (in both senses of that word) if players and teams negotiated face to face.[25] For that matter, pessimists might ask if agents tend to screw things up, squeezing value from their clients and missing deal-enhancing opportunities.

Although these are reasonable questions, they posit a model of the negotiation process that may be inappropriate in this context. Instead of reasoning backward from the fact of final agreement to infer a latent zone of agreement, this chapter offers an alternative view of the process. As a consequence, it also poses a somewhat different set of questions. Specifically, it argues that when these negotiations begin, the reservation prices of teams and players are often far apart. Furthermore, agents and general managers often recognize that when they sit down to bargain, there may be no ZOPA. Such expectations would surely influence the ensuing negotiation process.

▨ AN ALTERNATIVE FRAMEWORK:
FROM ZOPA TO NOPA

Imagine a situation where a player's minimum acceptable salary is more than the maximum that his team is prepared to pay. Agreement would be possible only if at least one of those parties subsequently revises its reservation price (or if sufficient value can be created to bridge the gap by trading on other issues). Figure 8.3 illustrates such a case, with the line P"T" representing a set of mutually unacceptable outcomes. The continuation of the line, above the horizontal axis, describes outcomes that would satisfy the player but that are even less acceptable to the team. Continuation of the line in the other direction, to the right of the vertical axis, shows salaries that the team would pay but that would be rejected by the player. The outcomes along P"T" itself represent unacceptable compromises, with each side favoring nonagreement over any available option. We might call this the NOPA line for "no possible agreement."

There are compelling reasons to believe that this model more accurately depicts player contract negotiations. One is the peculiar nature of BATNA in professional sports, specifically the fact that the team and player are usually locked together contractually. The BATNA is not really "no deal"; it is the prospect of an agreement at a later

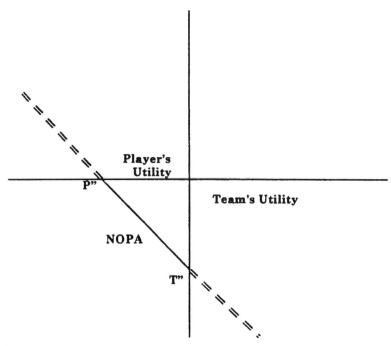

Figure 8.3. Failure to Agree, Requiring at Least One Party to Revise Its Reservation Price

point—when the other side finally comes to its senses or caves in. Players do not choose between a lucrative offer from the team and pumping gas at the local Kwikee Mart but, instead, choose between that offer and the expected result of continued bargaining.

Interlocked BATNAs are not unique to sports. They are a basic feature of labor-management negotiation, of course, though in other industries, parties' expectations are usually bound by common understanding of market conditions. It is understood that if wages get too high, the business will go bust; likewise, if they are too low, morale will suffer and the most productive workers will quit. In sports, by contrast, there is not the same kind of market discipline.

Comparability is a problem as well. The highest paid players are not necessarily the best performers, and their salaries become bones of contention in other negotiations. "Overpaid," says the general manager. "I should get more than he does," says the player. The breadth of pay ranges compounds the problem. One player may earn 10 or even 100 times as much as some of his teammates. Emotion is surely a factor as well. The same kind of ego and drive that allow an athlete to excel at the highest level of competition probably correlates with a high sense of self-worth. General managers struggling to keep up with an inflationary market may likewise tend to be a day late and a pound short in terms of anticipating what their players will require. Role bias is common in many settings; the culture of sports may be an ideal medium where it can breed.

The NOPA gap may be deepened if parties start thinking in terms of right or wrong, not just economics. Instead of coolly calculating what an arbitrator is likely to award in case of an impasse, a player may make pay a matter of principle, insisting on what he deserves. In turn, a general manager coping with escalating salaries may blame "unrealistic" players and "unethical" agents for the resulting red ink. Separating the people from the problem may be especially difficult in this kind of arena. Likewise, searching for underlying interests, creative options, and objective criteria may not get at the underlying dynamic of typical sports negotiations. In fact, there are several deep forces that tend to make the process adversarial.

First, the player's economic interests are inevitably bound up in his identity. Salary is important as wherewithal and as highly visible testimony to his worth, accomplishment, and standing relative to other athletes. To concede on salary is to admit one's shortcomings to the world and oneself.

Second, the potential for creative deal structuring to bridge gaps is real but limited. The primacy of the salary issue makes it almost impossible to separate the expansion of the pie from its division.

Third, as already noted, attempts to use "comparables" might actually drive the negotiators farther apart if each sees the other's as self-serving. A team's invocation of lower-paid players can easily be read as an insult. An athlete, in turn, who claims he is equal to the very best is seen as a greedy egomaniac.[26]

These contextual factors would be obstacles to interest-based negotiation even when a team is negotiating directly with a player.[27] If anything, they may be amplified when agents sit at the bargaining table in place of players; specifically, agents may often have even less incentive to consider interests, options, and neutral criteria as means to joint problem solving.

First, as to underlying interests, agents typically compete for players by ambitious claims about what they can win for their clients.

This is particularly true for an agent who is trying to get an established player to leave a rival agent. Stroking and flattering is at the heart of such courtship ("someone with your record deserves much more"), but the greater this seductive salesmanship,[28] the more the player's aspirations are likely to inflate. An agent can subsequently get trapped by such promises, of course, but they also can become self-fulfilling commitments.

Second, differences between the agent's interests and those of his client can further inhibit value creation.[29] For example, agents have scant interest in the player's personal relationship with the team and its management. General managers can find it frustrating to deal with an agent instead of the player if they are trying to address qualitative issues like their commitment to winning or the quality of life the community could provide him and his family. Agents, in turn, do not want their clients to be seduced by such intangible rewards, perhaps because no percentage comes back to them. With such communication blocked, some potential opportunities for value creation may be lost.

Third, the agent must also take into account the collective interests of his stable of clients—particularly when their long-term financial success will redound to him personally. It is true that the agent gets nothing in the short term from the specific player he encourages to hold out, but by thus signaling his own toughness, the agent may quickly make back any losses in other negotiations he is simultaneously conducting.

Finally, the fact that agents know that they may be called on to act as advocates when arbitration is a possibility may also make it hard for them to be dispassionate value creators at the bargaining table. (The same may be true for zealous litigators.) Even a clear-eyed agent may find it awkward to bring his client's sense of self-worth down to earth. The player who hears his own agent talking about his shortcomings and limitations may worry that he will be poorly represented if the contract ends up before an arbitrator.

In short, strong institutional and social factors promote hard bargaining on the part of sports agents. This may not be inevitable, but practices and attitudes captured in the quotations at the beginning of this chapter are consistent with a view of negotiation *not* as moves in or toward a zone of possible agreement but, instead, as responses to genuine gaps between the expectations of players and their teams.

Furthermore, if parties see the bargaining game as one in which they have to significantly change the other side's reservation price, then communicating one's own unwillingness to budge becomes critical. (Again, this is particularly important where the BATNA is not a pure walkaway but the expectation of cutting a more favorable deal sometime in the future.) The temptation to issue threats and ultimatums may well be strong. Such tactics may lead to an uncontrolled escalation of hostilities in which pride and face loom large. Even without personal animosity, it may be difficult to pursue interest-based negotiation when offers and counteroffers are volleyed back and forth in the press.

Contract negotiations in these situations are not conducted along a bargaining range, with the parties moving from extreme positions to some intermediate zone of possible agreement.[30] Instead, they constitute a dynamic process in which each side is trying to swing the line of *non*agreement (P"T") in its favor until it lies in acceptable territory.

Sports agents may be especially suited to this hardball task. As already noted, they have an ongoing professional interest in not appearing to be weak. Whereas a player might bargain once a year at most, agents build their reputations through multiple negotiations. Agents also offer tactical advantage. Because they do not suffer the consequences of a poor relationship, they can play the heavy, setting high demands and holding a player out while insulating the client from retaliatory threats.

Those who represent the players, however, are not the only agents in these transactions. The teams typically are represented by general managers (GMs) who are neither owners nor playing field coaches. The GMs have incentives and interests that are not perfectly parallel with those of others in their organizations, especially as they contend with conflicting mandates. They are hired to build winning (and popular) teams, but they also have to watch their budgets. Pushed to control costs on one hand, they also have to avoid alienating fans and the press on the other. Periodically, GMs are fired.

The perceived toughness of a GM depends in part on the priorities of his employer. Some teams essentially operate as corporate franchises, like the Disney Company's Mighty Ducks in professional hockey. General managers in such situations may have a budget just as would the heads of any other business units. Whenever they negotiate one player's contract, they must be mindful of what will be left for others on the team.[31]

Other general managers work for teams owned by wealthy individuals whose interests in profits may be dwarfed by a personal compulsion to be a "winner" or at least be in the media spotlight.[32] GMs with such bosses sometimes have to cope with players' agents going over their heads, directly or indirectly, to get the owner to sweeten the pot. This leaves the GMs playing the "bad cop" role, having taken a tough line that gets softened by their superiors. With corporate ownership, the reverse may be true: The GM may implicitly scapegoat the faceless bureaucrats who have locked him into a budget. Either way, hard bargaining can easily result.

Occasionally, one person holds the dual role of general manager and on-the-field coach.[33] The usual practice, however, is to separate these functions, in part because they require different skills but also because of the perceived advantage of having one person hammer out the contracts while leaving the other to build successful working relationships with the players.[34] This separation likewise may reinforce the tendency toward hard bargaining.

 SOME PROVOCATIVE DATA

Much of what we know about negotiating professional sports contracts and the role of agents in that process is necessarily anecdotal. Getting access to conduct a large-scale quantitative study would be difficult. Moreover, differences in both the economics of the various sports and their governing collective bargaining agreements would present challenging issues of research design. Even within particular sports, the wide variance in the financial condition of different teams and the important status differences among players raise tricky problems of comparability.

In 1995, however, David Lax, James Sebenius, and I conducted a negotiation program for virtually all the general managers of the National Hockey League (and many of their top assistants). As part of an exercise on prenegotiation preparation, we created a revealing experiment that avoided some of these research design problems.

Specifically, we randomly divided the 50 participants into two groups. One was assigned to act as agents for a talented college player who was about to turn pro. Those in the other group were cast in their familiar roles as general managers. The background information on the hypothetical player and the team had been constructed with the help of NHL officials; participants were given enough credible information to allow them to make judgments about appropriate contract terms. The player's record made him a promising prospect, someone who would surely get more than the league minimum but also not so overpowering that he could command the top amount under the newly imposed salary cap for rookies. The team, in turn, was described as an average NHL franchise in respect to win/lose record and financial performance. Agents and teams had identical information (though we did not mention this.)[35]

The situation, in short, replicated the kind of negotiations that these general managers regularly conduct. Moreover, the group had just experienced the first portion of a training workshop in which they all had negotiated a simple real estate simulation. In the debriefing, they had been introduced to concepts like BATNA and ZOPA.

To prepare for this next exercise, we asked participants privately to assess their broad interests and goals, consistent with their role instructions. Then we asked each of them to complete forms that had them identify the following information:

1. Their "walkaway" price; that is, the least they would accept if they had been assigned to be agents for the players or, if they were in the role of general manager, the most that they would pay;

2. Their target deal or aspiration;

3. Their expected first offer, if they had to make one; and

4. Their estimate of the likely walkaway price of the *other side.*

A few of the participants did not complete the entire form, but 47 out of 50 stated their prenegotiation walkaway prices. All but 7 of the 50 also estimated the walkaway price for their counterparts.

We randomly paired each "agent" with a corresponding "general manager." This matching took place before we had tabulated the responses to the prenegotiation survey. Results are presented in Table 8.1.

TABLE 8.1 National Hockey League General Managers and Assistant
General Managers (June 22, 1996)

Agent	Goal	Other	BATNA	ZOPA/ (Gap)	BATNA	Other	Goal	Team
A	?	?	200	60	260	283	233	I
B	600	400	550	(17)	533	667	?	II
C	475	416	383	(33)	350	500	350	III
D	550	250	500	(242)	258	350	258	IV
E	500	300	400	(157)	243	333	?	V
F	583	533	533	(166)	367	500	367	VI
G	?	?	450	(182)	268	200	?	VII
H	850	?	650	(184)	466	600	466	VIII
I	850	850	500	(192)	308	200	?	IX
J	725	666	600	(208)	392	392	384	X
K	?	?	483	(217)	266	333	266	XI
L	675	658	567	(242)	325	850	?	XII
M	?	400	600	(250)	350	350	?	XIII
N	850	850	650	(250)	400	267	?	XIV
O	850	600	500	(275)	225	263	192	XV
P	600	500	567	(317)	250	250	?	XVI
Q	750	800	700	(325)	375	375	225	XVII
R	850	700	700	(350)	350	400	325	XVIII
S	850	500	667	(364)	303	850	283	XIX
T	850	550	750	(417)	333	400	300	XX
U	850	500	850	(500)	350	500	300	XXI
V	850	467	850	(550)	300	?	275	XXII
W	850	500	850	(550)	300	200	275	XXIII
X	850	525	750	?	?	?	?	XXIV
Y	483	550	450	?	?	?	?	XXV

Goal = individual's target or aspiration level, Other = prediction about other side's BATNA; BATNA = individual's walkaway; ZOPA/(Gap) = difference between respective BATNAs.

These results are striking in several respects. First, in spite of the participants' firsthand knowledge of the market and their seemingly strong personal identification with the team's position, those who were asked to act as agents calculated a much higher value for the player (as reflected in their professed walkaway prices) than did those cast as general managers. Specifically, the median walkaway price stipulated by the 25 agents was $567,000. By contrast, the median maximum salary set by the 22 GMs was only $325,000—in spite of the fact that everyone was evaluating exactly the same information. That the so-called agents came in 74% higher testifies to the power of role bias, even when people have deep personal experience that seemingly should pull in the other direction.

Second, within each group there was wide variation in all the assessments. Most notable is the range of walkaway prices for the agents, from $200,000 to $850,000 (the then-existing rookie salary cap).[36] There was variation among the general managers as well, with the stingiest willing to pay $250,000 and the most generous, a maximum of only $533,000.

Third, the 22 random pairings of the parties produced only one prenegotiation ZOPA in which the least demanding agent was paired with the most tight-fisted general manager.[37] The frequency of ZOPAs is partly luck of the draw, but four was the maximum number of pairs with preexisting ZOPAs that we could have created. (Moreover, one of those four would have been a pairing which the walkaway prices of the parties was an identical $400,000.[38]) In short, these data strongly support the argument advanced earlier that sports contract negotiation often may begin not with an implicit zone of possible agreement, but with a gap between what the parties claim to be their walkaway prices.

Fourth—and most intriguing—is the fact that many of these experienced professionals clearly *expected* that there would be a gap between the most the team would pay and the least that the player would accept. This belief can be seen by comparing the walkaway figure that each person identified for himself and the estimate he made of the other side's likely walkaway. Twenty-one of 25 agents provided this information. Of these, in turn, 11 anticipated that the team would not be willing to meet their bottom line, while 8 were hopeful that there was room to bargain. Two of the agents, incidentally, stipulated the same number for their own walkaway and that of the team. (This makes certain strategic sense: If the agent's goal is to maximize dollars for his client, why set his own walkaway price at less than the team is thought willing to pay?)

Those representing the teams were even more pessimistic about the existence of a ZOPA. Of the 22 general managers who estimated the agent's likely walkaway, 14 assumed it would be higher than their own top dollar. Only 4 expected that there would be a ZOPA. Four others set equivalent amounts for their walkaways and the bottom lines for the agents. As a result, roughly two thirds of these people headed to the bargaining table with the expectation that there was no agreement presently possible, and half of the others assumed that there was utterly no room in which to move.

If this is a common expectation, the prevalence of hard bargaining should be no surprise. If a gap is anticipated, negotiation is less likely to be a game of discovering the ZOPA and making moves (either positional or principled) within it than a contest of getting the other side to budge. Given the interlocked BATNAs of teams and their players, a fundamental technique for getting the other party to move is signaling one's own unwillingness to do so. If this seems harsh, consider the consequences of the alternative: What is one side likely to do if it senses that the other may soon cave in? Hard bargaining tactics are a familiar way of exploding such perceptions.

When we randomly paired the participants in our experiment for the negotiations, 18 of the 25 matches involved people who had both set their own walkaway and estimated that of the other side. Of these 18, only 2 resulted in pairings where each expected that the other would meet his price. (In spite of their optimism, there actually were gaps of $192,000 and $250,000, respectively!) There were also 2 other pairings in which an agent expecting an overlap was matched with a general manager who thought the agent would just meet his bottom line.[39]

In more than three quarters of the pairings (14 of 18), at least one of the parties sat down to negotiate with the belief that the other side would *not* accept its own last best offer.[40] Pessimism also marked the pairings where we had incomplete information. In 5 of those 7, the party who provided information anticipated a NOPA situation. The presence of just one negotiator at the table who believes that there is gap between the parties' bottom lines is probably sufficient to trigger hard bargaining. Such a person may feel that he has little choice other than to force the other side to capitulate or to capitulate himself.

Our pairings were random, but regardless of the vagaries of chance, there were bound to be many negotiations where at least one side came into the process believing that the other side would have to be pushed (by persuasion or force) to meet his bottom line. In this experiment, the participants stipulated their own walkaways and that of the other side before knowing the identity of the person with whom they would deal.

Such is not the case in practice. Agents and general managers know each other, usually from prior experience and always by reputation. In other settings, such knowledge might soften demands and expectations, but if anything, the opposite may be true in professional sports, where relationships between agents and teams are often bitter and contentious.

CONCLUSION

The results from our prenegotiation experiment support the NOPA model of bargaining presented earlier in the chapter. In negotiations over player contracts, the process often begins with no zone of possible agreement. Deals are eventually cut when one or both sides reassess their nonagreement alternatives—typically continued bargaining in hopes that the other party will sweeten its offer.

Agreement is hardly inevitable: Witness the frequency with which cases go to arbitration. The device is often used even in baseball, whose arbitrators are empowered only to choose the team's offer or the player's demand. In theory, such a system should promote efficient negotiation, as each party seeks to put a number on the table that the arbitrator will see as at least a little more reasonable than that of the other side. Through a series of reciprocal moves, a team and a player should ultimately come together without actually having to resort to the arbitrator.

In the sports context, however, final offer arbitration has not worked as some expected. Rational incentives to settle apparently can be overwhelmed by emotion and a sense of right and wrong. Given the extraordinary salary levels, moreover, some players apparently feel that they have little to lose in the arbitration process. Whatever the ruling, they will be rich, so why not set their bottom line high? General managers likewise may have reason to dig their heels in, preferring to blame an arbitrator for a high award rather than to set a costly precedent themselves.

As was noted earlier in this chapter, sports negotiation may well be a special case in some important respects. It is worth contrasting the role of sports agents to that of literary or entertainment agents, for example. Although the latter are not necessarily held in any higher regard,[41] they function in very different markets. Although a big-name athlete may be contractually bound to play for a particular team until his seniority earns him free agent status, a Hollywood star or best-selling author is more of a "free agent."[42] Negotiations take place in an auction context where each side has to compare the proposal on the table with any number of other possible deals. Parties are not hand-cuffed together, so their BATNAs are not interlocked.

Money also matters in these venues, but there is often more room for creativity and value creation. Deals can be structured that mix certain guarantees with contingent payments;[43] rights to income from ancillary products likewise can be crafted.[44] The more complex and open-ended these transactions, the harder it may be to visualize strict bottom lines. If so, the parties may be less inclined to arrive at the bargaining table anticipating a NOPA. Self-fulfilling tendencies toward hard bargaining may thus be mitigated. The need to foster constructive personal relationships may affect positively the substance and tone of these negotiations as well. Unlike their sports counterparts, literary and theatrical agents have relationship interests that are more consistent with those of their clients. Just as an author must be able to work creatively with an editor (or an actor with a director), a talent agent has an ongoing interest in maintaining access and in packaging deals.

Hard bargaining still takes place in these contexts, of course. In negotiations over the next blockbuster book or movie, each side still may push the other to revise its original walkaway price. As others have cogently observed, the challenge is to create and claim value simultaneously, mindful that the tactics that advance one can undermine the other (Lax and Sebenius 1986).

Sports agency takes place in a context where the incentive to claim is particularly strong. There are surely many other contexts, however, where there is no zone of agreement when the parties first sit down to negotiate. Sometimes, those gaps can be overcome by careful identification of underlying interests and the generation of new options. Sometimes, people even may reconstruct their fundamental values. At the same time, however, we should not forget that another game also may be taking place, one in which the parties understand that their alternative to agreement is not walking away, but outlasting the other side. In the case of sports agents, this game is in the spotlight before an audience of fans, reporters, and other interested stakeholders. In other contexts, the game may be played far more subtly, yet it nonetheless goes on.

NOTES

1. Dell is a tennis promoter, sports agent, and lawyer; he is also a former player.

2. Falk (1995) includes a catalog of "strategies" like good cop/bad cop that really are hardball tactics.

3. Brian Burke, a graduate (1981) of Harvard Law School, is a former agent who subsequently became general manager of the Hartford Whalers. He is now the executive vice president of the National Hockey League (NHL).

4. See, for example, cases collected in Weiler (1993), Chapter 5, "Agent Representation of the Athlete." Several articles deal with ethical and fiduciary breaches by agents and proposed regulatory schemes for deterring them. See, for example, Cohen (1993) and Ehrhardt and Rogers (1988).

5. I must acknowledge the enthusiastic and insightful help of Pacey Foster of the Program on Negotiation, who gathered much of the background material. I am also grateful to PON Executive Director Marjorie Aaron for providing that support.

6. Joe Namath is remembered for brashly guaranteeing victory in the third Super Bowl—and delivering on his promise—but his biggest impact on professional sports came several years earlier, when he opted to sign a record-setting contract with the then-upstart American Football League instead of the established NFL.

7. There is irony in the fact that in the same period that union membership in the United States was declining by more than 50%, the only militancy to be seen was among highly paid athletes. While parents had seen autoworkers, teamsters, and mine workers out on strike, their children saw tackles and shortstops on the picket line.

8. After hitting 60 home runs in 1927, Babe Ruth demanded $100,000 in salary. When challenged that his pay would exceed that of President Coolidge, Ruth reportedly replied, "But I had a better year."

9. Several years ago, on the eve of the deciding game of the NHL's championship playoffs, a star forward is rumored to have demanded to renegotiate his contract then and there. The team insists that it did not capitulate

to his demands. Some knowledgeable observers are not convinced, however, and believe that the team actually capitulated.

10. Distance in the sense of objectivity may also be a virtue in cases where a player has an inflated view of his own worth, although this may be tough to sell to such a player.

11. Agents get from 4% to 10% of the salary that they negotiate, although one could argue that they really should be rewarded on the margin for improving deals. The question whether they should be compensated for time or results has been considered elsewhere. Each method has consequences in respect to the alignment of the agent's incentives with those of the principal. The late Bob Woolf wrote that when he was trying to sign Larry Bird as a client, Bird insisted on a lower percentage, arguing that it would take no more time or effort for Woolf to negotiate a big contract as opposed to a small one. According to Woolf's version of the story, he very much wanted Bird as a high-profile client, but after sleeping on it, he decided that a discounted rate would be "unfair" to the other athletes he represented. Bird was so impressed with his integrity, Woolf recalled, that the basketball player retained him at his normal rate. Bird says that the story is pure puffery and that he in fact got a special deal. The story suggests interesting issues regarding player-agent relationships that are not pursued in this chapter.

12. Perhaps this may explain why a high percentage of sports agents are lawyers. There are other legal services that an agent may deliver as well, among them tax, investment, and estate planning advice.

13. Players who were never picked in amateur drafts or players who are unconditionally released by their teams also fall into this category, but these constitute unusual cases.

14. See, for example, "Sally Soprano," a simulated negotiation available from the Case Clearinghouse of the Program on Negotiation at Harvard Law School.

15. Eric Lindros was the number one draft pick of the Quebec Nordiques (now the Colorado Avalanche) even though he had previously let it be known that he did not want to play in Quebec province. After many months of stalemate, and with the Nordiques facing the possible expiration of their draft rights, the team reluctantly traded him (or more precisely, the right to sign him) to the Philadelphia Flyers. Lindros was able to have his way only because he was universally recognized as a sure superstar.

16. John Elway was able to use the fact that he was a top baseball pick as leverage in negotiating with football's Denver Broncos. Baseball players Jake Gibbs, Bo Jackson, and Kirk Gibson were likewise fortunate.

17. A final offer procedure is used in baseball in which the arbitrator must pick either the player's last best offer or the team's; the arbitrator cannot impose his or her own judgment. Arbitrators in hockey are not so bound, but

teams now have the right to "walk away" from up to three unfavorable arbitrations in a two-year period.

18. Many general managers are ambivalent about multiyear contracts and weigh the benefits of building for the long term against possible loss of motivation. There may be hard bargaining over the expiration date, depending on where that will leave the player in respect to his free agency rights.

19. Contracts are insured, however, either by underwriters or by the team itself in the event a player is injured in the course of employment.

20. When that policy was in effect, a generous owner might "tear up" the contract of a player who performed beyond all expectations—an act of largesse that probably has seldom, if ever, been reciprocated by a player who has had a lousy year.

21. A hitter who gets a bonus for hitting a certain number of home runs may have a disincentive to bunt in key situations, for example. For that matter, a team that must pay someone a bonus for playing in a certain number of games may be tempted to use a substitute as that threshold looms.

22. Years after slugger Dave Parker left the Pittsburgh Pirates, the team unsuccessfully brought suit demanding that he return some of his salary on the ground that his subsequently admitted drug use was a violation of his contractual promise not to engage in immoral conduct.

23. Even if guaranteed salary is the sole issue, it is probably more accurate to speak in terms of utility as opposed to dollars, in the light of tax implications and differing discount rates. Strictly speaking, even though the salary issue would be linear, the utility trade-offs might not be.

24. Exceptions sometimes occur when a player is signed again after a major injury. In such cases, the base salary may be quite small, with a big jump coming if the player makes the team or appears in a stipulated number of games.

25. For an argument that a lawyer-agent's deal structuring expertise can sometimes expand the pie, see Gilson and Mnookin (1995) and Gilson (1984).

26. Harry Sinden, long-term president and general manager of the NHL's Boston Bruins, refuses to "talk comparables" when he is negotiating player contracts. Some agents let him get away with this.

27. This point is compatible with (but not identical to) the Lax and Sebenius argument that a Gresham's Law of negotiations may operate, so that competitive bargaining tactics drive out cooperative ones (Lax and Sebenius 1986:3-41).

28. Although it is possible to conceive of a value-creating agent who tries to sell himself as a more creative negotiator than his competition, that may be much too subtle a pitch when others are simply promising bigger bucks.

29. Conflict of interest between player and agent can exist even when salary is the sole issue. For example, an agent short of cash and with a higher

discount rate than the player he represents might settle on the cheap (Mnookin, Peppet, and Tulumello 1999:49). If anything, however, the agent's need to establish a reputation as a tough bargainer may more frequently encourage holding out when a player perhaps really should sign.

30. Sometimes, of course, there can be big zones of agreement right from the start. In the mid-1970s, Derek Sanderson of the then-championship Boston Bruins talked to the owner of the Philadelphia franchise in the rival World Hockey Association. As Sanderson tells it, he was not seriously interested in leaving the Bruins and the established NHL. Thus, when the owner asked how much it would take to make him jump to the new league, Sanderson flippantly answered, "A million dollars a year." This was many times his current salary, but the owner immediately said, "No problem." Quick-witted, Sanderson said, "And a Rolls Royce." "It's yours," answered the owner. By the time they were done, Sanderson had negotiated a contract that was beyond his wildest expectations.

31. The same constraints ostensibly exist in salary cap sports like football and basketball, though it increasingly appears that such ceilings can be evaded.

32. George Steinbrenner of the New York Yankees is the prototype, though actually he has several partners.

33. It is interesting that, among the few people who hold dual roles, Bill Parcells of the New York Jets and Rick Patino of the Boston Celtics are regarded as tough negotiators. Parcells apparently sees coaching advantage in the fact that his players know that he also has hiring and firing power.

34. Long after Roger Clemens left the Boston Red Sox, he continued to vilify General Manager Dan Duquette in the press for poor treatment in earlier negotiations. He had no similar quarrel with anyone else in the organization.

35. Agents had green packets, and teams had orange ones. The narrative information for the teams gave the background of their organization first, whereas the agents' sheets began with data on their client. The information itself was identical.

36. It is possible that the less demanding agents were less subject to bias and may indeed have had trouble empathizing with the role they normally see as their nemesis. The agent with the lowest demand set a threshold that was barely half that of his most easily satisfied colleague.

37. This counts only the pairings in which both the agent and the general manager stipulated a walkaway figure in their prenegotiation forms. In three other matches, we do not know the walkaways of one side.

38. Instead of a ZOPA, this might be more accurately characterized as a POPA: a point of possible agreement.

39. Here the actual gaps were $208,000 and $325,000.

40. Of these 14, 5 involved two similarly pessimistic negotiators. Another 5 matched an optimist who believed there was a ZOPA with another person who did not. The 4 remaining matches paired someone who believed agreement was barely possible (because of identical walkaways) with a pessimist who expected a gap.

41. In a well-known quotation, the late humorist Fred Allen said that the minds of people who control television are "so small that you could put them in a gnat's navel with room left over for two caraway seeds and an agent's heart."

42. Such was not the case under the old studio system in Hollywood, in which actors were locked into long-term contracts that would oblige them to make a certain number of pictures. (United Artists was formed by Mary Pickford, Douglas Fairbanks, and Charlie Chaplin to break the power of the producers.) Likewise, even today publishers push for "option clauses" in their contracts that require their authors to give them subsequent books.

43. Book contracts typically provide authors with an advance against earnings, the latter being calculated by percentages that rise with sales. Best-selling author Stephen King recently signed an unusual deal in which he accepted what, for him, was a low advance (a paltry $1,000,000) in return for a 50% share of the revenues, much higher than the standard 15% cut.

44. Literary and theatrical agents provide some of the same kind of negotiation skill and strategic advantage to their clients as do sports agents. They can offer other benefits as well. First, they can provide access. A well-known agent can get a publisher or producer to read a new author's work. Having earned professional credibility (and perhaps won personal favors), these agents also provide value to those across the table by sifting through the talent pool. There really is not a comparable function for sports agents. In our sports-obsessed society, promising high school and college players get plenty of publicity. Scouts for professional teams swoop down on budding stars as fast as the agents do.

▨ REFERENCES

Burke, B. 1993. Negotiations involving agents and general managers in the NHL. *Marquette Sports Law Journal* 4(1):35-50.

Cohen, G. 1993. Ethics and the representation of professional athletes. *Marquette Sports Law Journal* 4(1):149-197.

Ehrhardt, C. W. and S. M. Rogers. 1988. Tightening the defense against offensive sports agents. *Florida St. University Law Review* 16(3):633-674.

Falk, D. B. 1995. The art of contract negotiation. *Marquette Sports Law Journal* 3(1):1-27.

Gilson, R. 1984. Value creation by business lawyers: Legal skills and asset pricing. *Yale Law Review* 94(2):239-313.

Gilson, R. and R. H. Mnookin. 1995. Foreword: Business lawyers and value creation. *Oregon Law Review* 74:1-14.

Lax, D. and J. Sebenius. 1986. *The manager as negotiator: Bargaining for cooperation and competitive gains.* New York: Free Press.

Mnookin, R. H., S. R. Peppet, and A. R. Tulumello. 1999. *Beyond winning: How lawyers and clients can create value in legal negotiation.* Unpublished manuscript, Harvard Law School.

Raiffa, H. 1995. Post-settlement settlement. *Negotiation Journal* 1(1):9-12.

Weiler, P. C. 1993. *Cases, materials, and problems on sports and the law.* St. Paul, MN: West.

Yasser, R. C., J. R. McCurdy, and C. P. Copelrud. 1988. *Sports law: Cases and materials.* 2d ed. Cincinnati: Anderson.

Unnecessary Toughness

Hard Bargaining as an Extreme Sport

Brian S. Mandell

Participants in a growing number of domains of negotiation—labor, family, corporate, environmental, and international—have discovered the many benefits of interest-based, mutual-gains bargaining. In the domain of professional sports, however, resistance to a more cooperative problem-solving approach to negotiation remains high. Hard bargaining continues to prevail in sports negotiation and crowds out possibilities and incentives for generating innovative approaches to value creation and relationship building, as Michael Wheeler argues in his chapter, despite opportunities for more creative and effective approaches to structuring deals.

What is it about the structure of professional sports negotiations and the particular institutional context in which these negotiations unfold that makes hard bargaining apparently so necessary and so rewarding? Is it the overbearing presence of zealous agents, with their strong financial and reputation-building incentives, that tends to favor an uncompromising, winner-take-all approach to deal making, as Wheeler suggests? Is it because the pool of athletes, often inexperienced and unsophisticated negotiators who are easily flattered and

263

manipulated by unscrupulous agents, comes to the table with hopes for wildly unrealistic salaries? Is it the shared presumption of players, agents, and teams that brinksmanship, stalemate, and capitulation are necessary prerequisites for effective agreements? Is it that, because of the brief lifespan of most professional athletic careers, efforts to leverage talent, an intangible asset, compel players and their agents to focus narrowly and greedily on very short time horizons? Although deal makers in the realm of professional sports like to wear the reputation of shrewd, hard bargainers as a badge of courage, a looser examination of their deal making may reveal room for contentiousness to coexist with creativity and problem solving. Theirs is a negotiation structure that needs refinement more than it needs fundamental repair.

HOW CONTEXT FRAMES AND REINFORCES A CULTURE OF IMPASSE BARGAINING

Negotiations between players, agents, and teams tend to be highly visible, contentious, and greed-driven interactions, with an optimistic focus on the eventual deal that inevitably will emerge. Best alternatives to negotiation include stalemate and capitulation by the other side or holding out for an offer from another league. Interactions among stakeholders have a ritualistic quality—threats, ultimatums, and extreme offers from players, agents, and teams, often transmitted through the media, and in a rising crescendo at critical seasonal junctures. This combative culture of noncooperation and inflammatory discourse is tailor-made for agents skilled in the strategic and psychological use of brinksmanship. After all, these tactics are what it takes, at least in the mythology of professional sports negotiation, to represent the "best of the best."

Aggressive bargaining behavior may be grounded for the most part, as Wheeler suggests, in the overriding belief among agents that, in this context, money is the salient distributive issue. Agents find little incentive to create value around less tangible issues that they cannot readily translate into higher contingency fees. To demonstrate their success in a relatively small, closed market, in fact, agents are likely to prefer one-dimensional contests of "show me the money."

Finally, as a result of two features of the professional sports context, agents operate with an extraordinary level of autonomy and authority. On one hand, the athletes they represent are frequently young, inexperienced, and lacking in sophistication. Although a dense communication network thrives among players, agents, and teams, many athletes are thus unprepared to calculate a best alternative to a negotiated agreement (BATNA) and are unaware of how best to structure an agent's mandate and incentives. On the other hand, agents have routine access to team managers and specialized knowledge both of the negotiation process and of the athletic market. They are therefore free to actively shape and manipulate the preferences of players eager to be auctioned off to the highest-bidding team.

With the need to demonstrate their ability to deliver enormous salaries, agents are ethically challenged as they seek to secure their reputations and attract additional business. Agents therefore exploit the context available to them. They aim, moreover, to sustain this milieu by ensuring that players depend on them to extract maximum rewards from teams unevenly disciplined in their assessments of athletic talent.

▓ HOW AGENTS' ROLES AND INCENTIVES SUPPRESS THE EXPLORATION OF INTERESTS, OPTIONS, AND NEUTRAL STANDARDS

The range of representational roles played by sports agents is bounded by league rules, norms, collective bargaining, and arbitration frameworks as well as by the degree of autonomy negotiated with principals. In the sports domain, agents are neither "champions" nor "visionary leaders" who generate creative options or transform the principal's interests and self-perception (as described by Joel Cutcher-Gershenfeld and Michael Watkins in Chapter 1 of this volume). Rather, without trust, the agent's task is more narrowly focused on advising players how to avoid the positional traps embedded in the structure of sports negotiations. This is not to suggest, however, that an agent never plays the role of "partner" with his or her principal. Agents do, as Cutcher-Gershenfeld and Watkins suggest, simultaneously represent their own interests (especially acting as principals) as well as those of players.

In linking roles to specific functions, sports agents—in the context of league sports—assume four distinctive roles. First, they act as "tension creators." By manipulating the zone of potential agreement (ZOPA) through continuous exaggeration of the worth of players to teams and by encouraging their principals at the same time to adopt more realistic expectations, agents generate a dramatic roller coaster atmosphere of high-stakes, sudden-death bargaining.

Having softened up the negotiating environment, agents are then free to engage in two other roles: "access creator" and "wealth creator." In the role of access creator, agents serve as matchmakers, bringing together players and teams who otherwise might not find each other. Although the market for any specific sport is relatively small, inexperienced players need to be properly packaged by agents and then given access to top bidders. Agents acting in the role of wealth creator draw on their own reputations as they seek to establish the worth of players, by separating out the very best from the next best, and so on. In short, agents help to create the market for new talent. Finally, once the battle with team managers is joined, agents serve in the role of "shield," a fourth distinct role, protecting players from suboptimal offers and from the mudslinging of hard bargaining.

HOW WEAKLY ALIGNED INTERESTS AND INFORMATION ASYMMETRIES GIVE AGENTS TOO MUCH POWER, AUTONOMY, AND COMMITMENT AUTHORITY

In the four roles described above, agents leverage their skills, knowledge, and reputations in ways likely to exacerbate rather than temper positional bargaining. This is especially the case because agents, paid by contingency fees, have every incentive to promise athletes higher salaries and to promote reputations for achieving the impossible.

This narrow and highly focused set of incentives for agents suggests further that less experienced and less sophisticated players exert little authority over the agents' more contentious bargaining strategies and tactics. Because players are not at the bargaining table, communication between players and teams is filtered by what agents choose to tell players. Agents may have little incentive to portray players' interests accurately to team managers or clients. Given the prevailing structures of the financial relationship between principals and agents (namely, contingency fees based on the salary negotiated), agents push for over-the-top deals employing only "partially open truthful exchange" (POTE) to achieve their goals. The fog of battle may have an unfortunate result, precluding players either from accepting earlier offers that fall within their range of reasonable deals or from considering potential trades, among other issues that could create joint gain. In addition, agents representing several players are likely to have little interest in making players their allies; they have every incentive to play athletes off against each other, highlighting the unique and distinctive value of each player to team managers. By contrast, players may be keen to have agents act as allies who protect and promote their interests on a consistently reliable basis.

 ## HOW AGENTS ADD VALUE IN SPORTS NEGOTIATIONS

From the preceding discussion, it could reasonably be argued that agents do more harm than good, engaging in a variety of contentious behaviors that do not help expand the ZOPA between principals. A closer examination of this domain reveals, however, that agents do add value in the small, complex market for athletic talent. To begin with, agents give saliency to athletes by packaging and converting talent into a commodity for sale to the highest bidder. In this connection, agents play an important screening role for teams. They separate the very best athletes from the next best ones and establish the worth of the top of the field. Such distinctions and clustering are critical for top players, who expect to command more compensation than their counterparts who are only close to the top. Most important, agents offer specialized knowledge of a given sports market. Not only do they intimately understand the particular needs of different teams, but they also know how to match the teams up with new talent as it enters the market, whether in a formal draft system or by other means. Then, once teams are ready to bid and deal for players, agents also demonstrate specialized knowledge of the "negotiation dance," whose common steps include impasse bargaining, preparing for arbitration, and the skillful exploitation of timing.

A sense of timing—generally knowing when to hold, fold, or close—is one of the skills most prized by agents and most valued by the players they represent. "There is a lot of risk in people trying to strike while the iron is hot. If you miss it, it will never happen again," observes sports marketer Lewis Jones, "but the question is when to strike and when to wait and when to pull back. It's a complicated business and not a lot of people know when to make those choices."[1]

During negotiations with teams, agents offer players distance and detachment. They ensure that players are insulated from the negative interpersonal fallout produced by hard bargaining. Distance from the table gives principals an opportunity to strengthen commitments to winning maximum rewards; players can remain unavailable and incommunicado. Detachment from developments at the table also gives athletes (via communication filtered by agents) an opportunity to set realistic expectations and to moderate inflated views of self-worth.

Finally, agents provide valuable information about the other side—especially about the possibility of finding a pretext for increasing a player's settlement demand. By playing out gambits in an effort to ratchet up leverage with the other side, they provide tactical flexibility.

▓ HOW AGENTS IMPOSE COSTS ON SPORTS NEGOTIATIONS

Ironically, when agents exploit information asymmetries with their principals, manipulate weakly aligned interests, engage in positional hard bargaining, and provide significant rewards for agent and athlete alike, they simultaneously reinforce the justification for and legitimacy of strategies and tactics of impasse bargaining. This approach, to paraphrase Roger Fisher, ends up being tough on the people and the problem. Unnecessarily tough tactics and inflexibility produce needless impasses and destroy the goodwill and trust (among players, agents, team managers, fans, and the media) needed to foster more effective value creation. In protracted negotiations, agents tend to focus narrowly on the process of closing agreements rather than on the benefits of enhancing the content of the agreements. Driven to show something for labor and sunk costs—of time, reputation, and forgone opportunities to represent others—the agent pushes for maximum concessions. In the midst of this pursuit, agents are likely to withhold critical information from players. To stiffen the client's resolve, an agent may, for example, fail to disclose the other side's willingness to extend a deadline or may resist agreeing to a deal that falls well within the player's range of acceptable offers. Using his presumed authority and flexibility, the agent may force the player to hold out. The athlete, in effect, becomes a hostage to the agent's current (and future) reputation as a shrewd, tough, and effective bargainer.

Such actions by agents, which undoubtedly stretch the limits of ethical behavior, reflect a misalignment of interests: Players and agents often have very different goals and aspirations. The great autonomy and authority typically given to sports agents exacerbates this misalignment of interests. Agents are free, for example, to cultivate close relationships with team managers and with other agents. When they value these relationships more highly than relationships with the players they represent, however, they may do so at the expense of getting more advantageous deals for players. Even more dangerous for unwary principals, agents enmeshed in coalitions with the other side may find themselves acting contrary to the interests of the player. As consumers of agents' services, principals need to know whom they are dealing with and just what kind of service they provide.

DON'T KILL ALL THE AGENTS, JUST SHORTEN THEIR LEASHES

Wheeler's chapter suggests that, on balance, although agents do exploit and reinforce positional bargaining between players and teams, they also produce some important value. Like entertainment agents and literary agents, sports agents also rank, package, and sell talent. Sports agency differs from agency in the other domains, as Wheeler argues, in degree rather than in kind. Having said that, we are still left with a prescriptive challenge.

What advice can we offer principals in the sports domain to allow them to achieve greater managerial control over their relationships with sports agents? And what advice can we offer sports agents about how to exercise their mandate and authority in ways likely to yield better outcomes for principals?

At the outset, it is worth arguing that the gains can be significant in the professional sports context for principals and agents who do not further complicate their relationship. Principals can have more opportunities to exercise greater authority over agents, provided they are willing to think harder about the kinds of monitoring and incentive mechanisms needed to enable agents to satisfy athletes' interests more fully, but negotiating one's own professional sports identity is a demanding task. "There's going to be a lot of people who are pulling at you," basketball player Magic Johnson counseled a rising young athlete. "You just have to be yourself—not who they want you to be."[2]

The twofold prescriptive challenge is to advise principals how to achieve greater managerial authority and control over their relationships with agents and to advise agents how to exercise their mandate and authority more effectively to achieve better outcomes for principals. Greater explicitness about preferences and interests will help both sides to achieve significant joint gains. Players who wish to insist that agents keep the identity and authority of the principal in sharp focus throughout the negotiation process can, for example, exploit the unwillingness of their agents to sacrifice either reputations or opportunities for business growth. Or players can develop robust monitoring and incentive mechanisms to more actively help in the task of managing the complicated social and monetary relationship with agents. Players need not passively wait for agents to deliver a negotiating victory from the jaws of defeat, an attitude that encourages agents habitually to dig deeper into the realm of no possible agreement (NOPA).

In a domain where agency is the norm, where stakeholders are agreement-driven, and where interests are regularly filtered through a dense information network, principals need to manage the risks of using agents more effectively. Players need their own screening devices to make better distinctions between strongly and weakly performing agents. Most fundamentally, principals must ensure that agents use their deal-structuring expertise to expand the pie—especially around such issues as multiyear contracts, performance incentives, no-trade promises, and deferred payment of salary.

As principals in the negotiations, players need to take the following steps as safeguards against agent incompetence, conflicts of interest, and blocking coalitions that undermine the satisfaction of interests. First, they must avoid giving vague instructions to agents, instructions that are inherently positional, impasse prone, and subject to early commitment. Players need to redirect agents beyond short-term gains toward the broader goal of satisfying underlying "quality of life" interests. Such redirection ensures that the player receives a larger share of the value created in negotiations than might otherwise be the case.

Second, players need to reduce the agent's authority to commit early in the negotiation process on the single issue of compensation. Participants would be foolish to forgo opportunities to generate new options that might better satisfy a wider range of tangible and intangible interests.

Third, players must get a better sense of how more of their interests can be satisfied, and they can do so by insisting on regular consultations with agents. The consultation process affords principals the opportunity selectively to share information about preferences with the agent and the opportunity to calibrate the scope of authority to be given to agents as negotiations proceed from one phase to the next. In this connection, principals can choose to increase the agent's authority to commit to an agreement only after a full exploration of interests and alternatives ensures that significant opportunities for creating additional value have not been overlooked.

Fourth, players must rethink the methods by which contingency fees are paid. The agent's compensation must be aligned more closely to the satisfaction of the multiple interests of principals. Finally, players must strengthen and verify the accuracy of communication by circumventing agents and communicating offers directly to team managers, who are the principals on the other side of the negotiation.

For agents, the tasks of strengthening interest alignment, building trust, and producing higher value outcomes are no less challenging. To safeguard their reputations and to increase the likelihood of representing the best of the best, agents need to do the following. First, they must reflect harder on their own independent interests; they must think beyond short-term gains to those relationship networks—with players and team managers—that can facilitate the creation of additional value. They must also be more mindful of how such relationships might conflict with the interests of principals. Second, they must insist on written instructions about the flexibility of the negotiating mandate and the scope of authority for making commitments. They must think of limited authority as a strategic asset, not a liability. Exercising authority in this way helps the agent avoid early positional traps and promotes a negotiation process that is less likely to set the agent up for failure and loss of credibility. Third, agents must insist that principals share more information and be more explicit about their preferences and interests as a precondition for creating more favorable deals. Finally, if principals demand a larger share of the value created in negotiations, payments and incentives should be structured to compensate agents for producing value around tangibles and intangibles alike.

If principals and agents choose to follow this prescriptive advice, an important transformation will occur for all stakeholders, including sports fans and the media. Although the destructive consequences of hard bargaining in professional sports will never be fully mitigated, opportunities to provide additional value need not be suppressed. The challenge, however, is for principals and agents to break free of old bad habits.

 NOTES

1. Jones, deputy media director at J. Walter Thompson in New York, is quoted on page 36 of *Business Week* in the April 18, 1997, cover story (Stagehill, R., G. de George, R. Melcher, B. Hyman, R. Grover, L. Himelstein, and A. Palmer, "Tiger, Inc." pp. 32-36).

2. Johnson's agent, Lon Rosen, describes this conversation between Johnson and Tiger Woods in the *Business Week* article cited in Note 1, p. 34.

PART III

Prescriptive
Implications

Major Themes and Prescriptive Implications

Lawrence E. Susskind
Robert H. Mnookin

When we began our year-long seminar "Agents in Negotiation," we had no idea how we would conclude. Our strategy was to consider agents as a "complicating factor," that is, as one of approximately half a dozen features that make a negotiation complex. Such factors might include the cultural diversity of the parties, the presence of neutrals, the gender of the parties, the scientific or technical complexity of the issues under discussion, and the number of stakeholding group—any factor, that is, that may require elaboration of the basic model(s) or theory upon which negotiation practice is based. We were also committed to bringing together as many disciplinary perspectives as we could. If we were going to enrich the basic theory of negotiation, including the work generated by the Program on Negotiation over the past decade and a half, why not reach out in as many directions as possible for assistance and advice? Our mission was to figure out how best to adapt or modify the interest-based model of negotiation that typically assumes two monolithic parties seeking to advance their own interests, to take account of problems and opportunities presented by the involvement of agents.

As our discussions evolved, three themes emerged. First, agents appear to have different roles to play and to add value in different ways, depending on the scope and content of the negotiation. The expertise offered by a lawyer, for example, representing his or her client in a contract negotiation is quite different from the "assistance" a diplomat provides to a country involved in a treaty negotiation or the added value a union negotiator contributes on behalf of the rank-and-file. We spent a considerable amount of time trying to parse the different roles that agents (or representatives) play.

Second, it quickly became clear that communications between agent and principal and among agents is crucial to exploiting the added value that agents can generate. We explored the advantages and disadvantages of "full and completely truthful" communications between agents and principals at various points in different kinds of negotiations. Ultimately, we discovered that the alignment of interests (and not just the quality and completeness of communications) was really what we were concerned about.

Third, there was agreement early on that the mandate(s) given to (or assumed by) agents can substantially add to or detract from their effectiveness. This generalization stood as seminar participants attacked it from their very different vantage points and as we tested its relevance in a wide range of practice situations.

The chapters in this volume examine these three themes in some detail. From our own standpoint, we are convinced (although others in the seminar may have reservations) that we can say some things with confidence about agents in negotiation. A number of my colleagues, who are more patient researchers and in less of a rush to squeeze out prescriptive advice, will be more than satisfied with the testable propositions that also appear in the final chapter of this book. On behalf of a more intrepid few, we are prepared to go a step farther and offer summary statements and prescriptive advice based on what we have already discovered about the three themes listed above.

ROLES PLAYED BY AGENTS

Agents play many roles in negotiation. The choice of the role they play ought to reflect the interests of the principal, the relative bargaining power of the principal vis-à-vis other principals, the skill and knowledge of the agent, and the agent's reputation. The agent should not be calling the shots, and principals should think long and hard about what they want from an agent before choosing someone to represent them in a negotiation. A lot depends on the match between the skills and style of the agent they select and the circumstances surrounding the negotiation—particularly the relative power of the parties. For example, if a principal has a weak best alternative to a negotiated agreement (BATNA) and his or her counterpart has a strong BATNA, it would be best to find an agent who has had experience (and success) operating in such a situation.

One key role of an agent, in almost any negotiation, is to expand the zone of possible agreement (ZOPA) between or among the principals as far as possible. This involves not just creativity and substantive knowledge about the issues under discussion but also good listening skills and a quality of mind that permits simultaneous exploration of many options. Agents who are good only in the competitive clinches and are afraid that any sign of cooperation will undermine their ability to walk away with the larger "piece of the pie" when it comes time to distribute value are not likely to succeed in expanding the ZOPA. Of course, an agent had better be able to ensure that his or her principal receives an appropriate share of any and all value created. The more inclined principals are to jump at the first offer, the more they need skilled "value claimers" as their agents.

The role an agent plays must take account of the authority assigned to that agent by the principal. The less authority ceded by the principal, the less responsibility the agent has for evaluating options or making decisions. An agent who is accustomed to wielding substantial authority throughout a negotiation probably would be the wrong person to select for an assignment involving little if any authority. A limited grant of authority does not necessarily limit an agent's creativity; however, the ground rules must be clear—both internally between the agent and the principal and externally between the agents and between the principals. Agents with limited authority can still work, especially at the early stages of a negotiation, to gather information and generate options for their principals. They can still help their principals analyze each option objectively.

In the final analysis, the role of the agent and the role of the principal are intertwined, or at least they ought to be. Most principals, from time to time, are forced to play the role of agents in that they, too, have constituents to whom they must account; they understand what is involved. Problems seem to emerge when agents are "one-trick ponies," unable to make adjustments to the needs of their clients or the circumstances, and their principals (but not their counterparts!) are intimidated by the agent's competitive style and reputation.

ALIGNMENT OF AGENT-PRINCIPAL INTERESTS

Principals can enhance the effectiveness of their agents by ensuring that agent-principal interests are carefully synchronized. Interests can be realigned by altering the incentives given to agents. Altering the instructions alone will not do it. Incentives can include more than a fixed fee or a share of the deal; they can encompass promises of future assignments as well as promises of the kind of publicity that can make or break an agent's reputation.

Complete alignment of interests between agents and principals is not necessarily helpful. Indeed, at the earliest (inventing) stages of a negotiation, nonalignment (or at least the appearance of nonalignment) may be advantageous. For example, if agents really throw themselves into brainstorming wildly different options (and the agents involved are looking out for their own interests even if those are somewhat different from their client's interests), they are more likely to end up with "packages" that fully exploit differences and leave their principals better off. Too many assumptions early on about what the principals will and won't accept can inhibit useful brainstorming.

In the international treaty-making arena, when top country representatives are empowered to do nothing more at a meeting than read preapproved statements (aimed at mollifying factions back home), the chances of generating real solutions to pressing global problems are minimized. When the same representatives are empowered to participate, on their own responsibility, in a brainstorming process in which no commitments are sought, their levels of creativity can be truly astonishing. When commitments must be ratified, nonalignment of interests between principals and agents in the final stages of a negotiation can undermine the prospects of agreement (or at least its likely implementation). Prior to that, though, less concern about complete alignment of interests can be a plus. We are not arguing that nonalignment is, in and of itself, an advantage; rather, experience has demonstrated that less concern on all sides about whether there is complete alignment can free the parties to be more creative.

It is sometimes advantageous for principals and agents to collude in presenting a "false nonalignment" of interests so as to maximize gains when value is being distributed. This is especially true when principals put substantial emphasis on maintaining long-term relationships with other principals but feel strongly that they do not want to be pushed to take less on the grounds that, by being greedy, they are threatening the relationship. Under these conditions, a principal would love to be able to say that he or she is staying out of it and leave the "nasty" part of the negotiation completely in the hands of the agent. Of course, this does not always work. A knowledgeable principal on the other side will say that the first principal should not let his or her agent make the important decisions and that the first principal will be held accountable anyway.

MANDATES GIVEN TO AGENTS

As the seminar progressed, we became more convinced that it is best to put the authority granted to agents in writing and to disclose these instructions to the other agents. It appears to be helpful for an agent to show another agent exactly what his or her mandate is. Whether these written instructions are accepted at face value, of course, is another matter. At the outset of a negotiation, it seems as if an agent is more likely to be effective if he or she has no explicit authority to make binding commitments on any substantive issue, especially if it is clear in the instructions that this is likely to change as the negotiation progresses. Principals, not agents, should have the final say over the choice of objective criteria used to argue for a particular distribution of value. Indeed, principals as well as agents have reputations at stake, and the choice of objective criteria has a lot to do with the kind of reputation that both the principal and the agent will create for themselves. Those who choose to supply no objective criteria at all—classic hard bargainers engaged in a test of will—earn a well-deserved reputation as unyielding and not very creative negotiators. In sum, the authority, autonomy, breadth, and adaptability of an agent's mandate should be carefully set to increase the size of the ZOPA, to maximize the likely implementability of the agreement, and to benefit the reputations of both the agent and the principal.

▦ PRESCRIPTIVE ADVICE TO PRINCIPALS VIS-À-VIS AGENTS

Although the same research findings can be used to generate advice to agents vis-à-vis principals, we really did not focus very much on that side of the equation. Instead, we concentrated almost entirely on the best advice we could give principals about dealing with agents. Moreover, the seminar as a whole did not try to reach consensus on the kind of prescriptive advice offered below. These notions are based on our understanding of the seminar discussions and the commentaries of our colleagues.

Presume that the agent on the other side may not be portraying his or her principal's interests accurately. If one assumes that an agent's interests diverge from the principal's interests, he or she will ask a lot more questions, evaluate what is heard in a different light, and press for more direct evidence that the other principal has, in fact, heard a proposal before accepting an agent's claim that it has been rejected. One might also frame offers or proposals in a contingent fashion. For example, one might propose multiple packages, each offering a lot more on one thing and less on several others, and ask the agent to indicate which is more attractive to his or her principal and why. One would do this before indicating which package is preferred and would not accept a mere rejection of all the packages. Rather, one would keep pressing for clarification by offering additional "if-then" options. My presumption is that an agent will feel obliged to take "if-then" offers back to the principal (even if the agent does not like one or another of them), because the potential upside of one or more of the "if-then" choices could be too good from the principal's standpoint for the agent to have rejected out of hand.

The more one assumes that there is a divergence between an agent's interests and his or her principal's interests, the more one is likely to rely on written summaries of discussions and written responses to proposals. In addition, one is likely to press for a face-to-face meeting with the other principal(s) before an agreement is finalized. When it comes time for implementation, the agent could be long gone, so it is necessary to see the other principal's reaction when one asks, point blank, for a personal endorsement of the "deal." Of course, this has implications for how to deal with an agent representing one's own interests as well. The principal should be there in person to ensure that everyone understands the final agreement as well as the obligations and commitments it implies. It is important to see written versions of offers and responses from the other side.

Try to find out the structure of the financial relationship between the agent and the principal on the other side. A principal should not be shy about asking directly what the financial relationship is between the other principal and his or her agent. After all, it is likely to directly affect the negotiation. It would not be surprising if the agent would not reveal this information. One might still want to put the question to the other principal (and risk being told the same thing again). In the book publishing business, agents receive a fairly standard rate of payment for helping to get a manuscript published. Does the fact that the rate is well known in the industry undermine or help increase the effectiveness of literary agents? We suspect it helps them. If both sides are aware of the structure of these relationships, it allows each side to better estimate the value of offers and proposals to the principals.

In most instances, a principal would be willing to share information about the nature of his or her financial arrangement with the other side's agent. It is not clear how the principal's interests are served by keeping this secret. If others do not agree, however, and asking directly does not produce what the principal wants to know, he or she might offer to exchange this information with his or her counterpart. If that does not work, the principal might be willing to reveal unilaterally the relevant information about his or her own case and hope this encourages the other side to do the same. If it doesn't, the principal would not be at much of a disadvantage. In fact, having revealed this information (which should help both parties), a principal might also be able to trade the revelation for something else later on in the negotiation.

Try to make the other agent an ally. The principal may not get to talk directly to the other side. In that case, the only person who can transmit a principal's proposals, along with the arguments to back them up, is the agent on the other side. If a principal treats this person as an enemy, the agent may misrepresent the principal's statements in an effort to "get even" or undermine the principal. If the principal tries to work around the agent, he or she may not only fend off such efforts but even may actively work to undermine the principal's chances of getting what the principal wants. In the end, there is no alternative but to treat the other agent as an ally.

What does this mean? First, an agent should not try to drive a wedge between the agent for the other side and his or her principal. Second, agents should treat one another as they would like to be treated themselves. Third, agents should help each other to meet their interests (to the extent possible) insofar as these are not inconsistent with the interests the agent is trying to meet. Fourth, each agent should negotiate in a way that seeks to enhance his or her relationship with the other agent and not just the principal. Finally, each agent should work to enhance, not undermine, the reputation of his or her counterpart.

In his preface to this volume, Abram Chayes suggests that everyone involved in any kind of negotiation is really an agent of some kind and not just a principal. That is, there are very few negotiators who do not have someone else to whom they are accountable. Everything presented in this book, therefore, actually can be construed not just as specialized advice to agents or to people involved in the complexities of agent-principal interaction but as general advice to everyone participating in any kind of negotiation.

Chayes's observation came as something of a revelation to the participants in our seminar. The more we savored his suggestion, the more it made sense. When we review the prescriptions above in light of this interpretation, it does not seem necessary to change or qualify anything. One should always assume that the person with whom one is negotiating with is an ally, not an enemy (at least until proven otherwise). Furthermore, it should be assumed that this person is the only one in a position to get the "powers that be" to accept the proposals of the other side. Each side should try to give the other the evidence and arguments it needs to get a "yes" from its second table (i.e., the people to whom they report but who are not part of the direct communications). In the final analysis, assuming that almost all negotiation is done on behalf of "others," it is crucial that we have a good idea of how to incorporate agents into a basic theory of negotiation.

Agents in Negotiations

Toward Testable Propositions

Terri Kurtzberg
Don Moore
Kathleen Valley
Max H. Bazerman

The chapters in this volume provide a fascinating set of ideas that we expect can vitalize a critical, yet underdeveloped, part of the negotiation literature—the role of agents. Our goal in this chapter is to funnel the wealth of ideas in this volume into a set of testable propositions that can build on and further develop the scientific study of the role of agents in negotiation. We hope that this organization will increase the likelihood that these chapters provide a springboard for research in this critical set of negotiation issues. The first step in our chapter is to *quickly* review existing empirical work on the effects of agents in negotiation and attempt to place the current work into the literature. After that, our focus turns to a synthesis that presents the ideas in the previous chapters as testable propositions.

Authors' Note: This research was supported by the Dispute Resolution Research Center, Northwestern University, Evanston, Illinois.

Agents are expensive. They add extra dimensions to the flow of information, they confuse issues of the "ownership" of ideas and of goals, and they can present conflicting interests. Indeed, the use of intermediaries in bargaining relationships has been shown to reduce the likelihood of transaction, increase the sale price, and increase the time to agreement (Yavas, Miceli, and Sirmans 1997). Why would any party facing a negotiation employ an agent, then? Summarizing a literature built from economic theory, Rubin and Sander (1988) have provided a comprehensive explanation for the benefits of hiring an agent as opposed to negotiating principal to principal. First, they argue, agents can lend expertise to both the specific subject matter and the process of negotiation in general. Second, agents may be strategically connected to certain situations and people so as to facilitate agreement and access to information. Third, agents afford a degree of detachment that can be difficult to maintain as a principal. Fourth, agents can be used in tactical ways, such as playing either side of a "good cop/bad cop" routine in which the decision-making responsibility is diffused among several parties. Additionally, research in a legal setting indicates that a prebargaining commitment of an agent can increase the credibility of a principal (Croson and Mnookin 1996) as well as lock a principal into a strategy of cooperation (Croson and Mnookin 1997). Even with these benefits, however, the use of agents is complicated and can sometimes be detrimental to the principal.

Much of the groundwork for the discussion of agents in negotiation situations has been laid through economic theories of the relationship between principals and agents. Economic agency theory discusses this relationship primarily in terms of the optimal contracts for aligning the interests of the agent and the principal. If the agent and the principal both act in their own self-interest as value maximizers, there will often be divergence between the outcome the agent would prefer and that which the principal would prefer. This divergence leads to costs on the part of the principal *and* the agent, costs necessary if the principal is to be willing to risk acting through the agent. Jensen and Meckling (1976) offer three sources of agency costs that extend naturally into agents in negotiations: (1) the monitoring expenditures by the principal, (2) the expenditures incurred by the agent in "guaranteeing" that she or he will act in the best interests of the principal, and (3) the actual loss incurred by having the agent negotiate in the place of the principal. An ideal contract minimizes these costs, increasing the net benefit of using agents. Designing ideal contracts is extremely complicated. Quite obviously, it is only when the benefits outweigh the costs that agents should be enrolled in negotiations.

Sappington (1991) points out that to the degree that the agent does not bear all the risk based on the outcome of the negotiated situation, it is not possible for the agent and the principal to have perfectly aligned incentives. In many cases, the agent's incentives follow a path of diminishing returns along which the proportional increase in benefits accrued by the agent for outstanding performance no longer outweigh the proportional increase in effort by the agent to attain such results. Conlon and Parks (1990) explore the potential presented by contingent pay agreements and find that the presence of a tradition of noncontingent pay anchors both the form and the amount of agent earnings. These contractual issues underlie the research done on agents in negotiation situations. Issues of cost/benefit and optimal contracts also underlie the research on agents in negotiation situations.

Bazerman, Neale, Valley, Zajac, and Kim (1992) found, in a simulated real estate negotiation, that the use of an agent increases the rate of impasse in negotiation, even where the agent does not get paid unless there is an agreement. In addition, they found that the use of an agent increased the selling price of a house, but not by enough to offset the cost of the agent—thus, the costs of the agent are effectively split between buyer and seller. Valley, White, Neale, and Bazerman (1992) asked how much information principals should share with agents. Their results show that the agent's awareness of the buyer's reservation price raised the settlement price, whereas knowledge of the seller's reservation price resulted in the lower settlement price. Because agents aligned themselves with the seller only when both buyer and seller revealed their reservation prices, Valley et al. (1992) concluded that it is most beneficial for buyers to remain as silent as possible about their true reservation prices.

Lax and Sebenius (1991) calculate payoff functions to describe the role of uncertainty in an agent's behavior. They illustrate how the agent's demands unambiguously increased with increases in uncertainty about either the principals' reservation price or the payoff function. In addition, the more risk averse the agent, the more demanding he became of his negotiation opponent. Increasing the levels of uncertainty also increased the likelihood of impasse. Murnighan, Cantelon, and Elyashiv (1997) explored the ethical complexities surrounding the role of the real estate agent. Consistent with the above findings, this research shows that agents tend to share information and facilitate agreements selectively. Agents' interests are not perfectly aligned with those of their principals. These authors note that this misalignment can lead to ethically questionable behavior on the part of the agents, such as hiding crucial information, despite the agents' legal obligations for disclosure.

Overwhelmingly, previous research points to the hazards associated with the use of agents. The current research agenda, developed from the chapters in this volume, attempts to map out more closely the reasons for such hazards. Current questions include the following: When do agents most successfully find integrative trade-offs? Under what conditions do agents claim more value for themselves? How much authority and autonomy is optimal? Such questions aim to describe the conditions under which the use of agents can be either beneficial or problematic.

 PROPOSITIONS

The chapters in this volume inspired us to go from the chapters toward testable propositions. Each author has contributed a unique perspective on the ways in which agents change the negotiation process, and these perspectives can be overlapped and combined in such a way as to inform new empirical research. The series of propositions that follows begins by identifying some of the basic roles that agents can play and establishing the potential effects of these roles on negotiated outcomes. Finally, the implications of each role can be deduced from the interaction between the role and the needs of the principal.

Cutcher-Gershenfeld and Watkins present several different continua along which an agent's role can be understood based on interest alignment, breadth of vision, and unification of internal interests. The first continuum runs from agent through partner to principal, depending on the degree to which the agent has interests that are aligned with those of the principal. The second continuum runs from agent through champion to visionary, depending on the scope of the agent's authority. The final continuum runs from agent through mediator to partisan, depending on the division of internal interests experienced by the negotiating parties. This chapter's use of these continua inspires a set of propositions on the consequences of interest alignment, amount of independent authority, and their interactions in producing negotiated outcomes.

Cutcher-Gershenfeld and Watkins (Chapter 1) argue that independent authority given to agents will be correlated with the tendency to explore creative alternatives. Agents free to explore novel solutions will do a better job at finding integrative trade-offs. Cutcher-Gershenfeld and Watkins, however, also see such agents, whom they call visionary leaders, as those most likely to fight a hard distributive battle and win concessions from opponents. This pair of predictions is particularly interesting in the light of evidence that negotiators who behave contentiously, wringing as much of the surplus as they can from their opponents, have a correspondingly more difficult time finding integrative trade-offs and making the trades that maximize the size of the pie (Neale and Bazerman 1991).

Proposition 1: Authority given to an agent will be positively correlated with ability to find integrative trade-offs.

Proposition 2: Authority given to an agent will be positively correlated with contentious behavior aimed at extracting new concessions from negotiating opponents.

The above propositions, if borne out, would point to a clear path for principals: Maximize the authority granted to your agent. This authority, however, will likely benefit the principal only to the degree to which the agent and principal have aligned incentives. Conflict between these parties will likely substantially change the nature of the division of the surplus created between the two parties.

Proposition 3: Conflict of interest between principal and agent will be positively correlated with the amount of surplus claimed by the agent.

A politician negotiating an international trade pact is an example of a visionary agent whose interests are closely, but not perfectly, aligned with those of the principal. Here, the negotiator is likely to place value not only on a pact that is good for her constituents but also on one that looks good and increases her chances of keeping her political job. Situations such as international negotiations, however, often function in an environment with multiple agents and no clear principal. In this case, it is often the shifting wind of public opinion that directs the interests of the agent.

In contrast, Nicolaïdis (Chapter 3) raises the additional complicating condition of situations in which there is more than one principal and these principals must first agree on preferences and priorities among issues and then must relate these instructions clearly to the agent. Nicolaïdis sees some of the same advantages as Cutcher-Gershenfeld and Watkins in granting authority to agents; however, she argues that the optimal amount of authority to grant an agent will depend on two things: the conflict of interest between principals and agents and the conflict of interest among principals. Giving too much authority to an agent carries with it different agency costs than does granting too little authority. Where there is a conflict of interest between principals and agents, increases in the agent's authority will be associated with the agent claiming more of the surplus (Proposition 3, above). Similarly, a conflict of interest among multiple principals can further complicate the guidelines established for the agent.

Proposition 4: Where there are conflicts of interest between principals, increasing the authority given to an agent will increase the likelihood that the surplus will be inequitably divided among multiple principals.

Where agents are given too little authority, they will be less likely to find integrative solutions that increase the size of the pie. In addition, when their hands are tied, agents may be more likely to reach an impasse despite a positive bargaining zone.

Proposition 5: Reductions in the agent's authority will be positively correlated with impasse.

Babbitt's (Chapter 4) discussion of international negotiations highlights the case of multiple principals as well. A foreign affairs agent must answer to multiple constituents, including the president, Congress, and public opinion. Because the agent will be held accountable by each of these parties, the agent will likely try to avoid alienating any one party through extreme decisions or concessions. Bold moves will not be supported if the agent is unable to assert a persuasive vision to multiple constituents, and integrative trade-offs will become more difficult, especially if they benefit some principals at the expense of others.

Proposition 6: The greater the number of principals, the less likely an agent is to find integrative trade-offs.

Babbitt's chapter also highlights the concern that arises when a foreign representative becomes too engrossed in the local culture, thereby losing perspective needed to negotiate on behalf of the original country. This implies that agents will make too many concessions to the other side and will decrease the surplus for the original principals. To avoid such problems, agents are moved around every few years. The implicit assumption here is that too much knowledge of one's opponent could become detrimental to the principals.

Proposition 7: There is a curvilinear relationship between the agent's knowledge of the opponent and surplus generated for the principal, such that agent performance is maximized at a moderate level of familiarity with the opponent. Agents who are either extremely unfamiliar or extremely familiar with the opponent will, by comparison, perform poorly for the principal.

King and Zeckhauser's (Chapter 7) discussion of legislators revisits the issues surrounding a complex set of principals. Because legislators are responsible for representing an entire constituency that may contain a wealth of perspectives, the agent role can be quite complicated. The task of selecting an agent is made more complex by the fact that candidates must be voted into office without knowledge of the issues they will face. Because legislators are rarely able to take direct orders from constituents moment to moment on all the issues that they face, they must act in what they believe to be the interests of their constituency. In this situation, King and Zeckhauser argue, voters will be concerned about the ideology of the candidate. This concern for ideology amounts to a desire to maximize the similarity between the interests of the agent and the interests of the principal.

Proposition 8: The less the agent is able to take direct orders from principals, the more concerned will be the principals with maximizing the similarity between their own interests and the interests of the agent.

One condition specific to this setting raised by King and Zeckhauser is the visibility of political negotiations. Allowing the public to watch the negotiation in progress can take its toll on the negotiation process. Constituents who see only a part of the process might look poorly upon compromising behavior on the part of their legislator. Strategic alliances and compromises that might improve the outcome in the long run might look bad when reported on the evening news. This fact, these authors argue, limits the kinds of solutions that are possible for an agreement. Negotiation over time will give way to issue-by-issue compromise. These arguments can be stated as testable propositions. Note that King and Zeckhauser treat an increase in the observability of the agent's negotiations as similar to the concept of reducing the authority granted to an agent (Propositions 1, 2, 4, and 5, above), with parallel consequences for negotiated outcome.

Proposition 9: Observable negotiations will limit the agent's search for solutions, and as such will be positively correlated with impasse.

Proposition 10: Observable negotiations will increase the priority placed on issue-by-issue, short-term goals rather than long-term interests.

Another interesting point highlighted by King and Zeckhauser in this political context is the presence of a deadline in the negotiation. Although many negotiations have deadlines, election dates are inflexible and are crucial to the political career of the legislator. Recent accomplishments will hold undue weight, especially if principals have short memories. As such, the approach of the election deadline can lead to a flurry of activity. Because politics requires compromise, the approach of deadlines is likely to increase the amount of negotiation, bundling, trade-offs, and compromising behavior.

Proposition 11: As a deadline approaches, agreements will contain more bundling of issues as agents increase the use of compromise and trade-off strategies.

Note that because political activity tends to be observed more closely as an election approaches, this prediction is at odds with Propositions 7 and 8.

Salacuse (Chapter 5) addresses the legal distinctions made to separate the different types of agent roles. He identifies three separate possibilities: the independent contractor, the employee, and the partner. Any of the three can be assigned to the task of negotiating on behalf of a principal, but the degree to which they have authority to make and execute decisions about agreements depends on their legal role. A partner has the most authority to make such decisions. This situation begins to resemble Nicolaïdis's discussion of multiple principals and the difficulties that arise in that condition. An employee, although the most costly option for the principal, is the most easily controlled. In Nicolaïdis's terms, then, the mandates are the most strict in this case, and the margin of maneuverability is the smallest. In terms of the continua presented by Cutcher-Gershenfeld and Watkins, an employee would act more like an agent and less like a partner or principal. Finally, an independent contractor requires the least specific mandates because the individual is hired primarily for expertise in the area in question and as such needs less specific direction. This freedom, however, leaves room for mixed motives to interfere with the issues already brought to the negotiation by the principals.

Another issue raised by Salacuse is that of multiple agents from a legal perspective. This model helps to explain situations in which the chain of command requires each party to delegate the role of agent to the next in command while still answering to the principal above. This long chain of command can diffuse the flow of information in such a way as to both hinder the negotiating agent's efforts and confuse the issues to the point at which negotiated agreements are not ratified by the original principal. Not only does the flow of information risk being altered in a long chain of passage, but Salacuse also notes that this distance increases the chances that an agent's own agenda will surface when the agent is removed from the principal. Therefore:

Proposition 12: The longer the chain of people between the ultimate principal and the negotiating agent, the lower will be the level of benefit claimed by the principal.

The distance between the principal and the agent effectively serves to create a very broad mandate and allows for the agent's personal agenda to interfere. Longer chains of people serve to confuse the information on preferences and priorities, as well as removing the principal from involvement in and control over the negotiation.

A final issue raised from this legal perspective is that of power. A principal is in a more powerful position over the agent to the degree to which (1) the personal relationship between them is professional and not personal, (2) the agent is easily replaced, (3) the agent is isolated from the networks of the competition, and (4) the agent actually provides all relevant information to the principal. In terms of outcome, then:

Proposition 13: Negotiation payoff to the principal will be higher to the degree that the principal has power over the agent.

Power allows the principal to narrow the mandate and restrict the margin of maneuverability and as such restrict the agent to negotiating only those issues that are relevant and prevent him or her from introducing independent agendas.

Fisher and Davis (Chapter 2) provide an analysis of the issues surrounding information exchange between principals and agents. The primary focus of this discussion centers around the question, What type of information should principals reveal to their agents? These issues mirror previous research done (Valley et al. 1992) on the effects of information sharing with agents. The prescriptions of Fisher and Davis are based on the following implicit propositions:

Proposition 14: Negotiation payoff to the principal will be higher to the extent that principals provide the agent with less information about their reservation level.

Proposition 15: Negotiation payoff to the principal will be higher to the extent that principals provide the agent with more information about the trade-offs that they are willing to make.

Basically, Fisher and Davis believe that principals tend to give away too much information relevant to claiming a pie and that they tend to give away too little information relevant to creating or enlarging a pie.

McKersie (Chapter 6) highlights two critical aspects of agency in the labor-management context. Both concern the "subprocess," or the level of negotiation in which a management agent or labor representative negotiates between his or her organization and the other negotiator. First, the principal-agent and agent-agent relationships are at odds with each other. The relationship between negotiators (both agents) is often of lasting duration, built on mutual trust and common experience and understanding. In contrast, the agents often face a precarious situation in their relationships with the principals, with the constant threat of being taken out of the position in the next round if the results are not to the principal's liking. Second, McKersie points out that the negotiators are usually the primary implementers and "enforcers" of the final agreement. McKersie argues that these aspects of agency in this setting create a specific set of incentives for the agents. He claims that the central characteristic of agency in the context of collective bargaining is that "the parties have a continuing relationship to manage and to preserve" (p. 193). This leads to testable propositions:

Proposition 16: The stronger and longer lasting the relationship between the agent-negotiators, the more the final agreement will reflect long-term interests rather than short-term gains.

Proposition 17: The greater the positive discrepancy between the strength of the relationship of the agents and the strength of the relationship between the agents and their respective principals, the more divergence there will be between the actual tenor of the negotiations and the reported tenor of the negotiations.

Proposition 18: When there is a discrepancy between the principal's stated preferences and the outcome of the negotiation, the agent will use comparable contract settlements to rationalize the differences.

Proposition 19: The stronger the relationship between the agents, the more likely it is that the agents will work together to present the agreement in such a way that it appears to meet both sides' interests, even if this is not objectively true.

Implicit in McKersie's chapter is the assumption that both principals and agents actually benefit in the long run from a strong, positive relationship between the negotiators. Rather than accepting this as an assumption, we assert that this, too, is a testable proposition:

Proposition 20: Negotiations between agents with strong, lasting relationships will have a positive long-term benefit for both sets of principals, relative to those carried out by agents with weaker ties.

In sum, McKersie believes that the relationship between the agents and between the agents and their respective principals is a primary determinant of behavior and outcome in labor-management negotiations. This leads to interesting propositions not only regarding labor-management negotiations but also on how personal relationships between negotiators affect behavior and outcomes in other settings.

Wheeler (Chapter 8) adds a specific context, that of sports agents' negotiations, to the discussion of the function of agents. His discussion draws attention to the situational norms, culture, and role scripts that influence the behavior of agents negotiating on behalf of athletes. The role scripts may be particular to the sports arena or potentially could be a more generalized occurrence. It is worth noting, however, that situational norms are likely to be significant predictors of negotiator behavior. Wheeler suggests that agents and principals are likely to behave in ways consistent with their expectations and role scripts, even when those behavioral guides are not normatively optimal responses to the situation.

Wheeler's chapter also highlights an interest that agents may care deeply about: their reputations. Here, it is likely that the interests of agent and principal will not be perfectly aligned. Agents who depend on their reputation bringing them new business will behave in ways that are likely to enhance their reputations, whether or not this behavior benefits the principals who hire them. Although Croson and Mnookin's (1997) research described the potential benefits to committing to an agent with a reputation for cooperation, it is also important to recognize the value of having an agent who is known to "drive a hard bargain" in some situations. When an agent maintains a reputation for toughness, the agent's reputation can function as a personal agenda that can have the same hindering effects on settlement as have been discussed above. Note the parallels between Wheeler's focus on agents' concern for reputation and King and Zeckhauser's discussion of the importance of observability of political negotiations.

Proposition 21: Agents who feel that their reputation is at stake as part of the negotiation will take more risks (i.e., display more contentious behavior) than agents without their reputation at stake.

Proposition 22: Agents who feel that their reputation is at stake as part of the negotiation will set higher reservation prices than agents without their reputation at stake.

Proposition 23: Agents who feel that their reputation is at stake as part of the negotiation will have higher impasse rates than agents without their reputation at stake.

Essentially, an agent's focus on personal reputation instead of the best interests of the client will make "walking away" more attractive than settling for a deal that involves concessions. This discussion is tempered, however, by the specific reputation for which the agent strives. A reputation as a tough negotiator will result in a significantly different set of behaviors than a reputation as a reliable deal maker. Such reputations can thus provide moderating conditions for various predictions as to agent behavior.

Clearly, many issues can get in the way of effective bargaining through an agent. When employing an agent, therefore, it is important for a principal to understand the importance of structuring the task in such a way as to minimize the involvement of an agent's personal agendas, which can cloud the issues and increase the likelihood of impasse. Before any of these prescriptions can be explained fully, however, further empirical research is needed to identify the mechanisms behind these potential effects. The next section of this chapter examines briefly what these empirical studies would look like.

▓ AGENTS IN NEGOTIATIONS: FUTURE EMPIRICAL RESEARCH

Where do research ideas come from, and how should they be tested? There are many answers and opinions to these questions. We argue that analytical reasoning, professional experience, real-world problems and issues, reading the existing literature, and qualitative research procedures are excellent ways to identify ideas worthy of further study. Once hypothesized, however, scientific prediction should be subject to rigorous empirical testing. In the context of negotiation, we argue that laboratory studies provide an excellent context for theory testing.

We see most negotiation teachers running experiments all the time. The simulations that dominate the teaching of negotiation provide a unique arena for manipulating one, two, or three independent variables, while holding other variables constant. Scoreable negotiation outcomes also provide clear dependent measures. Thus, we can imagine bringing the ideas developed in this volume into the classroom for instruction and rigorous scientific testing. We imagine the development of multiple-agent negotiations in which the independent variables described above can be manipulated and the dependent variables described above measured. Figure 10.1 outlines some key dependent and independent variables.

Many important negotiations within and between organizations employ agents. In fact, in the weightiest negotiations, representation by agents is more the rule than the exception. For example, buying a house is the average person's biggest purchase, and the negotiation almost invariably involves the use of at least one agent. In negotiating labor contracts, both individuals and organizations use agents, as do athletes and entertainment figures in the negotiation of extremely high salaries. The development of strong theories that illuminate the conditions affecting agent performance in negotiation are essential both to understanding the fundamental processes at work and to building prescriptive advice on how agents in negotiation can be used most effectively. We believe that the earlier chapters move the conceptual development in the right direction. We hope that this chapter provides the direction and inspiration to test the implications and predictions of the many ideas presented in the chapters of this book. Empirical testing of the various theories of agents in negotiation is essential if we are to discriminate useful theories from inaccurate theories.

It is important to note as well that agent-principal relations and incentives in actual applied settings do not entirely mimic the designs and exercises that we can create in a controlled laboratory setting. For

Potential Dependent Variables	Potential Independent Variables
Relative values of negotiated outcomes for principal(s) and agent(s)	Breadth of authority granted to agent
	Conflict of interest between agent and principal
	Number of agents
Joint value of negotiated outcome	Length or complexity of the communication hierarchy and the chain of command between principal and agent
Pareto efficiency of negotiated outcome	Number of principals
	Conflict of interest between principals
Impasse rates	Principal's power to control the principal-agent relationship (agent's autonomy)
Distribution of surplus between multiple principals	Type of information shared with agents
	Strength of relationship between agents and agent/principal
Reservation prices set by agent(s)	Length of relationship between agents and agent/principal
	Agent's reputation at stake (transparency, visibility)

Figure 10.1. Potential Variables, Dependent and Independent, in a Multiple-Agent Negotiation

example, situations in which agents must answer to multiple constituencies can create a level of complexity not explored in this type of research. In addition, it is difficult to simulate all the possible alternative agreements to any one deal. For the sake of manageability, negotiation cases often limit the acceptable versions of an agreement. Finally, negotiations performed in a classroom may inspire unique incentives of their own based on the classroom culture and the grade-based aspect of the environment. We hope that these contexts can provide us with a solid foundation for understanding the nature of such negotiation issues that can allow us to have insights into the more complex functioning of actual negotiation situations.

REFERENCES

Bazerman, M. H., M. A. Neale, K. L. Valley, E. J. Zajac, and Y. M. Kim. 1992. The effects of agents and mediators on negotiation outcomes. *Organizational Behavior and Human Decision Processes* 53:55-73.

Conlon, E. and J. M. Parks. 1990. Effects of monitoring and tradition on compensation agreements: An experiment with principal-agent dyads. *Academy of Management Journal* 33(3):603-622.

Croson, R. and R. H. Mnookin. 1996. Scaling the stonewall: Retaining lawyers to bolster credibility. *Harvard Negotiation Law Review* 1:65-83.

Croson, R. and R. H. Mnookin. 1997. Does disputing through agents enhance cooperation? Experimental evidence. *Journal of Legal Studies* 26:331-345.

Jensen, M. and W. Meckling. 1976. Theory of the firm: Managerial behavior, agency costs, and ownership structure. *Journal of Financial Economics* 3:305-360.

Lax, D. A. and J. K. Sebenius. 1991. Negotiating through an agent. *Journal of Conflict Resolution* 35(3):474-493.

Murnighan, J. K., D. A. Cantelon, and T. Elyashiv. 1997. *Bounded personal ethics and the tap dance of real estate agency.* Unpublished manuscript, Dispute Resolution Research Center, Kellogg Graduate School of Management, Northwestern University.

Neale, M. A. and M. H. Bazerman. 1991. *Negotiator cognition and rationality.* New York: Free Press.

Rubin, J. Z. and F. E. Sander. 1988. When should we use agents? Direct vs. representative negotiation. *Negotiation Journal* 7(4):395-401.

Sappington, D. 1991. Incentives in principal-agent relationships. *Journal of Economic Perspectives* 5(2):45-66.

Valley, K. L., S. B. White, M. A. Neale, and M. H. Bazerman. 1992. Agents as information brokers: The effects of information disclosure on negotiated outcomes. *Organizational Behavior and Human Decision Processes* 51:220-236.

Yavas, A., T. Miceli, and C. F. Sirmans. 1997. *An experimental analysis of the impact of intermediaries on the outcome of bargaining games.* Unpublished manuscript, University of Connecticut, Storrs.

Annotated Bibliography of Selected Sources

Pacey C. Foster
Jonathan R. Cohen

For readers interested in further pursuing the themes and issues raised in this volume, the following commentaries provide an introduction to the literature. This annotated bibliography is designed to be suggestive rather than exhaustive.

Ashenfelter, O. and G. Johnson. 1969. Bargaining theory, trade unions, and industrial strike activity. *American Economic Review* **59(1):35-49.**

In their pioneering study, Ashenfelter and Johnson use agency tensions to examine labor negotiations and empirically test conditions under which strikes are likely to occur. Using a three-party model (management, union leadership, and union rank and file), the authors obtain significant results in predicting industrial strike activity. At the core of the model lies the principal-agent tension between the union leadership and the union rank and file, leaders sometimes choosing to strike to adjust the expectations of the rank-and-file or to solidify their leadership positions.

Bazerman, M. H. and M. A. Neale. 1992. Negotiating through third parties. In *Negotiating rationally.* **New York: Free Press.**

Bazerman and Neale review some of the possible effects of involving a third party—such as a mediator, arbitrator, or agent—in a negotiation. All third parties, according to the authors, should be understood to have their own goals and frequently a strong interest in reaching agreement, but unlike mediators and arbitrators, agents have a vested interest in resolution because commission is often determined by how a pie is split. Agents may also possess more information than the principals they represent, whether because of more time spent with the other party or specialized knowledge, and they may use this information to promote their own interests. Drawing on evidence from their studies of real estate negotiations, Bazerman and Neale suggest that standard arrangements by which real estate agents receive a percentage of the contracted price tend to bias the agent in favor of the seller's interests and reduce the size of the bargaining zone. The authors find that selling prices are lower when an agent knows only the seller's reservation price and impasse rates are highest when an agent knows both parties' reservation prices. Selling prices and impasse rates are both higher in agent-assisted negotiations than in direct negotiations.

Bazerman, M. H., M. A. Neale, K. L. Valley, and E. J. Zajac. 1992. The effect of agents and mediators on negotiation outcomes. *Organizational Behavior and Human Decision Processes* 53(1):55-73.

Bazerman et al. describe two experiments that test the impact of agents and mediators on negotiated outcomes in real estate transactions. Their findings suggest that agents tend to (1) increase the sale price of homes, (2) increase the likelihood of impasse, and (3) receive a smaller percentage of the sales price as a commission when the bargaining zone is smaller.

Benton, A. A. and D. Druckman. 1973. Salient solutions and the bargaining behavior of representatives and nonrepresentatives. *International Journal of Group Tensions* 3(1-2):28-39.

This study considers the bargaining behaviors of representatives and nonrepresentatives in allocation scenarios that involve the distribution of both even and odd available sums. Drawing on experimental data, Benton and Druckman find that situations which only permit asymmetrical payoffs elicit more competitive behavior among group representatives than among individuals with no accountability to a constituency. They also observe that the possibility of salient outcomes based on equal concessions mitigates competitive tendencies among both types of negotiators and points to potential ways to alleviate some of the negative effects of role obligations within bargaining sessions.

Benton, A. A. and D. Druckman. 1974. Constituent's bargaining orientation and intergroup negotiations. *Journal of Applied Social Psychology* 4(2):141-150.

Benton and Druckman present experimental evidence that in negotiations where they are accountable to constituencies, representatives bargain harder if they have no information about their constituencies' interests or if they believe their constituency is competitive. In both cases, representatives bargain harder than nonrepresentatives. Competitive effects are mitigated if representatives believe their constituents are cooperative.

Burke, B. 1993. Negotiations involving agents and general managers in the NHL (National Hockey League). *Marquette Sports Law Journal* **4(1):35-50.**

This is a short summary of Burke's personal negotiation techniques and theory. Burke suggests that negotiators should adopt a "cordial but not warm" style, not look at their notes, involve the athlete in preparation, enter negotiation with alternatives, let the club make an initial offer, and become familiar with standard player's contracts, collective bargaining agreements, and the bylaws of specific leagues. He also suggests that agents should not promise endorsement income to their clients because this is available only to select athletes. Finally, he advises that agents not provide all-purpose representation but, rather, seek assistance on specialized issues like investment planning.

Cohen, G. 1993. Ethics and the representation of professional athletes. *Marquette Sports Law Journal* **4(1):149-197.**

This article provides a summary of the NBPA (National Basketball Player's Association) agent regulations, including information on how they were developed. In the 1980s, player concerns about agents' powers and fees led to regulations for agents in baseball and basketball. The article describes NBPA certification requirements, the standard player-agent agreement, fee structure, free market effects, and code of conduct. A section titled "Free Market" describes a players' negotiation analysis. The underlying premise of the NBPA regulations is that an agent owes a player his or her undivided loyalty.

Committee on Professional Responsibility. 1996. The evolving lawyer-client relationship and its effect on the lawyer's professional obligations. *The Record of the Association of the Bar of the City of New York* **51:443.**

Greater competition in the legal arena, increased costs of legal services, and recent advances in technology that facilitate heightened communication between an attorney and client have altered many clients' perception of their own role in a legal proceeding. Clients today, according to the authors, desire involvement in determining not only the objectives of a legal proceeding but also the means to those objectives, and clients and attorneys alike tend to define their relationship as a joint venture rather than a compartmentalized set of representational roles. This new relationship, however, poses a dilemma in that the client's increased involvement in the legal process and client-imposed limitations on the procedural means of representation have the potential to conflict with the lawyer's professional obligations to provide competent and zealous representation. After assessing the relevant codes and rules of professional responsibility, the authors conclude that an attorney should not be subject to discipline or malpractice liability for following the client's directions, as long as those directions are lawful, the client is adequately informed, and the course of action does not contradict the attorney's professional rules.

Croson, D. C. and R. H. Mnookin. 1996. Scaling the stonewall: Retaining lawyers to bolster credibility. *Harvard Negotiation Law Review* 1:65-83.

Agents provide opportunities for strategic interaction not directly available to principals. Croson and Mnookin explore a fascinating example of one such interaction: What should a plaintiff with a meritorious case do when her expected transaction costs of bringing suit exceed her expected recovery at trial? Might the defendant simply "stonewall" (i.e., refuse to pay anything), reasoning that the plaintiff will not sue because her net expected value from bringing suit is negative? Croson and Mnookin argue that through hiring a lawyer on a nonrefundable retainer, plaintiffs can "scale the stonewall" and extract a positive settlement. Put differently, a nonrefundable fee arrangement, or even the threat of it, can allow a plaintiff to make a *credible* threat to sue and thereby extract settlement.

Croson, R. and R. H. Mnookin. 1997. Does disputing through agents enhance cooperation? Experimental evidence. *Journal of Legal Studies* 26(2):331-345.

Applying the methods of experimental economics, Croson and Mnookin test implications of the model advanced by Gilson and Mnookin (1994) (see p. 306) that, by choosing lawyers with reputations for cooperation, clients can avoid excessive litigation. Based on simulated exercises using law students as subjects, they find that "self-interested clients would frequently choose cooperative lawyers if they could be confident that either (1) the other side would do the same or, (2) if the other side did not, they could switch representation."

Dee, P. T. 1992. Ethical aspects of representing professional athletes. *Marquette Sports Law Journal* 3(1):111-122.

Dee analyzes three kinds of codes that regulate agent conduct—a professional code (ABA Model Code), a sports industry code (Code of Conduct for NFLPA Contract Advisors), and a state regulation (Florida

Statutes). He identifies three kinds of behavior that are governed by such codes: (1) minimal standards of competence, integrity, and diligence; (2) improper conduct; and (3) parameters of solicitation. He compares and contrasts these three codes and argues that the conduct of sports agents is regulated by laws and codes that are not centrally codified.

Downs, G. W. and D. M. Rocke. 1994. Conflict, agency, and gambling for resurrection: The principal-agent problem goes to war (how constituencies can control interventionist chief executives). *American Journal of Political Science* **38(2):362-380.**

Working from the assumption that a political constituency has an interest in ensuring that its leaders act in accordance with its wishes, Downs and Rocke examine how—in the context of interstate conflicts—information asymmetries between the agent or political executive and the principal or citizenry may lead the latter to employ strategies to deter either overly passive or overly aggressive executives that have nonoptimal consequences. According to the authors, the dramatic, though effective, sanction of executive removal by electoral or forcible means plays a large part in shaping foreign policy in the short term and in establishing a precedent regarding the limits of citizen tolerance and the nature of citizen preferences for subsequent leaders in the long term. Drawing on historical as well as theoretical evidence, the authors find that a constituency which places a high value on an agent's fidelity to the wishes of her principal will base its use of removal sanctions on the results of the conflict in question, despite the fact that the quality of the agent's decision—which might even represent the citizenry's sentiments—may not be reflected in the conflict's outcome. A second, nonoptimal effect of regulating agents' actions through removal sanctions is a phenomenon known as "gambling for resurrection" in which an executive, threatened with removal based on an unsuccessful intervention in a conflict, will continue involvement in the conflict because it provides the only chance for the executive to avoid removal. Ironically, the more a constituency seeks to limit executive aggressiveness, the more it encourages its executive, who now has limited liability, toward an escalation of aggressive behavior. Downs and Rocke conclude their study with an assessment of the dangers of mistaking "gambling" behavior with overly aggressive behavior or vice versa.

Ehrhardt, C. W. and M. J. Rodgers. 1988. Tightening the defense against offensive sports agents. *Florida State University Law Review* **16:633.**

Ehrhardt provides a summary of the evolution and rationale for the use of sports agents. He proposes that negotiation inequities between team management and players led to the use of agents, which in turn led to large increases in player salaries. Agents add value by providing four primary services: (1) negotiation of contracts, (2) negotiation of endorsements, (3) financial advice and income management, and (4) legal counsel. The primary agency problems are income mismanagement, excessive fees, conflicts, and incompetence. These problems attracted attention from lawmakers, players' associations, and special interest groups who pushed for regulations. The article also summarizes recruiting tactics and recent state laws and suggests that state regulations are ineffective and difficult to enforce.

Enzle, M. E., M. D. Harvey, and E. F. Wright. 1992. Implicit role obligations versus social responsibility in constituency representation. *Journal of Personality and Social Psychology* **62(2): 238-245.**

Enzle et al. take issue with existing research on representative negotiation which suggests that representatives bargain more competitively and less flexibly than nonrepresentatives. In contrast, theory suggests that representatives, because they are responsible to constituents, will adopt strategies that maximize constituent gains—whether cooperative or competitive. Using a prisoner's dilemma game, they found that, compared with nonrepresentative dyads, dual representative or mixed dyads (1) made more cooperative choices, (2) better avoided synchronous competition, (3) better coordinated the selection of mutually beneficial cooperative strategies, and (4) achieved better economic results. They also found that when paired with unconditionally cooperative or competitive negotiators, nonrepresentatives reciprocated their opponent's strategy, matching competition with competition, and the converse. Surprisingly, representatives reciprocated only with competitive negotiators and exploited cooperative negotiators to obtain larger gains. This result could have been caused by differential surveillance of the representative and nonrepresentative teams, suggesting a potential confusion in the experiment. In general, their constituent responsibility hypothesis was supported.

Faber, D. M. 1993. The evolution of techniques for negotiation of sports employment contracts in the era of the agent. *University of Miami Entertainment and Sports Law Review* **10(1-2): 165-193.**

This article summarizes techniques and devices for the negotiation of sports employment contracts. Player techniques include holdouts, renegotiation, and leverage (e.g., comparative salaries, other offers, free agency, and arbitration publicity value). Management techniques focus on the use of leverage (e.g., pleading poverty, outspending the competition, leveraging the surroundings, and taking advantage of inexperience). Faber also summarizes player-favorable and management-favorable contract terms.

Falk, D. B. The art of contract negotiation. *Marquette Sports Law Journal* **3(1):1-27.**

Falk provides a detailed look at sports negotiation techniques including high-ball, low-ball, hard-ball, and "phantom" negotiation (i.e., with an agent not having authority); bluffing; and puffing. Although Falk does not explicitly address mutual gains negotiation, he does mention concepts found in the mutual gains literature including the importance of creativity and preparation. He suggests that agents structure the negotiation atmosphere to reflect their personal styles.

Fehr, D. 1993. Union views concerning agents: With commentary on the present situation in major league baseball. *Marquette Sports Law Journal* **4(1):71-87.**

This article focuses on the relationship between agents and unions in the sports industry. Agents in this industry are dependent on unions and conditions established by collective bargaining agreements (e.g., unions cede salary negotiation rights to agents). Fehr argues that agents are necessary because unions would not be as effective at bargaining individual salaries collectively. The article includes discussion of union and agent roles and fees.

Fisher, R. 1989. Negotiating inside out: What are the best ways to relate internal negotiations with external ones? *Negotiation Journal* **5(1):33-41.**

Negotiations between organizations implicitly involve three levels of positional bargaining: that among interest groups within the organization, between the representative and her organization, and between the representatives of the respective organizations. Fisher identifies four potential problems that arise from these multilayered negotiations: (1) a singular focus on commitment rather than interests, (2) an unvarying perception of the external negotiator over time, (3) the segregation of internal and external negotiations, and (4) the tendency among negotiators to appraise their own roles as being simply partisan. Situating his discussion in the field of international diplomacy, Fisher advises governments and their representatives to pay more attention to elements of a negotiation such as interests, precedents, relationships, and communication; to anticipate changes in the negotiator's role; to facilitate interaction between internal and external negotiations; and to recognize the negotiator as both a partisan advocate and a co-mediator.

Fraley, R. E., F. R. Harwell, and F. Russell. 1989. The sports lawyer's duty to avoid differing interests: A practical guide to responsible representation. *COMMENT* **11(2):165-217.**

This article summarizes conflict of interest issues for the sports agent (particularly attorneys). It explains an agent's duty to avoid conflicts of interest, focusing of application of the Model Rules of Professional Responsibility to sports representation. Situations that can lead to conflicts include (1) representing multiple clients with competing interests, (2) negotiating endorsements for players in the same sport, (3) surrounding fee arrangements with independent agent interests, (4) advising amateur athletes and planning to represent them professionally, (5) allowing player's association lawyers to negotiate for players, (6) negotiating for players and also managing their events, and (7) representation of players and coaches by the same agents. The article suggests that agents fully disclose potential conflicts to their clients and obtain consent from them. The most important issue to consider is whether a lawyer reasonably believes that a potential conflict will materially interfere with his or her independent professional judgment.

Gilson, R. J. and R. H. Mnookin. 1994. Disputing through agents: Cooperation and conflict between lawyers in litigation. *Columbia Law Review* **94(2):509-566.**

Litigation is often modeled as a prisoner's dilemma in which clients are trapped in an "arms race" of litigation expenditures, with lawyers the ultimate beneficiaries of that race. Such modeling, however, fails to consider the role of lawyers as agents. Gilson and Mnookin address that concern and obtain some fascinating insights. They argue that clients have a choice over what types of lawyers (i.e., "gladiatorial" vs. cooperative) they will hire and that, with attention to which lawyers they choose in the prelitigation phase, clients can potentially "solve" their prisoner's dilemma. More specifically, opposing parties who cannot credibly commit to avoiding highly litigious tactics directly may credibly do so indirectly through each hiring a lawyer with a reputation for cooperation. In this provocative essay, Gilson and Mnookin offer a scenario under which lawyers can be value creators for their clients during litigation.

Gould, M. T. 1992. Further trials and tribulations of sports agents. *The Entertainment and Sports Lawyer* **10(1):9-14.**

This short article explains that agents minimize the frustrations and inequities felt by self-represented athletes. Agent abuses arose from agent inexperience and/or incompetence, the lure of large financial rewards, and increasing competition. The article outlines four areas of agent abuse: (1) mismanagement of income, (2) solicitation of student athletes, (3) conflicts of interest, and (4) excessive fees. The article provides a brief overview of deterrence efforts and suggests that the lack of enforcement mechanisms limits the effectiveness of regulations. It also provides some suggestions for agents.

Gruder, C. L. and N. A. Rosen. 1971. Effects of intragroup relations on intergroup bargaining. *International Journal of Group Tensions* **1(4):301-317.**

Gruder and Rosen examine several of the ways in which intragroup relations, such as those between the representative of a bargaining party and the constituency, affect intergroup deliberations. Working within an experimental setting, the authors test the hypothesis that a representative's increased accountability to the constituency will amplify the representative's responsiveness to what is perceived to be the preferred bargaining style (fair and compromising, exploitative and demanding, or indeterminate) of the constituency. Although the anticipated interactions between the two variables of accountability and bargaining style do not occur, Gruder and Rosen find independent correlations between each of the variables and aspects of the intergroup negotiation, including the speed with which resolution was reached in the bargaining session, the number of agreements reached, and the size of concessions made.

Jones, M. and S. Worchel. 1992. Representatives in negotiations: "Internal" variables that affect "external" negotiations. *Basic and Applied Social Psychology* **13(3):323-336.**

Through simulations of labor-management negotiations, psychologists Jones and Worchel test the effects of several variables on an agent's perception of external negotiations. They find that (1) agents who are involved in formulating their group's strategy are more ready to accept their group's position; (2) agents who are new members of groups report less commitment to the group's position, less contribution to the prenegotiation discussions, and less satisfaction with their tasks than agents who are preexisting members of the group; and, somewhat surprisingly, (3) the possibility of the agent's reelection did not influence the agent's perception of the negotiations. They suggest that this third result may be an artifact of experimental design.

Kentucky bill seeks to regulate player agents. 1994. *The Sports Lawyer* 7 (November/December):7.

This article describes a bill designed to regulate player agents who solicit student athletes. This bill would prohibit agents from giving misleading or deceptive advice, offering benefits in exchange for representation, and entering sweetheart deals with colleges (e.g., offering incentives to employees).

King, E. V., Jr. 1993. Practical advice for agents: How to avoid being sued. *Marquette Sports Law Journal* 4(1):89-127.

King provides a firsthand account of issues that can lead to agent abuse. He suggests that, although their proximity to wealth can breed hunger, agents cannot get rich on their standard 3% to 4% commission. To increase their fees, agents feel pressure to provide services they are unqualified to give. King notes that multiservice, cradle-to-grave representation firms are particularly rife with opportunities for abuse. He suggests that contract negotiations are not the source of most agent abuses.

Lax, D. A. and J. K. Sebenius. 1986. Agents and ratification. In *The manager as negotiator: Bargaining for cooperation and competitive gain.* New York: Free Press.

Offering examples from managerial, legal, and political settings, Lax and Sebenius consider the costs and benefits of using agents in negotiations. Although the "perfect agent" might be understood as a surrogate or clone of the principal, the authors suggest that principals stand to profit just as easily as they may risk losses by employing representatives whose incentives, interests, bargaining behavior, propensity to take risks, perceived authority, and relationships with the other party or parties differ from their own. A negotiator who creates a real or feigned accountability may take advantage of some of the powerful situational dynamics of acting as an agent while reducing the negative effects of agent-principal asymmetries.

Lax, D. A. and Sebenius, J. K. 1991. Negotiating through an agent. *Journal of Conflict Resolution* 35(3):474-493.

Agents bargaining on behalf of principals, and particularly agents whose negotiated agreements require *ex post* ratification by their principals, often find themselves uncertain about their principals' reservation prices and even the agents' own nonmonetary payoff functions. Using a theoretical framework, Lax and Sebenius study the effects on bargaining behaviors and negotiated outcomes of these uncertainties and find that increased uncertainty regarding a principal's reservation price and the agent's payoff function will lead an agent to raise her reservation price, an effect magnified by increases in the agent's degree of risk aversion. The authors analyze the effects of this uncertainty in a variety of bargaining scenarios—including integrative bargains, distributive or "zero sum" bargains, optimal insistence prices in one-shot situations, and commitment games under different equilibrium concepts—and determine that increased uncertainty often, although not always, leads to a diminished likelihood of agreement.

Levmore, S. 1993. Commissions and conflicts in agency arrangements: Lawyers, real estate brokers, underwriters, and other agents' rewards. *Journal of Law and Economics* 36(1-2):503-539.

Drawing on case studies in a variety of industries, Levmore examines the trade-offs between risk and reward inherent in agency scenarios and proposes explanations for the variety of agency compensation arrangements. The study begins by considering both the uniformity of compensation or reward structures shared by an agent with multiple principals and the magnitude of this compensation. Uniform reward schemas such as flat commissions, the author suggests, decrease the agent's risk and promote joint revenue maximization among principals served by a common agent, thus reducing the conflicts among these principals. High, incentive-compatible, nonuniform, marginal commissions, although they appear to maximize profits for both the principal and the agent and to lessen principal-agent conflict, may actually (1) shift an unacceptable degree of risk to the agent; (2) result in competitive auctions among different agents, which ultimately become inefficient and costly for both the principal and the agent; and (3) when taken to the extreme of 100% commission, prove incompatible with the need for bilateral incentives. Having based this initial analysis on the real estate industry, Levmore broadens the scope of his inquiry into compensation arrangements, uniformity of reward schemas, and incentive structures to include a survey of the behaviors of lawyers, publishers, retailers, travel agents, underwriters, and other agents, taking into account the conflicts that arise both among principals of a single agent and among agents of a single principal.

Miller, G. P. 1987. Some agency problems in settlement. *Journal of Legal Studies* 16(1):189-215.

The traditional litigation paradigm of the attorney as the agent of the client is too simplistic, Miller argues, to account for scenarios in which an attorney effectively purchases an equity interest in the outcome of the case by entering into a claim-sharing arrangement, thus becoming a second agent of sorts. Because the standard economic model for settlements assumes that both parties function as unitary identities, Miller seeks to establish a new model that reflects the potentially conflicting interests that may underlie claim-sharing arrangements. Taking three different arrangements—the contingent fee, the hourly fee, and unallocated fee shifting—as the basis of his study, the author traces the effects on settlement incentives of the allocation to either the attorney or the plaintiff of responsibility over settlements. Miller finds that only the contingency fee with plaintiff control may lead to potentially optimal results for both attorney and client; the other five arrangements are putatively nonoptimal because they may induce the claimant—whether the attorney or the plaintiff—to act in a manner that is unfavorable to the claim as a whole. Miller concludes with recommendations for how claimants may structure their relationships with coclaimants to reduce the inefficiencies and conflicts of interest inherent in claim-sharing arrangements.

Mureiko, W. R. 1988. The agency theory of the attorney-client relationship: An improper justification for holding clients responsible for their attorneys' procedural errors. *Duke Law Journal* 4: 733-754.

Agency theory, according to Mureiko, fails to characterize adequately the attorney-client relationship, especially in cases concerned with assigning sanctions based on an attorney's procedural errors, and therefore has no place in judicial decisions. Although clients have long been held responsible for their representatives' substantive actions, it is only during the past century that courts have found—albeit inconsistently—clients culpable for their attorneys' procedural misconduct, despite court rulings that uphold an attorney's virtually unrestrained authority over procedural and strategic decisions. This contradiction, Mureiko argues, suggests that in procedural matters an attorney resembles an independent contractor more than an agent, because agency theory is unable to reflect a client's lack of participation in tactical choices. Although in standard agent-principal arrangements the principal may be found guilty of the agent's actions based on the relationship alone, Mureiko demonstrates that the application of agency theory in procedural misconduct rulings is often subject to policy concerns such as those involved in want-of-prosecution cases and discovery-abuse cases. Mureiko advocates the courts' abandonment of agency theory as a means to describe the attorney-client relationship for the sake of consistency, clarity of reasoning, and predictability.

Peters, E. 1955. *Strategy and tactics in labor negotiations.* **New London, CT: National Foremen's Institute.**

Based on his experience within the California State Conciliation Service, Edward Peters describes the inner workings of labor-management negotiations through rich, contextual accounts of those negotiations. His focus is not on conciliation but on strategy and tactics, topics most richly explored through particular examples. Moreover, Peters works not merely at relaying events but at extracting abstract principles from those events.

Pratt, J. W. and R. J. Zeckhauser, eds. 1985. *Principals and agents: The structure of business.* **Boston: Harvard Business School Press.**

A central work in the development of principal-agent analysis, this collection of essays illustrates the application of that branch of microeconomic theory to business concerns. The goal throughout is relevance to actual business practice. The volume begins with two essays that provide theoretical overviews of the economics of agency. John Pratt and Richard Zeckhauser focus on information, incentives, and agency structure. Kenneth Arrow discusses the development of principal-agent theory within the economic literature, highlighting the gaps between that theory and many common agency relationships observed in practice. The book then explores institutional and organizational responses to agency tensions. In the institutional arena, Robert Clark explores legal fiduciary duties as a response to agency tensions between firm stockholders and management. Frank Easterbrook addresses insider trading, more specifically whether the use by corporate insiders of material information not yet known to the market benefits investors. Mark Wolfson empirically examines agency tensions driven by informational asymmetries in the oil and gas industries, and Richard Epstein analyzes the paradigmatic ground of principal-agent tensions: labor and employment contracts. In the organizational context, Robert Eccles uses field research to examine the firm's internal transfer prices through the lens of agency, and Harrison White explores the importance of control to agency for a variety of organizations, business and otherwise, both past and present.

Professional Sports Agency. 1995. *The Sports Lawyer.* **Special edition on sports agent regulation. Fall.**

An editor's note briefly summarizes regulation initiatives. The editor claims that the variety among state regulations places undue administrative burdens on agents and questions the effectiveness of state laws. Other articles include a summary of key aspects of Florida's regulation initiative, the most strict in the country; a summary of the bylaws of the National Collegiate Athletic Association dealing with the use of agents; a discussion of state regulations addressing the recruitment of student athletes; a description of a North Dakota law regulating athlete agents; and a sample NFLPA Standard Representation Agreement.

Pruitt, D. G. and P. J. Carnevale. 1993. Determinants of demands, concessions, and contentious behavior (Chapter 4) and Group processes in negotiation (Chapter 10). In *Negotiation in social conflict.* **Pacific Grove, CA: Brooks/Cole.**

In these chapters, Pruitt and Carnevale discuss factors that can negatively affect negotiation behavior and outcomes. In the section on representation, they point out factors that affect the behavior of representatives in negotiation. For example, to the extent that agents believe that their principals are interested in winning, they will tend to bargain harder and concede more reluctantly. In the absence of information to the contrary, representatives tend to overestimate their constituents' desire to win; therefore, in most cases, they concede less and take longer to reach agreements than individuals negotiating on their own behalf. Another common factor is the eagerness of representatives to please constituents to whom they are accountable, a condition that can lead to a paradox: When representatives act tough to please their constituents, they often reach fewer agreements, thereby undermining their principals' interest in reaching an agreement. Another such factor is that surveillance of representatives may reinforce the constituent preferences they perceive. If agents believe that constituents favor compromise, surveillance will tend to push them in that direction.

Putnam, R. D. 1988. Diplomacy and domestic politics: The logic of two-level games. *International Organization* **42(3):427-460.**

In this article, Putnam analyzes the relationship between domestic politics and international relations. Taking into account the existing literature, he suggests that we need to move beyond the observation that domestic politics influences international relations and vice versa, and develop theories that integrate both these levels to discover when and how they affect one another. He discusses the politics of international negotiations, which are often conceived as two-level games, and the role of decision makers or chief negotiators in these negotiations, in which states must balance sovereignty and interdependence. Putnam breaks the negotiations down into Level I, the negotiation phase, and Level II, the ratification phase, and then defines "win-sets" for each level, suggesting that the size of each "win-set" and the degree of overlap between them are integral to the outcome of the negotiations. He also considers the behavior of an agent in circumstances involving voluntary and involuntary defection and the prospects for agreement. Putnam looks at the determinants of the "win-set"; details Level II preferences and coalitions, Level II institutions, and Level I negotiator strategies; and outlines the significant features of the links between diplomacy and politics.

Raiffa, H. 1982. Salary negotiations in professional sports. In *The art and science of negotiation*. Cambridge: Harvard University Press.

Raiffa notes that the introduction of free agency in 1977 led to dramatic increases in baseball salaries; slower increases were seen in salaries in football, where free agency was not allowed. He accurately predicted collusion among teams to reduce the effects of competition introduced by free agency and provides statistics on salary increases in baseball and football.

Rubin, J. Z., D. G. Pruitt, and S. H. Kim. 1994. *Social conflict: Escalation, stalemate, and settlement*. 2d ed. New York: McGraw-Hill.

Social psychologists Rubin, Pruitt, and Kim explore three fundamental stages of conflict: escalation, stalemate, and settlement. Defining conflict as the "perceived divergence of interest, or a belief that the parties' current aspirations cannot be achieved simultaneously," the authors argue that most conflicts, from the intrafamilial to the international levels, pass through these common stages. They also describe basic strategies parties adopt in response to conflict: contending, yielding, and problem solving. Although their backgrounds are in social psychology, their approach is by no means limited to that discipline. They support their views with thorough references to research from many fields as well as descriptions of specific instances of conflict. In short, this book provides both a fine introduction to the study of conflict and an excellent overall treatment of that subject.

Rubin, J. Z. and F. E. A. Sander. 1988. When should we use agents? Direct vs. representative negotiation. *Negotiation Journal* 4(4): 395-401.

Rubin and Sander outline the distinctive features, benefits, and risks of negotiating directly versus negotiating through representatives. Although an agent's impact may vary according to whether the situation is competitive or collaborative in nature, the authors suggest that agents often lend a principal substantive knowledge, process expertise, emotional detachment, and the possibility of tactical flexibility. The use of representatives might also negatively influence a negotiation because agents add structural complexity and increase the likelihood of miscommunication between parties. Agents may fail to share a principal's goals or standards, introduce their own agendas into the negotiation, lack an emotional engagement with the situation, and, consciously or not, encourage a more adversarial negotiating climate.

Slusher, A. E. 1978. Counterpart strategy, prior relations, and constituent pressure in a bargaining simulation. *Behavioral Science* 23(6):470-477.

In simulations of labor-management bargaining, Slusher tests three hypotheses: (1) a shift in strategy by the bargaining counterpart from competitive to cooperative will produce "more later cooperation and more positive attitudes by the bargaining representative" than the reverse shift, (2) representatives under more constituent pressure are more competitive, and (3) where "conflictual prior relations exist, a constituent with strong feelings about his recommendations is preferred." The experimental results support each hypothesis. Perhaps most interesting is the implication of these results for the question of whether negotiators should begin with "easy" issues and work up to "tough" ones, or vice versa. Slusher suggests that if negotiators care most about their overall level of cooperation, they should follow the former approach, but if they care most about their future relationship, they should try the latter.

Smith, W. P. 1987. Conflict and negotiation: Trends and emerging issues. *Journal of Applied Social Psychology* 17(7):641-677.

Smith presents a concise overview of recent developments in the study of conflict and negotiation. His section on representative bargaining summarizes significant experimental findings. He points out that accountability and surveillance are two of the most important variables in the study of representative negotiation. In the absence of surveillance, agents tend to be sanctioned by their principals based on outcomes. Where observation is possible, agents may also be evaluated based on their tactics. In general, absent information about constituent expectations, agents bargain harder than they would on their own behalf. Increased accountability and/or surveillance increases this effect. Bargaining toughness will be mitigated when agents know that they are trusted by their principals, when they know their principals prefer conciliation, or when there is an ongoing relationship between the agents. Finally, Smith observes that the effect of intragroup dissension on the behavior of agents is not well understood.

Uphoff, R. J. 1992. The criminal defense lawyer: Zealous advocate, double agent, or beleaguered dealer? *Criminal Law Bulletin* **28(5):419-456.**

In 1967, Abraham Blumberg questioned the traditional concept of a criminal defense lawyer as a zealous advocate, suggesting instead that defense lawyers have come to act as double agents serving both sides of the plea-bargaining process. Uphoff argues that theoretical formulations of the defense lawyer as either a zealous advocate or a double agent do not coincide with the actual practices of criminal defense attorneys. After considering the systemic variables that affect the behavior of defense attorneys and the response of defendants to plea offers in three different samples, he proposes that "beleaguered dealer" would more adequately describe the role of defense counsel. Uphoff concludes his study with detailed recommendations for how indigent defense services may be restructured so as to enhance the zealousness of defense attorneys in the face of economic and procedural constraints.

Valley, K. L., S. B. White, M. A. Neale, and M. H. Bazerman. 1992. Agents as information brokers: The effects of information disclosure on negotiated outcomes. *Organizational Behavior and Human Decision Processes* **51(2):220-236.**

This article describes the results of an experiment testing the impact of availability information about the parties' reservation prices on the final sale or size of the agent's commission in a real estate transaction. Findings show that sale prices are highest when an agent knows only the seller's reservation price and lowest when only the buyer's reservation price is known. Valley et al. hypothesize that knowledge of only one reservation price serves to anchor the negotiation closest to that price. There was no support for the hypothesis that increased knowledge about reservation prices will increase the size of an agent's commission; however, the authors found that commissions were higher than the surplus generated for principals, suggesting a need to reevaluate the costs and benefits of agent use in this context.

Weiler, P. C. 1993. Agent representation of the athlete. In *Cases, materials, and problems on sports and the law.* **St. Paul, MN: West.**

This chapter provides a good general review of the legal issues surrounding representation of athletes. It defines the primary role for agents as negotiating employment terms with secondary roles including endorsement negotiation, revenue management, and tax planning and explains the prerequisites for becoming a sports agent. The chapter includes information on the role of agents vis-à-vis collective bargaining agreements, salary caps, and so on. The author offers examples of breakdown in agent-client relationships revolving around standards of competence, fee structures, conflicts of interest, and recruitment of college athletes and summarizes the emergence of sports agent regulation.

Weiler, P. C. 1993. Agent representation of the athlete. In *Statutory and documentary supplement to cases, materials, and problems on sports and the law.* **St. Paul, MN: West.**

This volume contains regulations such as the NBPA Regulations Governing Player Agents, Minnesota statutes, California Labor Code, Florida statutes, and the NCAA Constitution.

Yasser, R. L. 1994. *Sports law: Cases and materials.* **2d ed. Cincinnati: Anderson.**

Chapter 8, "Representation of Professional Athletes," describes the seven functions of a sports agent and five common areas of agent abuse. It also examines the duties imposed on agents by common law, statutes, and regulations and applies Model Rules of Professional Conduct to typical categories of agent abuses. Chapter 9, "Negotiation of Contracts," suggests that a mutual gains approach is particularly important in sports negotiation and provides a summary of applicable negotiation theory. This chapter cautions that the desire to protect the client's relationship with the team after the negotiation can create a conflict for agents during negotiations.

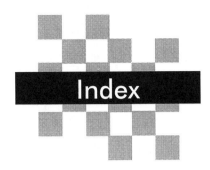

Index

Acceptance, of proposed settlement, 190-193. *See also* Ratification
Access creators, 266
Adam's Paradox, 149(n2)
Advocate, as role, 58
Agency:
  definition of, 158
  legal forms of, 161-169
  See also Agents
Agency costs, minimizing, 90-125
  commentary on, 127-132
  hypotheses on, 115-122
  See also Cost-benefit analysis
Agency law, 13-14, 157
  authority and, 160
  commentary on, 176-180
  consent and, 160-161
  control and, 159-160, 162, 168, 178, 180
  costs, benefits, and, 165-168
  fiduciary relationship and, 158-159, 168
  forms of agency and, 161-169, 177-180
  model for, 158-161, 170-174
  See also Power
Agency strategic dilemma, 105-109, 130
Agent-agent relationship:
  bonding in, 186, 189
  enhanced nature of, 281-282
  perception of differences in, 189
  personal relationships and, 200, 201, 202
  propositions on, 293, 294
Agent-partisan continuum, 9, 32-33, 43, 46, 137, 286

Agent-principal continuum, 9, 27-29, 286
Agent-principal relationship.
  See Principal-agent relationship
Agent-visionary continuum, 9, 29-31, 43, 286
Agents:
  advice on, 3-5, 17, 280-282
  alliances with, 174, 281-282
  alternative, 173-174
  as facilitators, 153
  as principals, 184, 198-199, 277-278
  as process managers, 153-154
  benefits of, 284
  categories of, 13
  chain of, 171-172, 291
  community of, 144, 146
  compared to representatives, 27
  everyone in negotiations as, x, 282
  fees of, 241, 266, 271, 285
  hazards in use of, 286
  interest configurations and, 109-118
  key issues concerning, 3-8
  long-term tenure for, 182, 196-197
  networks of, 174
  reputations of, 239, 295
  training of, 147
  transparency of, 154-155
  types of, 161-169, 177-180
  See also Principal-agent analysis; Principal-agent relationship; Representatives
Agents, effects of, 17-18
  literature review on, 284-286
  propositions on, 286-297

Agents, multiple:
  agency law and, 159, 171-174, 179
  future research and, 296
  international negotiations and, 143-144
Agents, roles of:
  as theme, 276-278
  authority instructions and, 62, 77, 84
  commentary on, 52-58
  concurrent, 46
  conflict in, 145-146, 151-152, 183-184, 186
  continua of, 27-33
  multiple, and representation, 25-42
  propositions on, 286-297
  sequential, 42-46
  shifts in, 43, 45
Alignment, of incentives, 196-197, 199-202, 278, 285
Alignment, of interests. See Interests, alignment of
Anchors, party leaders as, 216-219, 228
Arbitration, 240, 247, 248, 255
Arrow, K., 3, 90
Article 113 procedure, 99, 100
Authority, 10-11, 12, 277
  agency law and, 160
  agent-visionary continuum and, 30
  commentary on, 81-85, 264-267, 269-271
  dilemma in, 61-63
  dimensions of, 60-61, 68
  flexibility, autonomy, and, 118-119
  interest alignment and, 117-118
  power and, 173
  propositions on, 287, 288
  quantity vs. timing of, 10-11
  rational allocation of, 81-85
  role, mission, and, 210-212, 215
  timing in, 10-11, 68-71, 82-84
  ZOPA and, 279
  See also Commitment; Instructions; Mandates
Authority, approach to:
  conventional, 59-60, 63-68
  optimal, 87-125
  principles on, 68-76, 82-83
  with added dimensions, 68-77
Autonomy, 12, 102-103, 279
  as attribute of mandates, 96-97
  commentary on, 264-265, 266-267, 269
  flexibility, authority, and, 118-119

Babbitt, E. F., 13, 288, 289
Baker, H., 216
Bargaining, hard, 236-250, 263-269
Barriers to Conflict Resolution, 3, 6-8
BATNA (best alternative to negotiated agreement):
  as critical factor, 5
  commentary on, 264, 265
  ZOPA, NOPA, and, 245-246, 252, 254
Bazerman, M. H., 11, 17, 285
Beliefs, disclosure of, 155
Benchmarks, 190-191
Benefits. See Cost-benefit analysis
Best alternative to negotiated agreement. See BATNA
Biases, as psychological barriers, 7
Bonding, in agent-agent relationship, 186, 189
Bosnia, 139-140, 144
Bottom lines, and authority, 74-75
Boundaries, for interests, 31
Brennan, W., 230
Bundling of issues, 290
Burundi, 144

Cantelon, D. A., 286
Cardozo, B., 159, 161
Carter, J., 173
Caucuses, political, 214, 215-216, 220
Celebrities, 256
Chain of agents, 171-172, 291
Champion, as role, 30-31, 43, 44-45, 58
Chaney, R., 220
Change strategies, 193-194
Chayes, A. J., 282
Citizen principals, 204, 213. See also Constituents
Claiming value, 6-7, 37, 256
Closure stage, 69
Clout, 172-173
Coalitions, fluid, 205-206, 207
Coercion, and agency law, 161, 168
Cognitive barriers, 7
Cohen, J. R., 16
Collective bargaining, 181, 186, 239, 240. See also Labor negotiations
Colluding, 32
Commerce Clause, 98, 99
Commitment:
  agency law and, 161
  as critical factor, 5-6
  as dimension of authority, 60-61

commentary on, 266-267, 271
mandate attributes and, 97
See also Authority
Committing phase, 56, 57
Communication:
    authority and, 60-61, 70-71, 82
    crucial nature of, 276
    technology for, 149
Community of agents, 144, 146. *See also*
    Networks
Comparability:
    in internal negotiations, 191
    in sports negotiations, 246, 247
Complex agency, 179. *See also* Multiple
    agents
Compliance risk, and authority, 62-63
Complicating factors, ix-xi, 136, 275
Compromise, failure to, 208-209
Confidentiality:
    of instructions, 74
    of principal's identity, 75-76
Conflicts of interest, 287, 288. *See also*
    Interests, alignment of
Congress. *See* Legislators
Conlon, E., 285
Consent, and agency law, 160-161
Conservative negotiators, 217. *See also*
    Extreme negotiators
Constituents:
    dimensions in representation of, 9-10
    elections and, 209-210
    heterogeneity of, 204-205, 212
    See also Interests; Principals
Constraints, and agent's mandate,
    94-98
Consultants, 167. *See also* Independent
    contractors
Contingency fees, 266, 271, 285
Contingent agreements, 56-57, 280
Contingent approval stage, 69
Continua:
    agent-partisan, 9, 32-33, 43, 46, 137, 286
    agent-visionary, 9, 29-31, 43, 286
    dilemmas and, 35-39
    internal negotiation, 188-193
    matrix of, 33-35
    principal-agent, 9, 27-29, 286
    See also Dimensions
Contractors, agents as, 13, 161-169, 178
Contracts:
    agency law and, 165, 174, 177-180
    ideal, 285, 286
    in sports, 237-250

Control:
    agency law and, 159-160, 162, 168, 178,
        180
    mechanisms of, 91, 95-98
    See also Power
Core values, disclosure of, 155
Cost-benefit analysis, 165-168, 177-179
Costs:
    minimization of, 90-125
    of hard bargaining, 268-269
    of not settling, 191
    of public scrutiny, 207
    sources of, 284-285
Creating value:
    barriers and, 6-7
    commentary on, 264, 267-268, 271-272
    internal negotiation and, 190
    transformation and, 37
    ZOPA, NOPA, and, 243, 248
Crocker, C., 137-139, 143
Croson, R., 284, 294
Cutcher-Gershenfeld, J., 9-10, 286-287,
    291

Dance of negotiation, 217, 221, 267
Davis, W., 10-11, 292
Dayton Accords, 139-141
Deadlines, 206, 290
Descriptive analysis, 3
Dilemmas:
    agency strategic, 105-109, 130
    in authority, 61-63
Dilemmas, in representation, 9-10, 26
    case on, 39-42
    commentary on, 53-58
    types of, 35-42. *See also* Flexibility;
        Transformation; Trust
Dimensions:
    of authority, 60-61, 68
    of interests, 9-10, 26-42
Diplomats, 144, 146, 147-148. *See also*
    International negotiations
Disclosure:
    authority for, 74-76, 83
    of agent's beliefs and values, 155
    of principal's identity, 75-76
Distance, 238-239, 268, 292. *See also* Prox-
    imity
Dole, R., 221
Duty, 161, 168, 180. *See also* Fiduciary re-
    lationship

Economic agency theory, 284
Effectiveness, 169, 270, 278
Efficiency, external. *See* External efficiency
Elections, 141, 204, 209-210
Elyashiv, T., 286
Employees, agents as, 13, 161-169, 178
Endogeneity, and methodology, 226-227
Entertainment agents, 256
Entrepreneurship:
    interest configurations and, 114, 121
    legislation and, 204
Epistemic community of agents, 144
Equity, internal. *See* Internal equity
Ethics, 265, 286
Europe, 140-141, 144
European Union, 87-88
    case on, 98-105
    interest configurations and, 110, 111
    mandate design and, 119-122
Exclusive competence, 99
Exogeneity, and methodology, 226-228
Exploration stage, 69
External efficiency, 11, 93-94
    commentary on, 129
    interest configurations and, 109-115
    See also Mandates
Extreme negotiators:
    in labor negotiations, 190
    in legislative negotiations, 217,
        218-221, 228, 229

Fairness, internal. *See* Internal equity
Familiarity, proposition on, 289
Fast track procedure, 87, 99, 100, 102,
    103, 121
Fees, 241, 266, 271, 285. *See also* Financial
    relationship
Fiduciary relationship, 158-159, 168, 180
Final offer arbitration, 255, 258-259(n17)
Financial relationship, 281. *See also* Fees
Fisher, R., 3, 10-11, 231, 292
Flexibility, 12
    as attribute of mandates, 95-96
    authorization stage and, 101-102
    autonomy, authority, and, 118-119
    in practice, 147, 148, 149
    instruction negotiation and, 188
    interest alignment and, 116-117
    legal forms of agency and, 178
    ZOPA and, 279
Flexibility dilemma, 10, 37-39, 42
    commentary on, 55-57
    definition of, 38

Fluidity, of coalitions, 205-206, 207
Foley, T., 220
Forcing strategy, 194
Ford Sterling Plant, 39-42
Fostering strategy, 194
Free agents, 239, 240, 256

General managers, 249-250, 251, 253, 254
Gephardt, R., 221
Getting to YES, 3-6, 48
Gilmour, J. B., 208
Gingrich, N., 212, 220, 221
Glaspie, A., 142-143
Golden triangle, 18(n2)
Groseclose, T., 215, 219, 220
Ground rules, 56
GTY. See Getting to YES
Guild, diplomatic, 146

Haig, A., 137, 138
Hard bargaining, 236-250, 263-269
Harvard University, 75-76
Heterogeneity of constituents, 204-205,
    212
High Representative for Bosnia, 139-140
Holbrooke, R., 140-141
Holding out, 238
Hotelling, H., 215
Hussein, S., 142

Ideology, of legislators, 213-222
If-then options, 280
Impasse bargaining. *See* Hard bargaining
Incentives:
    alignment and, 196-197, 199-202, 278,
        285
    chain of agents and, 172
    electoral, 209
    in sports negotiations, 241, 244, 264,
        265-266, 270
    information, preferences, and, 2
Independence, 147, 148, 149. *See also*
    Authority; Flexibility
Independent contractors, agents as, 13,
    161-169
Industrial relations, 25
Information:
    commentary on, 266-267, 268, 269, 272
    in chain of agents, 171, 172
    in practice, 147, 149
    legal forms of agency and, 169, 178

preferences, incentives, and, 2
propositions on, 292
See also Knowledge
Initial exploration stage, 69
Inside-outside tension, 145
Institutional barriers, 7-8
Instructions:
    approach to, adjusted, 68-77
    approach to, conventional, 59-60, 63-68
    commentary on, 81-85
    compliance risk and, 62-63
    dilemma of, 61-63
    judgment risk and, 64-67
    negotiation of, 188
    open, 74, 78-80, 83
    See also Authority
Intellectual capital, 239
Interests:
    advice on, 17
    boundaries for, 31
    compared to positions, 4, 11
    configurations of, 109-118, 128, 131-132
    conflict of, 287, 288
    dimensions in representation of, 9-10,
        26, 27-35
    dynamic nature of, 24-26
    fiduciaries and, 158-159
    legal forms of agency and, 169
    transformation of, 29-31
    ZOPA, NOPA, and, 247-248, 265-267
    See also Representation
Interests, alignment of, 169, 178
    as theme, 276, 278-279
    false nonalignment and, 279
    heterogeneity and, 204-205
    internal negotiations and, 188-193
    propositions on, 287, 288, 290
Intermediaries, network of, 145-146
Internal equity, 11, 93-94
    commentary on, 129
    interest configurations and, 109-115
    See also Mandates
Internal negotiation, 188-193
International negotiations, 12-13, 87-88
    cases on, 44-46, 98-105, 137-143
    challenges in, 135-149
    commentary on, 151-155
    communities in, 144, 146
    hypotheses on mandate design for,
        119-122
    in practice, advice for, 147-148, 152-155
    interest configurations in, 110, 111
    multiple agents in, 143-144

multiple principals in, 136-141
role conflicts in, 145-146
shifting mandates in, 141-143
International relations, 25, 92
Intraorganizational bargaining, 25, 182,
    188, 191-193
Inventing phase, 56
Iraq, 141-143
Israel, 228

Jensen, M., 284
Judgment risk, 64-67
Judicial opinion, 230-231

Kantor, M., 173
Kaufman, G. M., 12
Kiewiet, D. R., 216
Kim, Y. M., 285
King, D. C., 15-16, 289-290
Kissinger, H., 172, 174
Knowledge, 169, 178, 289. *See also* Infor-
    mation
Kurtzberg, T., 17
Kuwait, 142

Labor-management relations, 14-15,
    39-42
Labor negotiations, 181-184
    alignment of incentives in, 196-197,
        199-202
    alignment of interests in, 178, 188-193
    challenges in, 185-187
    commentary on, 196-202
    in sports. *See* Sports agents
    perception of alignment in, 197
    perception of differences in, 189, 198
    stages for managing internally, 188-193
Law. *See* Agency law; Legislators
Lax, D. A., 53, 250, 285
Leadership, in political parties, 214-222,
    227-229
Learning, 68, 70-71
Legislators, 15-16, 203-205
    as delegates or trustees, 207-208
    commentary on, 226-233
    crucial elements for, 206-210
    elections and, 204, 209-210
    failures to compromise by, 208-209
    ideology of, 213-222
    methodology for study of, 216-222,
        226-227

party leadership and, 214-222, 227-229
politics and, 205-210
public scrutiny of, 206-208
role-authority-mission space of,
    210-212, 215
visionary role of, 211-212, 214
Literary agents, 256
Lofgren, Z., 205
Lott, T., 220
Loyalty, 158, 159

Mandate dilemma. *See* Flexibility
    dilemma
Mandates:
    agency strategic dilemma and, 105-109
    as theme, 276, 279-280
    attributes of, 95-98, 101-105, 115-119
    commentary on, 127-132
    criteria for, 93-94
    interest configurations and, 109-118
    iterated, 96, 129
    optimal. *See* Optimal mandates
    shifting, 141-143
Mandell, B. S., 16-17
Margin of maneuverability, 94-95
    agency strategic dilemma on, 105-109
    interest configurations and, 109-118
    mandate attributes and, 95-98, 115-119
Martinez, J., 13
Mayer, F., 94, 117
McCubbins, M. D., 216
McKersie, R. B., 14, 25, 182, 293, 294
Mechanisms of control, 91, 95-98
Meckling, W., 284
Media, the, 206-207, 237
Median citizen, 213
Median leader, 215-221, 228
Mediators:
    in international negotiations, 137, 145,
        152
    representation theory and, 32, 38, 43,
        58
Miceli, T., 284
Middlemen, political leaders as, 215
Mission, role, and authority, 210-212, 215
Mitchell, G., 220
Mnookin, R. H., 3, 6, 17, 97, 284, 294
Modern Operating Agreement (MOA),
    41-42
Moore, D., 17
Multiple agents:
    agency law and, 159, 171-172, 173-174,
        179

future research and, 296
in international negotiations, 143-144
Multiple constituents, 91-93. *See also*
    Two-level games
Multiple principals, 11-12
    agency costs and, 127
    in international negotiations, 136-141
    proposition on, 289
Murnighan, J. K., 285
Mutual gains approach, commentary on,
    52-58

National Football League, 237
National Hockey League, 250
Neale, M. A., 285
Negotiation:
    complicating factors in, ix-xi, 26, 275
    dance of, 217, 221, 267
    future empirical research on, 295-297
    key issues in, 3-8
    literature of, 2-3, 25
    on behalf of others, 282
    overlapping domains of, 3
    structure, people, context, and, 177
    two-person simplification of, ix-x
Negotiation, stages in, 14
    authority and, 69-70
    commentary on, 56
    internal negotiations and, 188-193
    mandate attributes and, 95-98
Negotiation theory, adjustment of, 9-12.
    See also Authority; Representation;
    Two-level games
Negotiator's dilemma, 53
Netanyahu, B., 228
Networks:
    of agent alliances, 174
    of intermediaries, 145-146
    See also Community
News media, 206-207
Nicolaïdis, K., 11-12, 288, 291
Nixon, R. M., 172, 174
No possible agreement. *See* NOPA
NOMINATE scores, 219-221
NOPA (no possible agreement), 16
    as alternative model, 245-250
    prenegotiation experiment and, 254,
        255

Obedience, 161. *See also* Fiduciary rela-
    tionship
Objective criteria, 4-5, 279

Objective standards, 231
Objectivity, and distance, 238-239
Observable negotiations, 206-208, 290
Open meeting laws, 206
Operational control, 96
Optimal contract, 179
Optimal mandates, 88, 93-94
  commentary on, 128-132
  hypotheses on, 115-119
Option generation stage, 69
Options, 4, 265-266, 280
Organizational barriers, 7-8
Organizational model, 161
Organizational proximity, 164
Organizational structure, 170-172
Organizational theory, 25
Organizing campaigns, for unions, 187
Oslo peace process, 44-46
"Other side":
  agents and. *See* Agent-agent
    relationship
  authority instructions and, 62-63, 77
  principals and, 280-281

Pareto optimality. *See* External efficiency
Parks, J. M., 285
Partially open truthful exchange. *See*
  POTE
Partisan-agent continuum, 9, 32-33, 43,
  46, 137, 286
Partners:
  as legal form of agency, 161, 163-169,
    178
  role of, 13, 28-29, 43, 45, 58
Party leaders, 214-222, 227-229
Patton, B. M., 3, 231
People-problem separation, 3-4
Peres, S., 44-46, 228
Political party leadership, 214-222, 227-
  229
Politics, 15, 290-291
  fluid coalitions and, 205-206, 207
  legislation and. *See* Legislators
  party leadership and, 214-222, 227-229
  shifting mandates and, 141, 143
Poole, K., 219
Positions, compared to interests, 4, 11
POTE (partially open truthful exchange), 267
Power:
  commentary on, 266-267
  definition of, 172

dynamics of, 157, 160, 172-174, 180
law and, 13, 179-180
proposition on, 292
See also Agency law; Control
Preferences, information, and incentives, 2
Principal-agent analysis:
  central elements of, 2
  central question in, 1-2
  complicating factors in, ix-xi, 136
  golden triangle of, 18(n2)
  in negotiation context, 90-98
  political applications of, 204. *See also*
    Legislators
  real-world negotiations and, x-xi, 24
  See also Agents
Principal-agent continuum, 9, 27-29, 286
Principal-agent problem, 24
Principal-agent relationship:
  agency law and, 157-172, 174-180
  as critical factor, 5
  authority in. *See* Authority
  essence of, 61
  financial aspect of, 281
  internal negotiations and, 188-193,
    197-200
  intertwined roles in, 277-278
  orientation in, 185
  power dynamics in, 157, 160, 172-174
  proposition on, 293
  time horizons in, 185-186
Principal-principal relationship, 280-281
Principals:
  advice for, 3-5, 17, 280-282
  as agents, 184, 198-199, 277-278
  citizens as, 204, 213
  dimensions in representation of, 26,
    27-35
  effectiveness of, 278
  election of, 141
  identity of, 75-76
  interest configurations and, 109-118
  See also Constituents
Principals, multiple, 11-12, 127
  international negotiations and, 136-141
  proposition on, 289
  two-level games and, 91-93
Principals, roles of:
  agents' roles and, 277-278
  authority and, 61-62, 76-77
  representation theory and, 27-29, 58
Problem-people separation, 3-4
Process:
  as a variable, 232(n2)

management of, 153-154
restructuring, 193-194
Proximity, organizational, 164. *See also*
  Distance
Psychological mechanisms, 7, 108
Putnam, R., 92, 111

Rabin, Y., 44-46
Raiffa, H., 105, 217, 218
RAM space. *See* Role, authority, and mission
Ratification, and agency law, 160. *See*
  also Acceptance
Ratification dilemma. *See* Transformation dilemma
Ratification stage, 69
Reagan, R., 137, 138, 139
Real estate agents, 286, 287
Reporting, and authority, 70-71, 82
Representation, 9-10
  cases on, 39-42, 44-46
  commentary on, 52-58
  complexity in, 23-26, 47
  descriptive, 213
  dilemmas of, 35-42
  dimensions of, 9, 26, 27-35
  in practice, 47-48, 53
  in theory building, 48-49
  nature of, 49
  roles in, 25-49
  See also Autonomy
Representational matrix, 33-35
Representatives:
  challenges for, 26
  compared to agents, 27
  definition of, 27
  roles of, 25-46, 52-58
  See also Agents
Reservation values, and authority, 74-75
Reserve clause, 237
Restatement (Second) of Agency, 158, 162
Restructuring processes, 193-194
Risk management, 270
Rogers, H., 205, 210, 211
Role, authority, and mission (RAM), 210-
  212, 215
Role conflicts:
  in international negotiations, 145-146,
    151-152
  in labor negotiations, 183-184, 186
Rosenthal, H., 219
Ross, L., 3, 6
Rubin, J. Z., 284

Salacuse, J. W., 13, 14, 291
Sander, F. E., 284
Sappington, D., 285
Search problem, 113
Sebenius, J., 53, 177, 250, 285
Sequential mandates, 96, 129
Sequential roles, 42-46
Shared competence procedures, 100,
  104. *See also* Article 113 procedure
Shields, agents as, 266
Shifts:
  in labor-management relations, 183-184
  in mandates, 141-143
  in roles, 43, 45
Shultz, G., 137, 138, 139
Sigelman, L., 207, 208
Simulations, 296
Sirmans, C. F., 284
Social contract, 185, 197
South Africa, 137-139
Sports agents, 16-17, 235-237
  advice on, 269-272
  commentary on, 263-272
  compared to celebrity agents, 256
  context for, 237-241, 264-265
  costs imposed by, 268-269
  negotiation analysis of, alternative,
    245-250
  negotiation analysis of, standard,
    242-245
  prenegotiation experiment on, 250-255
  roles of, 265-266
  value added by, 267-268, 271-272
Strategic barriers, 6-7
Strategic control, 95
Strategic dilemma, agency, 105-109, 130
Strategic miscalculation, 113
Strauss, R., 173
Structural barriers, 7-8
Structure:
  legal, 177, 180. *See also* Agency law
  organizational, 170-172
Suboptimality, 109, 111, 114, 115. *See also*
  Optimal mandates
Sunshine laws, 207
Supreme Court, 230, 231
Surplus, 287, 288, 289
Susskind, L. E., 10, 17

Tactical barriers, 6-7
Technology, 143, 148, 159
Template development stage, 69

Tension, 6-8
    creators of, 266
    in agency strategic dilemma, 108
    inside-outside, 145
    See also Dilemmas
Theatrical agents, 256
Time horizons, 185-186
Timing:
    adding value and, 267-268
    in authority instructions, 10-11, 68-71,
        82-84
Trade negotiations. *See* International ne-
        gotiations
Training, 147, 148
Transformation dilemma, 10, 36-37, 41
    commentary on, 54-55
    definition of, 37
Transformed interests, 29-31
Treaty power, 98, 99
Truman, D., 215
Trust:
    fiduciaries and, 158, 159
    interest configurations and, 113, 114
    interest understanding and, 183
    role conflicts and, 145
    working, 145
Trust dilemma, 10, 35-36, 40-41
    commentary on, 53-54
    definition of, 36
Tversky, A., 3
Two-level games, 11-12
    agency strategic dilemma and, 105-109
    hypotheses on, commentary on, 131-132
    hypotheses on, generation of, 115-119
    hypotheses on, testing of, 119-122
    interest configurations and, 109-118
    international negotiations and, 98-105,
        119-122
    principal-agent framework and, 92-93
Type I errors, 112
Type II errors, 112

Uncertainty, role of, 285
Unions:
    in sports, 237
    lobbying against, 186-187
    negotiations and. *See* Labor
        negotiations

United Nations, 139-140
United States:
    interest configurations in, 110, 111
    multiple agents and, 144
    multiple principals and, 137-141
    shifting mandates in, 141-143
    Supreme Court of, 230, 231
    trade authority in, 87-88, 98-105, 110,
        111, 119-122
Ury, W., 3, 231

Valley, K., 15, 17, 285
Value. *See* Claiming value; Creating
        value
Values, core, 155
Visionary-agent continuum, 9, 29-31, 43,
        286
Visionary, role of, 29-31, 58
    for legislators, 211-212, 214
    types of, 212

Walking away, 244, 295
Walton, R., 14, 25, 182
Watkins, M., 9-10, 286-287, 291
Wealth creators, 266
Wellstone, P., 211
Wheeler, M., 16, 250, 294
White, S. B., 285
Williamson, O. E., 165
Wilson, R., 3
Wilson, W., 223(n2)
Wizards, 153
Written instructions, 74, 78-80, 83, 271, 279
Written summaries, 280, 281

Yavas, A., 284

Zajac, E. J., 285
Zeckhauser, R. J., 15-16, 289-290
ZOPA (zone of possible agreement), 16,
        277
    commentary on, 266, 267
    in standard analysis, 242-245
    NOPA alternative to, 245-250
    prenegotiation experiment and, 251-254

About the Authors

Eileen F. Babbitt is Assistant Professor of International Politics and Director of the International Negotiation and Conflict Resolution Program at the Fletcher School of Law and Diplomacy, Tufts University. Her research interests include preventative diplomacy, postsettlement peace building, and roles for third parties in protracted intergroup conflicts. She is currently editing a book on the reframing of protracted conflicts and implications for intervention, as well as initiating research projects on trust building and on negotiating self-determination.

Max H. Bazerman is the J. Jay Gerber Distinguished Professor at the Kellogg Graduate School of Management of Northwestern University. From 1998 to 2000, he is the Thomas Henry Carroll Ford Visiting Professor of Business Administration and Marvin Bower Fellow at the Harvard Business School. His research focuses on decision making, negotiation, and the natural environment. He is the author or coauthor of more than 100 research articles as well as the author, coauthor, or coeditor of nine books, including *Smart Money Decisions* (in press), *Judgment in Managerial Decision Making* (4th edition, 1998), *Cognition and Rationality in Negotiation* (1991, with M. Neale), and *Negotiating Rationally* (1992, with M. Neale).

Abram J. Chayes is Felix Frankfurter Professor of Law, Emeritus, Harvard Law School, and Co-Director of the Project on International Compliance and Dispute Settlement. He is a member of the Steering Committee of the Program on Negotiation at Harvard Law School. In the 1980s, he represented Nicaragua in the World Court case against the United States concerning the Reagan Administration's policy of support for the contras. He is the author of *The Cuban Missile Crisis: Inter-*

national Crisis and the Role of Law (1974; 2nd edition, 1987) and coauthor of *The New Sovereignty: Compliance With Treaties in International Regulatory Regimes* (1995, with Antonia H. Chayes).

Jonathan R. Cohen is Assistant Professor at the University of Florida Levin College of Law in Gainesville. Trained as a lawyer and an economist, he is currently writing about ethical dimensions of negotiation and lawyering. His recent publications address the use of apology in legal disputes, the roles of rationality in negotiation, and theological implications of human cloning.

Joel Cutcher-Gershenfeld is Visiting Associate Professor at MIT's Sloan School of Management. He is also Co-Chair of PON's Program on Negotiations in the Workplace. He has recently coauthored a book on the global diffusion of new work systems, titled *Knowledge-Driven Work: Unexpected Lessons From Japanese and U.S. Work Practices,* and is coauthor of a forthcoming book on organizational learning. He has coedited three other books on training and public policy and is the author or coauthor of more than 60 articles or book chapters. Currently, he is co-leading research on the implementation of new work systems for MIT's Lean Aerospace Initiative, the employment implications of instability in the aerospace industry, the status of collective bargaining in the United States (for the Federal Mediation and Conciliation Service), and the global diffusion of ADR principles (for the Society of Professionals in Dispute Resolution).

Wayne Davis is Practice Manager at Fidelity Consulting, an internal management consulting unit of Fidelity Investments. He has been associated with the Harvard Negotiation Project for more than 15 years as a teacher, researcher, and developer of negotiation curricula and supporting teaching materials. His current focus is on intraorganizational negotiations and on the impact of "competition at Internet speed" on organizational behavior.

Roger Fisher is Director of the Harvard Negotiation Project, Williston Professor of Law Emeritus at Harvard Law School and coauthor of *Getting to YES: Negotiating Agreement Without Giving In* (2nd edition, 1991). His latest book, *Getting It Done: How to Lead When You're Not in Charge* (1998), was coauthored by Alan Sharp with John Richardson.

He is concerned with developing concepts and tools that help practitioners deal with their differences in a less costly and more effective manner. He is the founder and Senior Advisor to Conflict Management, Inc., and the nonprofit Conflict Management Group.

Pacey C. Foster is a doctoral candidate in organization studies at the Wallace E. Carroll School of Management at Boston College. He is the former associate director of the Program on Negotiation at Harvard Law School and has worked in alternative dispute resolution for more than 10 years. His current research and practice interests include negotiation pedagogy, integrating negotiation and action research methods, and exploring the social mechanisms underlying conflict behavior in organizational networks.

Gordon M. Kaufman is Professor of Operations Research and Management at the Sloan School of Management at MIT. His major interests lie in the mathematical modeling of negotiation processes and in teaching competitive decision making. His current research involves testing hypotheses of Internet negotiation.

David C. King is Associate Professor of Public Policy at Harvard University, where he teaches about the U.S. Congress, interest groups, and political parties. His books include *Turf Wars: How Congressional Committees Claim Jurisdiction* (1997) and *Why People Don't Trust Government* (1997), which he coedited with Joseph S. Nye and Philip D. Zelikow. His current research explores the causes and consequences of political polarization.

Terri Kurtzberg is a Ph.D. candidate in organization behavior from the Kellogg Graduate School of Management at Northwestern University, as well as a Research Associate for the Ernst and Young Center for Business Innovation. Her background includes a B.A. in psychology and an M.A. in education from the University of Chicago. Her primary research focuses on creativity in organizational and negotiating work teams. Other research interests include knowledge transfer and learning, conflict resolution, and the effects of electronic media on communication and negotiation effectiveness.

Brian S. Mandell is Lecturer in Public Policy and Chair of Harvard University's Wexner-Israel Fellowship Program and Pew Faculty Fellow and Senior Research Associate at Harvard's Belfer Center for Science and International Affairs. His current teaching and research address the theory and practice of negotiation, emphasizing third-party facilitation and consensus building in protracted policy disputes. He writes about international mediation and is completing a book on new approaches to conflict management. Before arriving at Harvard, he taught at the Norman Paterson School of International Affairs at Carleton University in Ottawa. Previously, he was a strategic analyst for the Canadian Department of National Defence specializing in United Nations peacekeeping and the implementation of arms control treaties.

Janet Martinez is a Senior Associate and Program Manager at the Consensus Building Institute. She teaches—at MIT and Harvard University—graduate and executive courses in negotiation, public policy, and international dispute resolution in the private, nonprofit, and public sectors. A lawyer and mediator, she has published cases, simulations, and articles on negotiation and consensus building. Her two current research interests are international dispute settlement system design (based on an analysis of the World Trade Organization) and the use of "parallel informal negotiation" in international trade and environment institutions. She is currently a Ph.D. candidate at MIT.

Robert B. McKersie is Society of Sloan Fellows Professor of Management Emeritus at the MIT Sloan School of Management. His research interests have been in labor-management relations, with particular focus on bargaining activity. With Richard Walton, he coauthored *A Behavioral Theory of Labor Negotiations* (1965). Subsequently, he focused his attention on the subject of productivity (authoring a book with Lawrence Hunter titled *Pay, Productivity and Collective Bargaining*) and participated in a multiyear project at the Sloan School that resulted in the award-winning book by Thomas Kochan and Harry Katz titled *The Transformation of American Industrial Relations*. More recently, he has returned to the subject of the bargaining process and coauthored, with Richard Walton and Joel Cutcher-Gershenfeld, *Strategic Negotiations*. He continues to do research on strategies being pursued in different industries to bring about more effective organizational arrangements. The auto, steel, and transportation sectors are of special interest.

Robert H. Mnookin is Chairman of the Steering Committee of the Program on Negotiation, Director of the Harvard Negotiation Research Project, and the Williston Professor of Law at Harvard Law School. His major interest is in studying barriers to the negotiated resolution of conflict and how to overcome them. His most important new project is a book on how lawyers can create value through negotiation.

Don Moore is a doctoral student at the Kellogg Graduate School of Management at Northwestern University. His research interests lie in decision making and negotiation. His dissertation is on the role of time pressure in negotiation.

Kalypso Nicolaïdis is Associate Professor of Public Policy at the John F. Kennedy School of Government at Harvard University. She teaches courses on negotiation, international institutions, the European Union, and nationalism. She is also currently a University Lecturer at Oxford University. Her research combines her interests in the sources of cooperation in regional and multilateral settings, the interface between trade and regulation issues, and the dynamics of bargaining under complexity. She is completing a book on the principle of mutual recognition and the lessons that can be drawn from Europe for the rest of the world.

Bruce M. Patton is Deputy Director of the Harvard Negotiation Project and a founding director of CMI/Vantage Partners LLC, an international consulting firm that helps organizations build and sustain important internal and external relationships that can make differences and conflict a source of creativity and competitive advantage rather than a drag on productivity. He is also the Thaddeus R. Beal Lecturer on Law at Harvard Law School, where he teaches the Negotiation Workshop he pioneered with Roger Fisher. He is the coauthor, with Fisher and William Ury, of *Getting to YES: Negotiating Agreement Without Giving In* (2nd edition, 1991) and the coauthor, with Douglas Stone and Sheila Heen, of *Difficult Conversations: How to Discuss What Matters Most* (1999).

Jeswald W. Salacuse is Henry J. Braker Professor of Commercial Law at the Fletcher School of Law and Diplomacy, Tufts University. He specializes in international negotiation, international business transactions, and law and development. He has written numerous books and articles on various aspects of law and international relations, including *Making Global Deals—Negotiating in the International Marketplace* (1991), *International Business Planning: Law and Taxation* (with W. P. Streng, 1982), *An Introduction to Law in French-Speaking Africa*, *Nigerian Family Law*, and *The Art of Advice* (1994).

Lawrence E. Susskind is Ford Professor of Urban and Environmental Planning at MIT, President of the Consensus Building Institute, and Director of the Harvard-MIT Public Disputes Program. His major interest lies in multiparty dispute resolution, particularly in the public policy arena. His most important new project is the development of strategies (such as parallel informal negotiation) that can be used to generate more creative (i.e., value-generating) options in diplomatic contexts. He is the senior author of *The Consensus Building Handbook* (1999), which spells out alternatives to Robert's Rules of Order for all kinds of groups and ad hoc assemblies that wish to operate by consensus.

Kathleen Valley is Associate Professor at the Harvard Business School. Her professional focus is on personal and professional relationships and their effects on negotiation processes and outcomes. Her latest project is *Fight, Play Fair, or Work Together: Mutually Developed Scripts in Negotiations*, a theoretical and empirical investigation of the ways in which social closeness and contextual differences affect the "script" that evolves during a negotiation.

Michael Watkins is Associate Professor of Business Administration at the Harvard Business School. He teaches and does research at the intersection between leadership and negotiation, exploring how leaders negotiate and negotiators lead. He recently completed a study exploring how new leaders coming into top management positions should manage their first 6 months on the job. This research will be published by Harvard Business School Press as *Right From the Start: Taking Charge in a New Leadership Role*. He is working on a book on international negotiations tentatively titled *Negotiating in a Complex World*.

Michael Wheeler is Professor of Management at the Harvard Business School. He is the author or coauthor of six books and numerous articles in scholarly journals and the public press. His research focuses on negotiation and dispute resolution, notably in the context of environmental policy, facility siting, and real estate development. He is the coeditor (with Deborah Kolb) of *Negotiation Journal* and has been a member of the Steering Committee of the Program on Negotiation at Harvard Law School since 1984. His current research focuses on complexity, specifically, the theoretical and practical implications of the fact that interests, BATNAs, and even the parties themselves often change in the process of negotiation.

Richard J. Zeckhauser is the Frank P. Ramsey Professor of Political Economy at the John F. Kennedy School of Government at Harvard University. He also teaches in the Law School and the Economics Department at Harvard. His research starts from the observation that uncertainty and strategic behavior are pervasive in our world; his major research interests are the challenges of making wise decisions under uncertainty and effective structures for relationships, whether between firms, individuals, or nations. He is currently studying how corporations and stock analysts manipulate earnings and earnings estimates, the game plan of elite colleges and their applicants in the minuet of early admissions, and how health insurance is and should be structured.